# Kingdom Rhetoric

# Kingdom Rhetoric

*New Testament Explorations in Honor of Ben Witherington III*

Edited by
T. MICHAEL W. HALCOMB

WIPF & STOCK · Eugene, Oregon

KINGDOM RHETORIC
New Testament Explorations in Honor of Ben Witherington III

Copyright © 2013 Wipf and Stock Publishers. All rights reserved. Except for brief quotations in critical publications or reviews, no part of this book may be reproduced in any manner without prior written permission from the publisher. Write: Permissions. Wipf and Stock Publishers, 199 W. 8th Ave., Suite 3, Eugene, OR 97401.

Wipf & Stock
An Imprint of Wipf and Stock Publishers
199 W. 8th Ave., Suite 3
Eugene, OR 97401

www.wipfandstock.com

ISBN 13: 978-1-59752-528-2

Manufactured in the U.S.A.

*To Ben Witherington III, a scholar, rhetor, and churchman, who has helped advance God's Kingdom throughout the world.*

*And in memory of Christy Ann Witherington, Ben and Ann's "Sweetpea" and "Purple Girl."*

# Contents

*In Honor of Ben*  |  ix

## SYNOPTIC GOSPELS

1. Perfection of Disciples in Matthew's Gospel: An Examination of a Central Concept in Matthean Kingdom Ethics  |  3
   —David R. Bauer

2. Text as Witness: The Surprising Conjunction of Jewish and Greco-Roman Rhetoric in Mark 12:1–37  |  21
   —Judith Odor

## LUKE-ACTS

3. The Exhortation to Monotheism in Acts 15:15–17  |  47
   —Craig S. Keener

4. Luke, Paul and the Law  |  71
   —Robert Brian Kidwell

## JOHANNINE LITERATURE

5. Reconsidering the Puzzle of "Earthly Things" in John 3:12  |  89
   —Joseph R. Dongell

6. With God on Our Side: The Rhetoric of Economics in Revelation  |  113
   —Jason A. Myers

## PAULINE EPISTLES

7. Paul's Prophesying Isa 28:11 in Context: The Signs of Unbelievers and Believers in 1 Corinthians 14  |  133
   —Fredrick J. Long

8 "Do Not Be Conformed to This Age": Rom 12:1–2 in Light of Environmental Determinism | 170
—T. Michael W. Halcomb

## GENERAL EPISTLES

9 Centering the Decentered Self: 1 Peter and Identity in the 21st Century | 197
—Ruth Anne Reese

10 Who's Stumbling on the Stumbling Stone? A Reassessment of 1 Peter 2:4–10 in Light of a Dynamic Understanding of Holiness and Election | 216
—Susann Liubinskas

# In Honor of Ben

As the title of this book indicates, this work was written to honor Ben Witherington III. I, Michael Halcomb, started thinking about this project as I finished up my PhD coursework at Asbury Theological Seminary. Not knowing what the future holds, I wanted to be able to honor my doctoral supervisor before the possibility of leaving Asbury was upon me. I'm grateful that I've had the chance to do that, and I'm especially appreciative of each of the authors who have contributed to this festschrift.

One of the unique things about this book is that it is a collaborative effort from the New Testament (NT) department at Asbury[1]. Essays are offered by five NT faculty and five NT students who have gone through or are currently working through the program. This book is divided into five sections which cover the breadth of the NT canon, with one senior and junior scholar each offering an exploration of a specific NT passage. To hearken back to the title, these "explorations" are done in the spirit of Ben's works, which, as we all know, also cover the whole of the NT canon.

This work is also somewhat unique in that it is not a celebration of a birthday or the end of a career. This is purposeful. Ben is almost always "in the know," and so I thought it best to catch him off guard. Indeed, it is something of a miracle that he never caught wind of this work. We all know that it is difficult for scholars to keep quiet about their research. Yet, the contributors to this volume have been stellar in that regard.

For those who know Ben, they will know the last year or so has been quite a difficult one for him and his family. On Wednesday, January 11, 2012, Christy Ann, the daughter of Ben and Ann, passed on unexpectedly. As a friend of Ben's, I know that these have been incredibly trying times for the Witherington family. Today, there exists a scholarship fund in Christy's

---

1. Throughout the remainder of this book the abbreviation NT will be used to denote New Testament, including instances when it is in the title of an English work. Similarly, OT will denote Old Testament.

name, The Christy Ann Witherington Scholarship Fund, at Asbury Theological Seminary, and readers should be aware that one hundred percent of the proceeds from this book will go to that scholarship fund to assist female students in Asbury's biblical studies program.

While many do know Ben as one of the most prolific NT scholars of the last few decades, they might be unaware of just how devout he is as a churchman. For example, he has been discipling and teaching a group from the New Covenant class at Centenary United Methodist Church (Lexington, KY) for nearly a decade. Two years ago Ben was instrumental in bringing me to that class, which I have been leading on Sunday mornings ever since. It is a truly unique Sunday school class and without a doubt, one of the most intelligent groups of believers I have ever worked with in a church setting. Certainly, Ben has had something to do with that. I am thankful for the opportunity to teach the New Covenanters and am grateful for the contribution they made to help this book to reach its final form.

It is my hope that readers of this volume will be encouraged in their explorations and research of the NT. Likewise, I hope this work will display some of the innovative and insightful work coming out of Asbury's still young PhD program. So as not to steal the thunder of each essay here in the preface, I will abstain from offering my own overview and interpretation of these entries and leave that exploration to you. As editor, I have endeavored to allow each author to channel his/her own creative energy. In that regard, each essay speaks for itself. As a collection of works, however, we hope that these essays honor Ben and help advance the Kingdom of God just as his own publications have.

Finally, on behalf of all of the contributors to this volume, I say thank you to Ben for his fidelity to the Body of Christ, his vigor in research and publishing within the academy, and his example of a life well-lived as child of God. John Wesley once said, "Light yourself on fire with passion and people will come from miles to watch you burn." We as contributors, along with many across the world, have had the opportunity to watch Ben's passion illuminate God's truth and we look forward to the years ahead in which we will get to see that flame burn everstrong.

Michael Halcomb
Pentecost 2013

# SYNOPTIC GOSPELS

# 1

# Perfection of Disciples in Matthew's Gospel

*An Examination of a Central Concept in Matthean Kingdom Ethics*

**David R. Bauer**

It is a singular honor for me to contribute this chapter to the book celebrating the ministry of my dear friend Ben Witherington. Ben has been a warm, encouraging, and supportive colleague since he joined the faculty of Asbury Theological Seminary in 1995. It goes without saying that he has been a most productive scholar. His contributions to NT studies are notable in terms of their scope, their number, and their quality. In his personal and professional life Ben has embodied the ideals of discipleship in the Kingdom; and Ben has always approached NT interpretation from the perspective of Christian discipleship. Accordingly, I have chosen to explore a central (yet often overlooked) aspect of Matthew's presentation of the life of discipleship within the Kingdom: the perfection of disciples.

In his magisterial commentary on Matthew Ulrich Luz declares that "perfection is of fundamental importance for Matthew."[1] And Léopold Sabarin, commenting on Matthew's reference to perfection in 5:48 (and its relation to the "golden rule" in 7:12), insists that "le verset et la regle d'or de 7:12 constituent sûremont pour Mt. les affirmations par excellence du Jesu sur l'ethique der Royaume..."[2]

These assertions are supported by an examination of the role of perfection within Matthew's Gospel itself. The term appears three times in the Gospel. In 5:48 (where it occurs twice) it brings to a climax the discussion of the "greater righteousness" that is necessary for entrance into the Kingdom.[3] In 19:21 Jesus declares to the rich young man that perfection is required for discipleship and for entrance into eternal life. Both of these references are unique to Matthew; the parallel passages in the other synoptics lack the term. Indeed, the adjective "perfect" (τέλειος) appears in the Gospels only in Matthew.

But in spite of assertions by certain recent commentators regarding the centrality of perfection in Matthew's Gospel, and in spite of the abovementioned considerations of the importance of perfection from the Gospel itself, most scholars have given scant attention to the Matthean concept of perfection. And most scholars who have attended to perfection in Matthew have pursued a redaction-critical investigation rather than focusing upon the ways in which the Gospel itself, in its final literary form, causes the reader to construe the meaning and significance of this concept.[4] Moreover, a majority of scholars have tended to interpret the two occurrences of perfection essentially in isolation from one another, rather than exploring fully

---

1. Ulrich Luz, *Matthew 8–20*, Hermeneia: A Critical and Historical Commentary on the Bible (Minneapolis: Fortress, 2001), 513.

2. Léopold Sabourin, *L'Evangile selon saint Matthieu et ses Principaux Paralleles* (Rome: Biblical Institute Press, 1978), 73. ["The verse and the golden rule of 7:12 certainly constitute for Matthew the most significant affirmations of Jesus pertaining to the ethic of the Kingdom..." Author's Translation]

3. Alexander Sand, "Das Evangelium nach Matthäus," In *Regensburger Neues Testament* (Regensburg: Friedrich Pustet, 1986), 121. There is general agreement that the sixth antithesis, of which 5:48 is a part, brings to a climax the list of antitheses that begins in 5:21; the principle of the motive of love, i.e., the desire to deal with persons in terms of redemptiveness (which is the explicit focus of 5:43–49), stands behind Jesus' "but I say to you" statements in the preceding antitheses. See, e.g., Robert H. Gundry, *Matthew: A Commentary on His Handbook for a Mixed Church under Persecution*, 2nd ed. (Grand Rapids: Eerdmans, 1994), 100; Robert Guelich, *The Sermon on the Mount* (Waco, TX: Word, 1982), 235–36.

4. For the values of redaction criticism in biblical studies, and its limitations, see David R. Bauer and Robert A. Traina, *Inductive Bible Study: A Comprehensive Guide to the Practice of Hermeneutics* (Grand Rapids: Baker Academic, 2011), 228–32, 393–99.

their complementary relationship. In this chapter, I will employ a literary-theological approach that focuses upon the final form of the text and that takes into account also historical background and the broader context of the NT canon insofar as the Matthean text invites such exploration. I will argue that perfection stands at the center of Matthean ethics, since in both passages where the term appears it develops the central command to love the neighbor and addresses the Matthean emphasis on the fulfillment of the law; that the occurrences at 5:48 and 19:21 are consistent with one another and complement one another; and that Matthew presents this perfection as realizable for Christians, as essential for discipleship, and as required for entrance into the future Kingdom at the Great Assize. In addition, this article will develop the meaning and significance of perfection within the world of Matthew's Gospel.

## PERFECTION ACCORDING TO MATTHEW 5:48

Two primary issues confront the interpreter of 5:48a: "You therefore must be perfect." The first pertains to the meaning of the adjective "perfect" (τέλειοι). The second involves the significance of the inflection of the verb usually translated "you must be" (ἔσεσθε).

### The Meaning of "Perfect" in 5:48

Lexicographers agree that τέλειος carries the ideas of (a) "having attained" the end or purpose" or (b) "complete,[5] "wanting nothing necessary to completeness."[6] It is necessary to determine which of these two aspects of τέλειος Matthew envisages in this passage. In this regard, it is important to note that Matthew compares (ὡς) the τέλειοι of the disciples in 5:48a to the τέλειος of "your heavenly Father" in 5:48b, which Matthew in turn links to the activity of "your Father who is in heaven" in 5:45. There in 5:45 Matthew presents the Father as doing that which results in the good or welfare of persons in general without regard to their righteousness or wickedness,

---

5. Frederick W. Danker, *A Greek-English Lexicon of the NT and Other Early Christian Literature*, 3rd ed. Revised and edited by Frederick William Danker. Based on Walter Bauer's *Griechisch-deutsches Wörterbuch zu den Schriften des Neuen Testaments und der frühchristlichen Literatur*, 6th ed. Kurt Aland and Barbara Aland (Chicago: University of Chicago Press, 2000), 995.

6. Joseph Henry Thayer, *Greek-English Lexicon of the NT: Coded with the numbering System from Strong's Exhaustive Concordance to the Bible* (Peabody, MA: Hendrickson, 1996), 618. See also *TDNT*, s.v. "Τελιος," by Gerhard Delling, 8:67–77.

which because he is the God of righteousness and the personal epitome of righteousness[7] indicates also that he acts for their good without regard to their attitude toward his person. The conclusion for the meaning of τέλειος in 5:48 is clear: Perfection involves actions that promote the good or welfare of *all* persons, irrespective of their righteousness or wickedness and without regard to the attitude of those persons toward the one who is perfect.

Moreover, Matthew connects this all-inclusive redemptive activity to the notion of universal love. Matthew makes this connection by linking 5:48 to Jesus' instructions in the antithesis of 5:43-45, where Jesus admonishes love to the enemy and the persecutor. Matthew forges this link between Jesus' commands in 5:44-45 and that of 5:48 through the (double) scenario of 5:46-47. Here the Matthean Jesus presents the inadequacy of a partial love (5:46) and a limited greeting (5:47) in contrast to the necessity of love towards all (including the enemy) in 5:43-45 on the one hand, and in contrast to the necessity of perfection in 5:48 on the other. Moreover, 5:46-47 supports both the admonitions in 5:44-45 (γάρ) and the demand of 5:48 (οὖν). Thus, 5:46-47 serves as the bridge connecting the two exhortations of Jesus in 5:43-48.[8] All of these considerations require the conclusion that the τέλειοι of Mt. 5:48a involves *completeness* in the scope of love, i.e., active

---

7. E.g., Matt 5:20; 6:33; 20:4; cf. 19:17.

8. These considerations, incidentally, point to the structural conclusion that 5:48 belongs primarily with 5:43-48, and does not encapsulate the teaching of all the antitheses in general throughout 5:21-47 in such a way as to separate it out from 5:43-47 specifically, as argued by some. See, e.g., Alan Hugh McNeile, *The Gospel according to St. Matthew: The Greek Text with Introduction, Notes, and Indices* (London: Macmillan, 1938), 73; Rudolf Schnackenburg, "Die Vollkommenheit des Christen nach den Evangelien," *GuL* 32 (1959), 424; Joachim Gnilka, *Das Matthäus-evangelium*, Herders theologischer Kommentar zum Neuen Testament (Freiburg: Herder, 1988), I:196; Jacques Dupont, "L'appel à imiter Dieu en Matthieu 5,48 et Luc 6,36," *RevB* 14 (1966), 154. Most recent commentators consider that 5:48 belongs primarily with 5:43-48 while also encapsulating the "I say to you" statements throughout 5:21-44; but typically they do not explicate precisely how this double functioning works. This view is accurate insofar as one recognizes that the discussion regarding love in 5:43-48 brings to a climax the preceding antitheses. A careful analysis of the antitheses reveals that Jesus' "I say to you" statements express the motive or attitude of relational redemptiveness, i.e., love. (The only exception may be the discussion regarding oaths in 5:33-37; but here Jesus appeals to the principle that the disciple's life is to accord with God's work in creation, which is picked up and developed in 5:44-45.) Thus, 5:48 stands as the climax to the climax and consequently relates directly to 5:43-48 and indirectly (through the "love-climax" function of 5:43-48) to the whole of 5:21-42. See, e.g., Craig S. Keener, *A Commentary on the Gospel of Matthew* (Grand Rapids: Eerdmans, 1999), 205; R. T. France, *The Gospel of Matthew*, New International Commentary on the NT (Grand Rapids: Eerdmans, 2007), 228; Peter Fiedler, *Das Matthäus-evangelium*, Theologischer Kommentar zum Neuen Testament (Stuttgart: Kohlhammer, 2006), 155.

well-wishing[9] over against the other major possibility for the meaning of τέλειος, viz., that of realizing the end or purpose. This latter concern plays no role at all in Matthew's understanding of perfection.[10]

But if the perfection of 5:48 involves completeness in terms of a comprehensive scope of love, and especially love towards enemies,[11] it is important to explore, at least briefly, the exact nature of the "enemies," and the meaning of "love" in Matthew's Gospel.

It is possible that Matthew envisions here primarily *religious* enemies, i.e., those whose animosity is actually directed toward Christians as an expression of the hostility these persons hold toward the God whom Christians worship and serve. Evidence exists for this conclusion. For one thing, the "neighbor" in the OT passage quoted in the antithesis of 5:43 (Lev 19:18) meant there "fellow Israelite" or fellow member of the covenant people of God, over against the heathen (enemies).[12] Thus, 5:43 suggests that the OT taught love towards the fellow member of the covenant community but hatred of the religious outsider. Moreover, in 5:44 the Matthean Jesus draws a parallel between the enemies of the disciples and "those who persecute [the disciples]," i.e., those who are outside of God's community, the church, and who abuse Christians for the sake of Christ (e.g., 5:11). Further, Matt 5:47 declares that it is entirely inadequate to limit greetings to the brother or sister, i.e., fellow member of the community of God (cf. 12:47; 18:15, 21), again suggesting that the issue is a perfection that overcomes religious enmity. In addition, the Gospel as a whole understands opposition primarily in religious over against personal terms (e.g., 9:35—11:1; 23:34–36; 24:1–51). Finally, the reference to "hate your enemies" in 5:43, a phrase that does not explicitly appear anywhere in the OT, is very possibly an allusion to Ps 139:22: "I hate them [God's enemies] with a perfect (LXX Ps 138:22: τέλειον) hatred; I count them as my enemies."[13] Thus, perfection

---

9. As described by James Moffatt throughout his monumental study, *Love in the NT* (London: Hodder and Stoughton, 1929).

10. Schnackenburg, "Vollkommenheit," 420.

11. For a rather complete survey of the history of interpretation up to 1982, see Guelich, *Sermon on the Mount*, 224–227.

12. W. D. Davies and Dale C. Allison, Jr., *A Critical and Exegetical Commentary on the Gospel according to Saint Matthew, Vol. 1, Introduction and Commentary on Matthew I–VII*, International Critical Commentary (Edinburgh: T. & T. Clark, 1988), 550.

13. Note that according to this OT passage righteousness is expressed through perfect hatred of the enemy of God. Thus, the Matthean Jesus insists that the presence of God's enemy calls forth not a perfect hatred but a perfect love on the part of the righteous one. For other views on the provenance of this statement on hatred, see, e.g., W. D. Davies, *The Setting of the Sermon on the Mount* (Cambridge: Cambridge University Press, 1966), 245–52. Davies himself thinks the statement reflects the influence of

in 5:48 might involve doing good to those who hate God and his Church, and who are actively attempting to destroy the work of God in the world.

But, on the other hand, it is possible that Matthew has primarily *personal* enemies in mind. Enemy (ἐχθρός) is often used in the NT, including Matthew (e.g., 13:28; cf. e.g., Lk. 6:27-31) of personal opponents. Further, Jesus talks about proper response towards personal enemies in 5:38-42, which leads directly to the climactic passage 5:43-48. Finally, Jesus commands that disciples are to do "more" than love those who love them (5:46), thus suggesting personal animosity on the part of others towards the disciples. Therefore, perfection in 5:48a might involve doing good to those who oppose disciples personally, not on the basis of their participation in God's community.

Yet it is unnecessary to force an absolute Either-Or between these two construals of the enemy. Indeed, the parallel construction in 5:46-47 suggests that both personal and religious animosity are involved in these enemies who are to be the recipients of perfect or complete love. Jesus' scenario in v. 46 involves personal enemies, while his scenario in v. 47 involves religious enemies. Thus, the perfection of 5:48 is comprehensive in terms of the type of enemy in view; it has to do with loving both personal and religious (God's) enemies.[14]

But what is the meaning of "love" in Matthew's Gospel? In the Gospel as a whole love is understood as that which produces good or welfare for others. Matthew describes it in terms of the "golden rule" (7:12), since the Matthean Jesus describes both the golden rule and the command to love the neighbor in the same terms: "this is the law and the prophets" (cf. 22:40). Indeed, for Matthew love is the fulfilling of the law and the prophets (22:37-40).[15] Hence, a complete love points to complete obedience to God's will and complete fulfilling of God's law.

Matthew's understanding of perfection as a comprehensive love that alone fulfills God's will suggests that such love is an essential component of discipleship, for obedience to God's will is the mark of discipleship in Matthew.[16] In addition, Matthew demonstrates the necessity of this "perfect love" for discipleship by linking perfection to sonship to God. We note that Matthew structures v. 48 according to a comparison between the perfection of disciples and that of *your heavenly Father*. And we note, too, that the

---

Qumran, which in my judgment is a highly unlikely possibility.

14. Thus also Keener, *A Commentary on the Gospel of Matthew*, 203.

15. See Richard Hays, *The Moral Vision of the NT: A Contemporary Introduction to NT Ethics* (San Francisco: Harper Collins, 1996), 101; and Victor Paul Furnish, *The Love Command in the NT* (Nashville: Abingdon, 1972), 30-34.

16. E.g., 5:17-20; 7:21-23; 12:46-50; 19:16-22; 21:28—22:14.

purpose of the command to love enemies and persecutors is, according to v. 45, "that you may be *sons* of your *Father* who is in heaven."[17] In Matthew, sonship of persons to God always indicates true discipleship and participation in the Kingdom; to be a son is to be a disciple and to participate in the Kingdom, not to be a son is to be excluded from the Kingdom (e.g., 12:50; 13:43; 21:31).

In fact, the structure of the segment 5:17-48 provides additional support for the absolute necessity of this perfection or comprehensive love for discipleship, and indeed for entering into the Kingdom both in its present, realized form, and in its final, consummated form.[18] It is most natural to take 5:17-20 as comprising general claims that Matthew develops or "spells out" in 5:21-48.[19] This movement from general to particular is manifestly the case with 5:20, since this verse speaks of the necessity of a "righteousness that exceeds that of the scribes and Pharisees" for entrance into the Kingdom; and this exceeding righteousness is given particular expression in the commands of Jesus in the antitheses of 5:21, 27, 31, 33, 38, 43, and in the climactic command of 5:48. Consequently, 5:48 is a specific expression of the "exceeding righteousness" that is necessary for entrance into the Kingdom. The connection between the perfection of 5:48 and the "exceeding righteousness" of 5:20 that is necessary for entrance into the Kingdom is further suggested by the link between the adjective περισσόν ("more") in 5:47 and the verbal form of the same word, περισσεύσῃ ("exceed"), in 5:20. According to 5:47 the failure to do "more" points to a fundamental inadequacy that can be met only by fulfilling the demand of 5:48 to be perfect. Obeying the command to be perfect, then, involves the doing of the "more" (περισσόν) and thereby practicing that "exceeding" (περισσεύσῃ) righteousness that is necessary for Kingdom participation.[20]

17. Often the NT indicates that sonship is constitutive of likeness: Because one is a son therefore he is like his father (e.g., John 1:18; 14:9; Heb 1:1-3; 1 John 3:1-10). In Matt 5:43-48 Jesus employs a converse logic, indicating that likeness is constitutive of sonship: If you are like the Father you are therefore sons of the Father.

18. In Matthew the language of entering into the Kingdom is used both of participating in the Kingdom as it has already come in the ministry of Jesus and of participating in the Kingdom in its final, consummated form. See 7:21; 18:3; 19:23; 23:14.

19. See Jack Dean Kingsbury, "The Place, Structure, and Meaning of the Sermon on the Mount," *Int* 41 (1987), 138-39; Davies and Allison, *Matthew I-VII*, 481, 501-502; Adolf Schlatter, *Der Evangelist Matthäus* (Stuttgart: Calwer, 1948), 151-165; Daniel J. Harrington, *The Gospel of Matthew* (Sacra Pagina; Collegeville, MN: Liturgical, 1991), 90-91; France, *The Gospel of Matthew*, 178-228.

20. The necessity of this perfection for discipleship implies, of course, its realization. Matthew will later indicate that its realization is made possible by the power of God (cf. 19:21 with 19:26). Schnackenburg, "Vollkommenheit," 421-423, points out that the realizability of perfection by the power of God was the view of perfection in

## The Significance of "You must be"

I mentioned above that the second issue in the interpretation of 5:48a, in addition to the meaning of the adjective τελειος, involves the inflection of the verb ἔσεσθε. Although most English translations render this verb as an imperative, it actually stands in the future active indicative. A general agreement exists among grammarians and commentators that we should take this verb as an "imperatival future."[21] The "imperatival future" refers to a use of the future tense in NT Greek in which the indicative is used with an imperatival sense, in distinction from the employment of the imperative mood.

There is less agreement about the *significance* of Matthew's use of this imperatival future. Many commentators assert that the future tense carries with it the promise of realization, i.e., Matthew employs the imperatival future to suggest that within this command there is an element of prediction that gives assurance that this command will be realized (through the power of God).[22] This interpretation is especially prominent among German

---

the OT, among the rabbis, and among the Qumran community. For a different perspective, see Paul Gaechter, *Das Matthäus Evangelium* (Innsbruck: Tyrolia, 1962), 198–99; and Donald Hagner, *Matthew 1–13*, Word Biblical Commentary (Dallas: Word, 1993), 136, who insists that "the perfection in view here is a goal toward which disciples are called to strive, but not one they will fully achieve in this life. The Christian will thus always have occasion to pray for the forgiveness of sins, as Jesus taught his disciples to pray (6:12)." Hagner's interpretation assumes that the comparison ("as") involves being perfect to the same degree as God is perfect over against being perfect in the same way that God is perfect, viz., by the practice of all-inclusive love. Matthew's insistence upon the requirement and thus the realizability of the fulfillment of this command implies that Matt 5:48 envisions the same kind of inclusive love, not the same (absolute) degree. Obviously, the perfection of disciples in analogy to the Father's perfection is not ontological (a matter of perfection of being), but modal (a matter of a mode of action, a way of behaving). See Paul Johannes du Plessis, ΤΕΛΕΙΟΣ: *The Idea of Perfection in the NT* (Kampen: Kok, 1959), 168–173.

21. H. E. Dana and Julius R. Mantey, *A Manual Grammar of the Greek NT* (New York: Macmillan, 1927), par. 178(3); A. T. Robertson, *A Grammar of the Greek NT in Light of Historical Research* (Nashville, Broadman, 1934), 874; F. Blass and A. Debrunner, *A Greek Grammar of the NT and other Early Christian Literature* (Chicago: University of Chicago Press, 1961), par. 362; Daniel B. Wallace, *Greek Grammar Beyond the Basics: An Exegetical Syntax of the NT* (Grand Rapids: Zondervan, 1996), 569–70. Wallace notes that the imperatival future is uncommon in the NT outside of Matthew. See also Keener, *A Commentary on the Gospel of Matthew*, 205; Hans Dieter Betz, *The Sermon on the Mount*, Hermeneia: A Critical and Historical Commentary on the Bible (Minneapolis: Fortress, 1995), 321.

22. See, e.g., Schlatter, *Der Evangelist Matthäus*, 197; Walter Grundmann, *Das Evangelium nach Matthäus* (Berlin: Evangelische Verlagsanthalt, 1981), 180; Alfred Plummer, *An Exegetical Commentary on the Gospel according to Saint Matthew* (London: Robert Scott, 1909), 88; Betz, *Sermon on the Mount*, 321.

commentators who often simply assert this meaning of the future without citation of evidence.

An examination of the actual use of the imperatival future in Matthew reveals, however, that the distinguishing feature of the imperatival future for Matthew lies elsewhere. Specifically, Matthew typically employs the imperatival future when he is quoting or alluding to an OT passage.[23] Thus, by using this form Matthew gives notice to the reader that he is quoting or alluding to an OT passage. This inflectional notification is important, because there is no OT passage that corresponds to the whole of 5:48. But Matthew is almost certainly *alluding* to Lev 19:2 ("You shall be holy, for I the Lord your God am holy"), which has the same structure and general sense as 5:48,[24] and combines this allusion to Lev 19:2 with a *quotation* of the brief phrase [ἔση] τέλειος ("you shall be perfect") from Deut 18:13. Matthew employs the imperatival future to alert the reader that he is alluding to OT passages, and thus to encourage the reader to think of Lev 19:2 and Deut 18:13.

The significance of this Matthean notification of intertextuality lies in its invitation to the reader to construe 5:48 in light of these two OT passages,[25] and especially Lev 19:2.

---

23. This significance of the imperatival future is clearly indicated in this segment, where we note the contrast within the antitheses between the imperatival future employed in the "you have heard that it was said" statements from the OT and the imperative mood in the "but I say to you" statements. But this use of the imperatival future is found throughout Matthew's Gospel; see, e.g., 19:18-19; 22:37-39. There may be a very few exceptions, a most notable exception being 6:5, where the very same word ἔσεσθε appears in a statement that is not taken from the OT. But the imperatival future in 6:5 is explained by the fact that Matthew might very well use the same form of the same word in 6:5 in order to link 6:5 with 5:48, suggesting that 6:5 is a negative counterpart to the positive command of 5:48. Although 5:48 belongs primarily with 5:17-47, the verses at the end of 5:17-48 (especially 5:45-47) are transitional to 6:1-18; note the connections between "your Father" in 5:45, 48 and the same phrase in 6:1, 4, 6, 14, 18, and the connection between "reward" in 5:46 and the same word in 6:1, 2, 5, 16. See John Nolland, *The Gospel of Matthew*, New International Greek Testament Commentary (Grand Rapids:Eerdmans, 2005), 270-71.

24. The command to be holy in Lev 19:2 was held both in Jewish tradition and in early Christianity (cf. 1 Peter 1:14-16) to be central to the godly life and to the self-identity of God's community. See Krister Stendahl, *The School of St. Matthew and its use of the OT* (Philadelphia: Fortress, 1968), 136-138; Schnackenburg, "Vollkommenheit," 424.

25. The implied reader of Matthew's Gospel knows the OT and is intended to consider the original wording and contexts of OT passages that Matthew quotes or references. See R. T. France, "The Formula-Quotations of Matthew 2 and the Problem of Communication," *NTS* 27 (1980/81), 233-51; Robert H. Gundry, *The Use of the OT in St. Matthew's Gospel with Special Reference to the Messianic Hope*, Supplements to Novum Testamentum (Leiden: Brill, 1967), 205-15; C. H. Dodd, *According to the Scriptures: The Sub-Structure of NT Theology* (London: Nisbet, 1952). For the purposes

A comparison between Matt 5:48 and its *Vorlage* reveals a number of editorial changes. For one thing, the "holy" (MT קְדֹשִׁים; LXX ἅγιοι) of Leviticus becomes the perfect (τέλειοι) of Matthew. This change suggests a Matthean emphasis upon τέλειοι and indicates that perfection, as elaborated in this context, is as central to the self-identity of the Christian community as holiness was for the self-identity of the people of Israel. Matthew seems to be attempting to define holiness here by perfection.[26] "Perfect" is thus the meaning of "holy" for the new eschatological community. That which makes the community distinct or separate (which is the essential meaning of holiness in the OT[27]) is perfection, i.e., all-inclusive love. Therefore, for the eschatological community of God, holiness is not to be construed in terms of personal distance or separation from the ungodly or those outside the community of faith. By defining holiness in terms of perfection, as delineated in this context, the Matthean Jesus is insisting that it is constituted by a profound commitment to active love towards the enemy and the outsider. It thus requires personal engagement. Holiness as perfection, then, must not be understood as relational separation ("with whom we associate") but rather as functional separation ("what we do/how we behave"). The very functional separation (or moral difference) of the eschatological community from the behavior patterns of those outside the community requires an intimate relational connection, a redemptive personal engagement. The life of those on the outside is not characterized by a deep, self-sacrificial love[28] that extends to the enemy and persecutor. The eschatological community is separate from the outsider precisely by being connected with the outsider through affective redemptive activity.

In addition, "the Lord your God" (MT יהוה אלהיכם; LXX κύριος ὁ κύριος ὁ θεὸς ὑμῶν) becomes "your heavenly Father" (ὁ πατὴρ ὑμῶν ὁ οὐράνιος), a change that emphasizes the comparison involved in the likeness implicit within the Father-Son language (cf. 5:45). This emphasis upon likeness is indicated by the change from "for" (MT כִּי; LXX ὅτι) of Leviticus to the correlative conjunction "as" (ὡς) here.[29] This change may suggest that the possibility and demand of this perfection comes from a new quality and

---

of our study of Matt 5:48 it is unnecessary to enter into the vexing problem of the text-form Matthew employs when quoting or alluding to OT passages; the changes Matthew introduces in 5:48 over against the original reading of Lev 19:2 apply to both the Hebrew and Septuagint texts. See Gundry, *Use of the OT*, 73–74.

26. Schnackenburg, "Vollkommenheit," 425.

27. See, e.g., *TDNT*, s.v. "Ἅγιός," by Otto Procksch; cf. Norman H. Snaith, *The Distinctive Ideas of the OT* (New York: Schocken, 1964), 20–50.

28. This anticipates our discussion of "perfect" in Matt 19:21.

29. Dupont, "L'appel," 140.

power that stems from the eschatological relationship of sonship to God through Jesus Messiah the Son of God.[30] In other words, it now involves not only submission to a God who demands, but a relationship with a Father that makes this kind of likeness possible. This consideration may suggest, then, that now is available a new possibility of likeness that was not realizable (or at least envisioned) in the passage from Leviticus.

Moreover, in the OT passage the emphatic "I" (MT אני; LXX ἐγώ) is used of God, while in Matthew the emphatic "you" (ὑμεῖς) is used of the hearers. This change suggests that in Matthew the emphasis is not upon the distinct character of Yahweh (as opposed to other gods in the Leviticus context), but upon the distinct character of the eschatological community as opposed to Gentiles, tax collectors (5:46–47), hypocrites (6:1–18), and scribes and Pharisees (5:20), all of whom stand outside the kingdom (5:17–20). It is arresting that Matthew implicitly but clearly lumps the scribes and Pharisees with Gentiles and tax collectors. The intended audience of Matthew would recognize that in terms of commitment to compliance with God's law the scribes and Pharisees existed at the opposite end of the spectrum from Gentiles and tax collectors. Like the Qumran community, the Pharisees tended to view perfection as flawless compliance to legal commandments.[31] But the Matthean Jesus has argued throughout 5:17–48 that fulfillment of God's will has nothing to do with legal compliance, and in fact that an attitude and behavior of compliance merely to the letter of the law will result in judgment (5:22a, 25) and hell (5:22c, 29–30). On the contrary, fulfillment of God's will involves transcendent and transformed[32] motivation of profound love that is expressed in a quality of behavior that does not simply go beyond what the letter of the law required but is of a different order than legal compliance. Thus, the whole notion of perfection before God is radically re-interpreted.

As mentioned above, 5:48a is dependent also upon Deut 18:13: "you shall be perfect before the Lord your God." The point of contact between

---

30. Note the correspondence throughout Matthew's Gospel between Jesus as υἱὸς τοῦ θεοῦ (1:21, 23, 25; 2:15; 3:17; 4:3, 6; 8:29; 11:27; 14:33; 16:16; 17:5; 21:37–38; 22:2; 24:36; 27:40, 43, 54) and disciples as υἱοὶ τοῦ θεοῦ (5:9, 45; 7:9; 9:15; 13:38; 17:25–26), and between God as Jesus' Father (7:21; 10:32–33; 11:25–27; 12:50; 15:13; 16:17, 27; 18:10, 14, 19, 35; 20:23; 24:36; 25:34, 41; 26:29, 39, 42, 53; 28:19) and God as the disciples' Father (5:16, 45, 48; 6:1, 4, 6, 8–9, 14, 18, 26, 32; 7:11; 10:20, 29; 13:43; 23:9). It is through discipleship to Jesus the Son of God, which involves doing the will of the Father, which makes it possible for persons to become sons of God (e.g., 12:46–50).

31. Keener, *A Commentary on the Gospel of Matthew*, 205; Emil Schürer, *The History of the Jewish People in the Age of Jesus Christ*, revised and edited by Geza Vermes, Fergus Millar, and Matthew Black, 4 vols. (Edinburgh: T. & T. Clark, 1979), II.381–404.

32. This anticipates our discussion of 19:21.

this statement and Mt. 5:48 is the phrase "you shall be perfect" (MT: תִּהְיֶה תָּמִים; LXX: τέλειος ἔσῃ; note that the Deuteronomy passage employs the singular form of the verb[33]). The command to be perfect here is placed within the context of admonitions to obey God's law and warnings against pagan practices. The emphasis is thus here, as also in Lev 19:2, upon a kind of existence towards God ("be") that expresses itself in the fulfilling of the law. This consideration suggests that "perfect" in Matt 5:48 involves the fulfilling of the law, a conclusion supported contextually by the overarching theme that pervades the whole of 5:17-48, viz., the disciples' relationship to the commandments of God. Matthew seems to have drawn this connection between perfection and the fulfilling of the law from the OT itself, for the OT employs perfection (both LXX τέλειος and MT תמים and לֵב) in the sense of a heart undivided towards God that leads to complete obedience to God's will (especially as expressed in the law).[34] Yet the OT understands this obedience to God's law not absolutely but rather dynamically and interpersonally. Thus, 1 Kgs 15:14 describes Asa's heart as perfect, although "the high places were not taken away" (as required by the law).[35] Asa was perfect towards God in terms of heart attitude, i.e., having a heart that was fully committed to God and to the obedience of God's will as expressed in the law of God, even though Asa's actual performance was not flawless.[36]

Before leaving this discussion of Matt 5:48 we should say a word regarding the parallel passage in Luke 6:36: "Be merciful (οἰκτίρμονες) even as your Father is merciful." The term Luke employs speaks to the motivation, or underlying attitude, of Christian love in contrast to inferior motives often at work in relationships with others (e.g., the desire to reciprocate [6:32-33], the hope to receive back or perhaps gain social standing in a client-patron environment [6:34]); Christian love stems rather from a profound sense of

---

33. The shift from the singular of Deut 18:13 to the plural here is explained by the desire to relate the command of 5:48a to that of 5:44, where the demand of Jesus stands in the plural (ἀγαπᾶτε) in contrast to the singular of what "you have heard" (ἀγαπήσεις and μισήσεις, v. 43). In the antitheses of 5:21-42 both the traditional injunction and Jesus' new demand are in the singular; only in 5:43-48 do we find the distinction between the singular of the traditional injunction and the plural of Jesus' new demand. This consideration reinforces the conclusion that 5:48 belongs primarily with 5:43-47.

34. *TDNT*, s.v. "Τέλιος," by Gerhard Delling, 8:67-77; Schnanckenburg, "Vollkommenheit," 426. See esp. the use of this idea in the Deuteronomic History, e.g., 2 Sam 22:26; 1 Kgs 8:61; 11:14; 15:3, 14; cf. also 1 Chron 28:9.

35. Deut 12:1-14; 17:14-29; cf. 2 Kgs 18:4; 23:4-20.

36. This example from Asa underscores a key distinction between the Greek understanding of perfection as virtue expressing absolute flawlessness over against the Hebrew understanding that expresses the dynamic concept of full or complete integrity of relationship. See esp. Schnackenburg, "Vollkommenheit," 420; Ulrich Luz, *Matthew 1-7: A Commentary* (Minneapolis: Augsburg, 1989), 346.

oneness with the other who is in need. Thus, the Lucan passage develops the attitudinal basis or motivation for all-inclusive love, while the Matthean version emphasizes the comprehensive character of a love that corresponds to God's own loving.

## PERFECTION ACCORDING TO MATTHEW 19:21

The word "perfect" (τέλειος) is used once more in this Gospel. In 19:21 Jesus says to the rich young man: "If you would be perfect, go sell what you possess and give to the poor, and you will have treasure in heaven, and come, follow me." The reader of Matthew's Gospel comes to this reference to τέλειος after encountering the concept at 5:48 and is expected to construe this reference in light of the earlier one.[37] This reference thus takes up the meaning of 5:48 and serves to develop and clarify that earlier occurrence. The following observations are relevant.

First, as in 5:48, τέλειος is again placed in the context of the command to love one's neighbor. The very presence of the command to love the neighbor in this passage is arresting, since Jesus here quotes the commands of the second tablet of the Decalogue, which deal with social responsibilities, omitting the tenth commandment (regarding coveting) and adding the love command, which of course did not belong to the Decalogue at all but appears rather in Lev 19:18. In a sense it is not surprising that the Matthean Jesus should bring these commands relating to social responsibilities to a climax with the law of love, since Jesus will affirm in 22:36-40 that upon the commands to love God and the neighbor hang "all the law and the prophets." Indeed, by bringing the antitheses in 5:17-48 to a climax with the demand to love others Jesus had already suggested that all of God's demands are fulfilled in the performance of love. All of these considerations underscore the consistent link Matthew forges between "perfection" and "love," and particularly between the fulfillment of God's law through love and the notion of perfection.

It is to be observed, however, that the command to love one's neighbor functions quite differently here in 19:16-22 than it did in 5:43-48. In Matt 5 the command to love the neighbor is cited as an example of the righteousness of the scribes and Pharisees and is thus judged to be wholly inadequate in the face of Jesus' admonition to love the enemy and the persecutor. The

---

37. The significance of the reader's process of construing later references in light of earlier ones ("primacy effect") is helpfully described by Meir Sternberg in *Expositional Modes & Temporal Ordering in Fiction* (Baltimore: The Johns Hopkins University Press, 1978), 102-104.

immediate context of 5:43-48 defines the "neighbor" as "those who love you" (v. 46) and as "your brother or sister" (v. 47). But Jesus' revelation in 5:43-48 of the will of God that lies behind the letter of the command to love the neighbor results in an expanded understanding of the "neighbor." After the expansion and clarification of "neighbor" that the Matthean Jesus offers in 5:43-48 subsequently in the Gospel of Matthew the "neighbor" is no longer restricted to those who love the disciple but includes now all those who are close, i.e., those to whom the disciple is able to express active well-wishing. The command to love the neighbor has thus been expanded in 5:43-48, and this expanded understanding of the neighbor is assumed in 19:16-23 as it will be assumed again in 22:36-40.

Second, from the context it is clear that this perfection is required for discipleship (19:21c), for eternal life (19:16), for entrance into the Kingdom (19:23), and for salvation (19:25). This passage, read carefully, indicates that this perfection is essential to discipleship and required of all Christians for entrance into the Kingdom of God both in its present realized and in its future consummated form, although the language here of "having eternal life" and "entering into life" suggests that the emphasis in this passage is upon participation in the future, consummated Kingdom.[38] This perfection is not, therefore, to be considered an "evangelical counsel," reserved for persons who wish to adopt a higher or more exalted spiritual path.[39]

---

38. Matthew consistently employs "eternal life" to refer to the blessings the righteous will receive on the Day of judgment; cf. 7:14; 18:8-9; 25:46. See Hagner, *Matthew 14-28*, 557.

39. This point is argued effectively by J. M. R. Tillard, "Le propos de pauvreté et l'exigence évangélique," *NRT* 100 (1978), 207-232, and represents the majority opinion of contemporary commentators; e.g., Luz, *Matthew 8-20*, 514, 519-20; Gnilka, *Das Matthäus-evangelium*, II:164-165; Sabourin, *L'Evangile saint Matthieu*, 255-256; John P. Meier, *The Vision of Matthew: Christ, Church and Morality in the First Gospel* (New York: Paulist, 1979), 140; France, *The Gospel of Matthew*, 736. Contra J. Galot, "Le fondement évangélique du voeu religieux de pauvreté" *Gregorianum* 56 (1975), 441-467; Erich Klostermann, *Das Matthäus-Evangelium*, Handbuch zum Neuen Testament, nr. 4 (Tübingen: Mohr, 1927), 159. The consideration that perfection seems to be a general, threshold requirement for discipleship in Matthew should not blind us to the fact that almost everywhere else in the NT τέλειος is employed in the sense of a higher level of the Christian life, i.e., a level of spiritual maturity not experienced by all Christians (see 1 Cor 2:6; 14:20; Eph 4:13; Phil 3:15; Col 1:28; 4:12; Heb 5:14; James 1:4, 17, 5; 3:2; 1 John 4:17-18). Incidentally, elsewhere in the NT this term is often connected to love, as in the Matthean passages. The use of "perfect" language in the rest of the NT thus relates well to John Wesley's doctrine of Christian perfection as a second, higher stage of the Christian life expressing a life driven by pure love; see esp. John Wesley, *A Plain Account of Christian Perfection* (London: Epworth, 1952; from the 6th ed., originally published in 1789).

Third, the "perfection" is to be achieved by this man through the selling of his possessions and the giving of all the proceeds to the poor. The reference to "treasure" (θησαυρός) in this passage (v. 21) forms a linguistic link to θησαυρός in 6:19-21: "Do not lay up for yourselves treasures on earth . . . but lay up for yourselves treasures in heaven . . . For where your treasure is, there will your heart be also."[40] Thus, treasure is linked to heart-commitment. As readers construe 19:21 in light of 6:21 they will recognize that Jesus is here suggesting that the ultimate motive of this man's life (his "heart") involved the acquiring of possessions for himself over against any *serious* concern for the welfare of others (serious in the sense of genuine cost). In his relation to possessions, which according to the Sermon on the Mount indicates heart attitude, he placed himself first over against others, and especially others in need. He thus fulfilled, "you shall love your neighbor as yourself" in terms of the letter of the commands in the second tablet of the Decalogue, i.e., in a manner similar to the "righteousness of the scribes and Pharisees" expressed in the "you have heard" statements of the antitheses of Matt 5:17-48, but not in terms of the spirit of the commands, which involves heart attitude and the fulfillment of the will of God that lies behind the letter of the commands[41] and that through an embracing of the motivation of love transcends the commands as legal ordinances.[42] Here, then, perfection involves an attitude of love (ἀγάπη) that sacrifices the luxuries, comforts, and prerogatives of the self for the sake of the needs of others. This consideration explains, incidentally, why the Matthean Jesus omits reference to the tenth commandment, that dealing with covetousness. Coveting expresses the desire to acquire for oneself, to grasp to own. We may infer that if Jesus had included the command regarding covetousness the man would not have been able to answer as he did: "all these I have observed from my youth."

Therefore, the statement in 19:21 confirms the close relationship between "perfect" and "love" and between "perfect" and the fulfillment of the law. It further suggests that "perfection" is required for participation in the

---

40. Nolland, *The Gospel of Matthew*, p. 792, helpfully notes that while 6:19-21 speaks of the accumulation of possessions 19:21 describes the disposal of possessions. In this and in other ways the two passages thus connect with and complement one another.

41. Hagner, *Matthew 14-28*, 558; Schnackenburg, "Vollkommenheit," 429; Gnilka, *Das Matthäus-evangelium*, II:164; Keener, p. 205.

42. The notion of the necessity of doing "more" than obedience of the commandments as legal ordinances observed without reference to the motivation of relational redemptiveness is found both in 5:43-48 where the term "more" explicitly appears (v. 47) and here in 19:21 with the question from the rich young man, "What do I still lack?" (v. 20).

Kingdom, for discipleship, for eternal life, and for salvation.[43] And it indicates, in addition, that the means of the accomplishment of this perfection is the power of God (19:25-26), which apparently is made accessible by receiving the proclamation of the Kingdom through repentance and faith (Matt 3:1-10; 4:17; 21:28-32),[44] and thus experiencing a spiritual transformation that the Gospel of Matthew describes in terms of a good tree that produces good fruit (3:7-10; 7:15-23; 12:33-37). Moreover, this "perfection" completes that which is lacking in the fulfillment of the law, especially the law of love.[45] In 19:21 "perfect" has to do with completeness in the *depth* and quality of love (attitude of genuine cost and sacrifice), even as "perfect" in 5:48a has to do with completeness in the *scope* of love. Moreover, Matt 5:48 and 19:21 complement one another by describing distinct challenges to the life of perfection. The challenge to perfection in 5:48 is external: hateful attitudes and actions on the part of others. But the challenge to perfection in 19:21 is internal: desire to find security in the accumulation of possessions, expressing a life centered on hoarding for the security of the self (which expresses a profound distrust in the goodness and power of God, 6:19-34) over against a sacrificial love for the neighbor.

## CONCLUSION

The basic meaning of perfection in Matthew is complete or whole. In Matt 5:48 it indicates a completeness or wholeness in the scope of love. It appears in connection with the command of Jesus in 5:44: "you must love your enemies and pray for those who persecute you." Thus, "perfect love" stands

---

43. We should emphasize again that we are referring here only to the way in which Matthew employs the concept of perfection. A survey of τέλειος in the rest of the NT indicates that all of the other NT writers employ it in the sense of an advanced level of spiritual maturity. According to the rest of the NT it is possible to be a fully converted Christian and a true disciple while not yet being τέλειος. See note 39 above.

44. Davies, *The Setting of the Sermon on the Mount*, 94-95; Schlatter, *Der evangelist Matthäus*, 197.

45. The emphasis in our interpretation upon the connection between perfection and self-sacrificial love does not exclude another connection that Matthew makes in this passage, viz., the connection between perfection and the necessity to do away with all obstacles to discipleship, esp. the love of money. This necessity of putting aside all rival commitments to God and Christ is made by Matthew on several occasions, e.g., 10:38; 13:44-50; 16:24-28. But many commentators wrongly reduce the existential challenge of the rich young man to love of money in the face of the necessity of surrendering the whole life to God and ignore the importance of the admonition to give to the poor as an expression of love towards the neighbor. See, e.g., Hagner, *Matthew 14-28*, 558-59; Schnackenburg, "Vollkommenheit," 430.

over against the letter of the OT law (as Matthew understands it). No longer is love discriminating on the basis of racial/ethnic, religious, or personal attitudes; love finds motivation not in the prior attitude of the other, but in God's attitude towards all (5:45). Desire for sonship (i.e., to be like the Father and to participate in the Father's eschatological salvation) is the motivation for this perfection (5:45; cf. 5:48b). Moreover, since 5:43–48 climaxes this section that deals with the necessity for the disciples to fulfill God's law, and since love is the fulfilling of the law for Matthew (22:37–40), and since "perfect" relates both structurally and conceptually to the "exceeding righteousness" of 5:20, and since "perfect" had the meaning in the OT of being undivided towards God in the obedience to God's commands, "perfect" may involve also the attitude towards God that is undivided in compliance to God's will. Thus, "perfect" indicates not only complete love (in terms of inclusive scope), but also complete conformity to God's will expressed in Jesus' authoritative agapocentric (i.e., love-centered) interpretation of the law.

Perfection in 19:21 builds upon and complements the notion of perfection in 5:48. It reinforces the notion that perfection relates primarily to the love command and makes explicit the claim that perfection fulfills the commands of the law. Moreover, insofar as 19:21 links perfection positively with love towards the neighbor this second reference to perfection participates in the development throughout the Gospel of the Matthean notion of love towards the neighbor, from the negative appraisal of the moral inadequacy of love towards the neighbor in 5:43–48 to the central role of love towards the neighbor in the fulfilling of the entirety of the divine will in 22:36–40. Further, 19:21 expands upon the necessity of perfection for all disciples, a necessity that was suggested in 5:48 through the structure of the paragraph (5:43–48) and the segment (5:17–48); but 19:21 makes the requisite character of perfection more explicit and specific. In addition, 19:21 describes a challenge to the life of perfection beyond the challenge Matthew presented in 5:48. In 5:48 the life of perfection struggles against the negative and hateful attitudes of certain other persons; in 19:21 perfection is challenged by the desire to find security in the accumulation of possessions, expressing a life centered on love of self versus sacrificial love of neighbor. Moreover, 19:21 in its context addresses explicitly the existential dialectic of perfection in that it acknowledges the human impossibility of perfection but at the same time promises effective divine assistance. Perfection is thus a matter of God's gracious empowerment that comes through acceptance of the call of the gospel in the face of the moral impotence of humans who on the basis of their own power would find such perfection impossible to fulfill. Finally, 19:21 develops the notion of perfection as completeness of love in a way different from, and yet complementary to, that of 5:48. Whereas 5:48

describes perfection in terms of the *inclusive scope* of love, 19:21 presents perfection in terms of *profound depth* of love that leads necessarily to personal sacrifice, especially in the presence of need.

# 2

# Text as Witness
*The Surprising Conjunction of Jewish and Greco-Roman Rhetoric in Mark 12:1–37*

JUDITH ODOR

## ACROSS THE CULTURAL DIVIDE: QUOTATION IN MARK 12

AT FIRST GLANCE, MARK 12:1–37 presents a set of fairly straightforward examples of midrashic rhetoric. In this series of encounters, Jesus maneuvers various tests put to him by the religious opposition, each time coming out ahead by means of some very creative midrash. However, it should not be forgotten that this glimpse of Jewish rhetoric is also part of a carefully compiled and arranged selection in a Gospel generally thought of as Gentile, even Roman. Thus the series of vignettes offers an unusual opportunity to examine how an argument fundamentally Jewish in content and strategy becomes co-opted, as it were, with no explanation or interpretive helps, into a Gentile milieu and Greco-Roman rhetorical schema—and this with every apparent expectation of recognition and understanding on the part of the audience!

While such a cultural transplant could simply be labeled unfortunate or a demonstration of the Evangelist's lack of skill, the careful placement of these encounters and their climactic movement suggests otherwise. Instead of carelessness or lack of skill, the text is instead an excellent example of the author taking full advantage of a surprising overlap between Jewish and Greco-Roman rhetoric: their treatment of texts as witnesses. In fact, the principles and strategies employed by each rhetorical system echo again in the other, leaving the texts of Mark 12 transcendently free to witness to king and kingdom across the cultural divide.

## READING STRATEGIES

Before becoming immersed in questions of rhetoric and trajectories of influence, it is imperative to situate the text itself appropriately. Narrative accounts in the NT carry the unusual distinction of holding in tension two contexts within themselves: first, that of the original, historical event itself, and second, that of the literary presentation (including the author, audience, and the context of writing). This facet of historical narrative should not be overlooked, as the gap between the two contexts is frequently quite eloquent and may carry significant implications for one's reading of either context. There is value in assessing the text as both event and as literary product, and in allowing these two perspectives to speak into one's understanding not simply of the text but also of the internal and external forces that have shaped event and text. This is especially true for studies of the Gospels, since the cultural and thus the rhetorical context of the events themselves were quite different from the cultural context of the audience (here one thinks particularly of the Gospels of Luke and John, for example). For this reason, choosing a reading strategy that embraces both the cultural context of the events and of the literary work is significant.

### Context of the Event

When it comes to the study of the Gospels, there is no issue that implicates one's reading strategies of both the events and their literary presentation more than the question of genre. The 1992 publication of Richard Burridge's thesis on the genre of the Gospels provided definitive arguments and proofs that the Gospels were composed as and would have been considered by their original audiences to be ancient biography, or βίοι.[1] Reading the Gospels as

---

1. Richard A. Burridge, *What Are the Gospels? A Comparison with Graeco-Roman*

βίοι indicates that we may expect a high degree of historical accuracy—according to ancient biographical literary conventions—in Mark's accounts.[2] While Greco-Roman literary conventions allow the author to be creative in how he presented the Gospel, this creativity would have been limited to such issues as style, arrangement, and amplification according to the convention set out in the *progymnasmata*. Inventing events was considered entirely inappropriate in a historical work (Lucian, *Hist.* 24–25), and given the strong tradition of disciples memorizing and passing on the sayings of their teachers (Philostratus, *Vit. Soph.* 1.22.524; Seneca, *Ep. Lucil.* 108.6),[3] it is entirely appropriate to consider that the events and essential argumentation of the Mark 12 vignettes are historically accurate.[4] With this in mind we are free to read the events as occurring fundamentally as they are presented in Mark's Gospel.

Reading these accounts historically also carries implications for the players of the dramas. The Gospel presents Jesus' debate partners as directly connected to or commissioned by Temple leadership (11:27). This context strongly suggests that they may be assumed to be highly educated, being sent as representatives of the religious leaders and socially elite to test Jesus in his interpretation of Hebrew Scripture. The original context of the events of Mark 12, then, is Judean Judaism and the religious educated elite, though mention of the chief priests and Sadducees (Mark 11:27; 12:18) also indicates that these were the socially elite as well. Reading these debates according to the context of the event, then, suggests reading both the challenges and Jesus' responses in light of Jewish rhetorical stratagems.

## Literary Context

The cultural context of Mark's Gospel as a literary product is a somewhat different issue. In order to determine the context of the Gospel, one must answer the questions of who the audience is and when and where the audience may be located. Two preliminary points must be addressed prior to diving into a discussion about Mark's audience. First, regardless of the text, an author must have an audience in mind; thus it may be assumed that the

---

*Biography* (New York: Cambridge University, 1992). See also Craig Keener, *The Historical Jesus of the Gospels* (Grand Rapids: Wm. B. Eerdmans, 2012), 73–84.

2. Craig Keener, *The Historical Jesus of the Gospels* (Grand Rapids: Wm. B. Eerdmans, 2012), 79–84.

3. See also Keener, *Historical Jesus*, 147–150.

4. Keener, *Historical Jesus*, 73–84.

Second Evangelist also wrote to a particular audience. Second, this audience may or may not have comprised a specific community.

It must be recognized that the term "community" is fundamentally misleading, for its inherent ambiguity masks whether this community may be a single church of a few dozen, a community of churches of a few hundred followers, or a city-wide community comprised of many smaller churches and reflecting a wide variety of social, economic, ethnic, and religious backgrounds. For the purposes of this study, then, the term "community" will be avoided in favor of the realistic recognition that a text may be written for a specific, small audience, yet with much larger eventual audience in mind.[5]

In other words, Mark's Gospel may have been written for the immediate benefit of a small church or group of churches, yet the author may have—and in light of the established tendency of Paul's letters to be copied and distributed throughout the known world—written his Gospel with the larger church in mind.

## When was Mark's audience?

Determining the date of Mark's Gospel—and thus his audience—as accurately as possible calls for heavy reliance on the historical records of the early church. According to Papias (as recorded by Eusebius), Mark's Gospel is a creative arrangement of stories and sayings recounted by Peter (Eusebius, *Hist. Eccl.* 3.9). The reliance on and preference given in the first century to verbal eyewitness testimony,[6] though, begs the question of why Mark would decide to record Peter's testimony, effectively removing the original voice one step further from the audience. Given this cultural preference, it is quite possible that Peter's own death may have motivated Mark to commit to text a significant voice that had fallen silent. Church tradition places Peter's death in Rome in the 60s during Nero's infamous rule (Eusebius, *Ecc. Hist.* 3.1), situating the Gospel of Mark at some point in the mid-to-late 60s,[7] although some scholars prefer a later date after 70 CE due to the apocalyptic imagery found in Mark 13.[8]

---

5. Richard Bauckham, *The Gospels for All Christians: Rethinking the Gospel Audiences* (Grand Rapids: Wm. B. Eerdmans, 1988), 28–30. See also Marcus, *Mark 1–8*, 28.

6. Richard Bauckham, *Jesus and the Eyewitnesses: The Gospels as Eyewitness Testimony* (Grand Rapids: Wm. B. Eermans, 2006), 22–30.

7. Ben Witherington III, *The Gospel of Mark: A Socio-Rhetorical Commentary* (Grand Rapids: Wm B. Eerdmans, 2001), 31.

8. So Joel Marcus, *Mark 1–8: A New Translation with Introduction and Commentary*, (YAB 27; New York: Doubleday, 2000), 38–39, although Robert Stein considers that dating the Gospel by Mark 13 is a moot point since the Gospel was written to a Roman

## Where was Mark's audience?

This particular aspect of the Gospel's audience has been the subject of significant debate over the past century of scholastic interaction. The discussion has centered on whether Mark's immediate audience was located in Syria or in Rome. Arguments for a Syrian provenance or audience have centered on the underlying Semiticisms of the Gospel, the gratuitous details that are uniquely characteristic of Markan versions of Synoptic narratives,[9] and the apparent references in Mark 13 to the destruction of the Temple.[10] However, a general consensus has been building over the past generation of scholarship that both the provenance and audience of Mark's Gospel is Rome, precisely as the early church historians relate.[11]

As noted above, the Gospel's emphasis on persecution fits the Roman atmosphere of the 60s quite well. Also, the Latinisms scattered throughout the text strongly imply a Latin audience (e.g., 4.21; 6:27; 7:4; 12:14, 15; 15:15, 16, 39), as do translations of coin values into Roman currency (12:42).[12] In addition, arguments based on Mark's gratuitous detail speak for the provenance of the stories themselves, not necessarily the provenance of the text.[13]

Brian Incigneri also argues that the significance of cities in Mark's Gospel as well as the idealization of country life—which was was common social theme in Roman literature—are both frequently overlooked markers indicating a Gospel tailored to a Roman audience.[14] Finally, Clement of Alexandria provides a tantalizing witness to a tradition that describes the impetus for writing the Gospel:

> When Peter was openly preaching the Gospel in Rome, in front of certain imperial *equites*, and furnishing for them many testimonies of Christ, Mark, a follower of Peter, having been petitioned by these men . . . wrote the Gospel called "According to Mark" from the things which were spoken by Peter.[15]

---

audience and not to a Palestinian Jewish community; see Robert H. Stein, *Mark*, Baker Exegetical Commentary on the NT (Grand Rapids: Baker Academic, 2008), 14–15.

9. Brian J. Incigneri, *The Gospel ot the Romans: The Setting and Rhetoric of Mark's Gospel* (Leiden: Brill, 2003), 65–69, 96–97.

10. Marcus, *Mark 1–8*, 38–39; Incigneri, *Romans*, 116–127.

11. Witherington, *Mark*, 26–28; Incigneri, *Romans*, 96–107; Stein, *Mark*, 11–12; Marcus, *Mark 1–8*, 33–37.

12. Stein, *Mark*, 11–12; Incigneri, *Romans*, 98.

13. Incigneri, *Romans*, 65–69.

14. Incigneri, *Romans*, 70–77.

15. Michael Peppard, *The Son of God in the Roman World: Divine Sonship in its*

While the accuracy of this tradition is impossible to fully ascertain, it speaks strongly for a consistent tradition of the Roman provenance and audience of the Gospel. This consistent tradition and the in-text features briefly discussed above together present a compelling argument in favor of Mark's Roman audience.

### What might Mark's audience have known about Judaism and the Hebrew Scriptures?

The question of the rhetoric found in Mark 12 rises directly out of considerations of his audience. After all, if Mark wrote to a predominantly Gentile audience, then the Jewish themes, references, and Scripture quotations beg the question of his audience's level of competence with the Jewish culture and Jewish Scriptures. Clearly Mark does not expect his audience to understand Aramaic, since he translates every instance of the language in his Gospel. In addition, he expects his audience to be ignorant of purity practices of first-century Palestinian Jews.[16] However, he references and quotes the Hebrew Scriptures without explanation and frequently without introduction, indicating that his original audience is quite familiar not only with Torah (12:29–30) but also with the Prophets (1:2–3) and the Writings (12:36).

Mark's assumption of their knowledge of the Hebrew Scriptures reflects NT evidence, which suggests that these gatherings may have been modeled after synagogue meetings, with teaching (Acts 20:7; 1 Cor 14:19, 29–36; Col 3:16), reading of Scripture (Jas 1:22; Col 4:16; 1 Thess 5:27; Acts 13:15), prayer (1 Cor 11:4–5; 14:14, 16), singing (Eph 5:14, 19–20; Heb 13:15; Col 3:16; 1 Tim 3:16), baptism as appropriate (Acts 2:41), the Lord's Supper (1 Cor 11:18–34), and almsgiving (1 Cor 16:1–2).[17] Obviously pertinent to this study is the reading of Scripture, which would include selected texts from the Hebrew Scriptures.

---

*Social and Political Context* (New York: Oxford University, 2011), 89–90. The excerpt is translated from Clement, *Adumbrationes* (Fragment 24, by Otto Stahlin, GCS 17:206 = Aland, *Synopsis*, 555 = Berol. Phill. 1665).

16. E.g., washing hands (Mark 7:3–4); although it must be noted that many consider Mark to have made a mistake here in that not all Jews washed their hands as Mark records. However, this may be a good example of the use of metonymy, especially with a view toward simplifying a complex situation for an audience unfamiliar with its cultural nuances. See also Witherington, *Mark*, 224.

17. Paul seems to describe the Lord's Supper as the focal point of a gathering (1 Cor 10:16–17; 11:20–29), but later describes a gathering that involves prophecy and interpretation (1 Cor 14:1–33); these may have been two aspects or events of a typical gathering.

In light of the evidence, then, even Gentile believers in predominantly Gentile churches would be familiar with the Hebrew Scriptures, and would quite likely be especially familiar with those sections affirmed by Jesus or significant to the Christian movement (Justin Martyr, *1 Apol.* 65, 67). Given the early church's tendency to read the OT in light of and as pointing toward Christ, those passages that appear to speak directly to Jesus' person, role, and ministry would be not only beloved but also function as especially authoritative witnesses affirming Christ and the faith of the church.

## QUOTATION IN JEWISH AND HELLENISTIC RHETORICAL TRADITIONS

As noted above, tracing the use of OT texts and their role in the rhetorical impact of the events and vignettes of Mark 12 must be accomplished according to the dual nature of the text: what the Gospel's audience would expect and understand (that is, against the backdrop of Hellenistic literature and what conventions guide and provide meaning for the use of quotation in a given text) and what Jesus' original audience would expect and understand (that is, against the backdrop of Jewish literature and what conventions guide and provide meaning for the use of quotation in a Jewish cultural context).

### Jesus and His Jewish Rhetorical Context

The task of reading Gospel events within their original Palestinian rhetorical context is somewhat complicated due to the lack of anything quite as handy as an extant first-century Jewish *progymnasmata*. Instead, one must search for rhetorical parallels in literature written prior to, within, or after the first century. Furthermore, given that the focus of this study is the rhetoric of Mark 12, there is no need to catapult ourselves directly into the whole of Jewish rhetoric and hermeneutics.

Instead, it is far more strategic (not to mention feasible!) to limit our exploration to the specific form of debate evidenced in these events. Although the responses vary in form—Mark 12:1–12 is a parable, 12:13–27 is halakhic in nature,[18] and 12:28–37 is closer to haggadah[19]—each story dem-

---

18. That is, being more concerned with appropriate interpretation of commandments; see Peter J. Tomson, Supp. to the *Journal for the Study of Judaism* 136 (Leiden: Brill, 2010), 140.

19. That is, being more concerned with exegesis of a particular text of the Hebrew Scriptures without focusing on the Law; see Michael Fishbane, *Biblical Interpretation in*

onstrates the same pattern: Jesus responds to his questioners and quotes Hebrew Scripture as the crux of his argument in the spirit of a proof or authoritative resolution to the debate.[20]

As regards literature written prior to the first century, neither the rhetoric of the OT nor that of the sages suggests the type of questioning and debate found in Mark's account. Yet while the OT does not record this particular style of debate, it does evidence significant inner-biblical exegesis[21] and "self-referential allusions."[22] This intertextuality demonstrates a long-standing hermeneutic of using Scripture to interpret Scripture, which is at heart precisely what Jesus is recorded doing. The additional elements of a Scripture quotation serving as the authoritative voice resolving a debate— especially a debate centered on proper interpretation of the OT—must derive from elsewhere.

Surprisingly, *elsewhere* does not seem to include either the Second Temple wisdom literature (written by the sages, the forerunners of the rabbis) or the Qumran manuscripts (whose authors used Scripture to affirm their vision of reality but not, it would seem, to serve as authoritative voices to conclusively establish their interpretation of religious law). Instead, this rhetorical use of quotation emerges much later, in rabbinic literature.[23]

As we turn to rabbinic literature it is critical to recognize that as we move from the Hebrew Scriptures to rabbinic literature, we encounter the trajectory of a developing rhetoric that itself moves through the sages and the early rabbis.[24] Furthermore, considering rabbinic parallels allows us to

---

*Ancient Israel* (Oxford: Oxford University Press, 1988), 281-283.

20. For a midrashic approach to these texts that underscores the use of Scripture in proving arguments, see Dale Miller and Patricia Miller, *The Gospel of Mark as Midrash on Earlier Jewish and NT Literature*, Studies in the Bible and Early Christianity 21 (Lewiston, N.Y.: Edwin Mellen, 1990), 278-292.

21. Michael Fishbane's analysis of ancient Jewish hermeneutics and intertextuality is especially illuminating here; Fishbane, *Biblical Interpretation*, especially 281-291.

22. Lyle Eslinger, "Inner-Biblical Exegesis and Inner-Biblical Allusion: The Question of Category," *Vetus Testamentum* 42:1 (Jan 1992): 47-58, 47.

23. Though the rabbinic literature extant today was actually written down a century (or more, depending on the text) after the first century, many of its traditions are of much earlier provenance; see Günter Stemberger, "Dating Rabbinic Traditions," pp. 79-96 in *The NT and Rabbinic Literature*, edited by Reimund Bieringer, Florentino Garcia Martinez, Didier Pollefeyt, and Peter J. Tomson, Supp. to the *Journal for the Study of Judaism* 136 (Leiden: Brill, 2010).

24. Seeing as we encounter Jesus at the midpoint between Hillel and the Patriarch, this concept of a trajectory also suggests that just as studying early rabbinical thought may bring enrich our understanding of Jesus and his teaching, so also may Jesus and his teaching in turn enrich our understanding of the development of Jewish rhetoric that we see come fully into its own in the later rabbinic literature. See Peter J. Tomson,

discern whether Jesus was anomalous in his argumentation or if both its form and function would have been familiar to his Jewish audience.

As it happens, there is no shortage of rabbinic parallels. For example, in his description of a sage, ben Zoma appeals to multiple OT texts precisely as Jesus does: as authoritative proofs not simply supporting but serving as final voices resolving the argument he makes (*Abot* 4:1). Likewise, Rabbi Joshua is recorded quoting Abraham's hospitality to guests (Gen 18:8) as a type defending Gamaliel's parallel generosity in serving his fellow rabbis at a banquet (*Bavli tractate Qiddushin 32b*). Also in *Qiddushin*, Rabbi Eliezer bar Sadoq quotes Job 8:7 to witness to his argument for the future flourishing of the righteous (*Bavli tractate Qiddushin 40b*). These argument types are fairly common in the tractates and, regardless of their date, bear witness themselves to the completion of the rhetorical trajectory that we find in process in the Gospel accounts.[25]

Thus Jesus' strategy is demonstrably in line with what we can determine regarding the development of Jewish rhetoric. This suggests that Jesus expected his audience to be familiar with his approach and to understand not just what he was saying but also what he was doing rhetorically. Yet the question remains: precisely what *was* Jesus doing in these debates? The bare minimum we may determine is obvious: these quotes, provided from an authoritative source, are given as incontrovertible proof of the validity of Jesus' argument.[26] The impact of the series of vignettes is also fairly straightforward: Jesus wins each debate, leaving his opposition stymied and humiliated.[27] These are, however, common-sense readings of the text and, while true, they are not exactly rooted in our understanding of first-century

---

"Halakhah in the NT: A Research Overview," pp. 135-206 in *The NT and Rabbinic Literature*, 190.

25. The study of Jewish rhetoric is hampered by the lack of Second Temple literature recording halakhic and haggadic debates. In addition, there is great need for a proper assessment of the extant literature to discern the full story of the development and movement of Jewish rhetoric during the Second Temple period. However, Richard Hidary provides an excellent analysis of classical rhetoric at work in the *sugyas* of Yerushalmi Berakhot; see Richard Hidary, "Classical Rhetorical Arrangement and Reasoning in the Talmud: The Case of Yerushalmi Berakhot 1:1," *AJS Review* 34:1 (April 2010): 33-64. His article was later expanded into a discussion of how Hillel's rules of interpretation intersect and, in fact, overlap with Cicero's rules of τοποι; see Richard Hidary, "Talmudic Topoi: The Hermeneutical Methods of Midrash and Greco-Roman Rhetoric," Paper presented at the 17th International Conference of the Jewish Law Association. New Haven, Conn. July 31, 2012.

26. Adela Yarbro Collins, *Mark: A Commentary*, Hermeneia (Minneapolis: Fortress Press, 2007), 563-64, 581; Stein, *Mark*, 555; Joel Marcus, *Mark 8-16* (N.Y.: Yale University, 2009), 831.

27. Witherington, *Mark*, 318-36.

Jewish rhetoric. The most that may be said is that Jesus stood firmly within the trajectory of developing Jewish rhetoric and wielded it well enough to soundly trounce all comers. Granted, this is Mark's account, but the schoolyard ambiance is not too far from the tone of his presentation.

As a final assessment of Jewish rhetorical use of quotations, this is less than robust, especially given that the abrupt introduction of Scripture in Jesus' response seems to indicate a shift in tone, an added dimension in this legal argumentation that is completely absent from the above analysis. The role of quotation as authoritative voice is undeniable, yet does this voice affirm the speaker or the argument, or both? Might it function more precisely as a sort of proof in a forensic debate or, from a different perspective, as an authoritative witness for a legal case? Without a thorough plotting of the rhetorical trajectory of Second Temple Judaism, these remain intriguing questions.

Yet as noted above, each text has two natures: the original event with its context, and the written text with its own context. Perhaps an analysis of the rhetoric of the text in its Greco-Roman context may shed some light—or at least provide some further thoughts—on Jesus' Jewish rhetoric. While it is highly unlikely that Hellenistic rhetoric was influenced by Jewish rhetoric, the reverse is contrarily quite possible, and even probable.[28] It is time to consider the relationship of Jewish and classical rhetoric more thoroughly, especially regarding the conjunction of the two in the Gospels.[29]

## The Rhetoric of Quotation in Hellenistic Literature

However, we must first examine the role of quotation in classical rhetoric before we may compare these two rhetorical systems. Assessing the mechanics of quotation in Hellenistic literature is an important step toward understanding the role it may take in Greco-Roman and, by extension, NT texts. First, a comparison between the two enables the modern reader to

---

28. Hidary's assessment of the Yerushalmi Berakhot reveals a concept of text echoing that of Cicero in his *De Inventione* 2.45–49. At the risk of oversimplification, the use of text in an argument is determined by its usefulness to the argument. The hermeneutic that the speaker applies to the text varies from literal to nonliteral according to the usefulness of the resulting interpretation. As for Cicero, texts serve as witnesses to the rabbi's argument. See Hidary, "Classical Rhetorical Arrangement," 57–9. See also Hidary, "Talmudic Topoi."

29. For an excellent treatment of Jewish and classical rhetoric at work in the OT quotations in Paul's letters, see Christopher Stanley, *Paul and the Language of Scripture: Citation Technique in the Pauline Epistles and Contemporary Literature* (New York: Cambridge University, 1992).

determine how well NT quotations fit Hellenistic conventions, and thus whether Greco-Roman literature truly is the appropriate context out of which to read these pericopes. Second, the ways in which NT quotations follow or challenge these conventions are clues to why an author chose a particular quotation and what he intends to communicate by its use.

### How did Hellenistic authors quote literary texts?

In his examination of literary conventions governing quotation in the first century, Christopher Stanley analyzes the citation practices of several representative first-century authors. The citations he focuses on are citations of Homer, since Homer was by far the most significant author in the Greco-Roman literary world, being significant not just because of his skill but by virtue of the fact that his *Iliad* and *Odyssey* became the cultural, spiritual, and literary cornerstone of the Hellenistic world. In fact, John Barton compares the Greco-Roman treatment of Homer to Jewish halakhic readings of Hebrew Scripture, both in method and in reverence.[30] Stanley's conclusions, then, carry significant implications for any study of quotation in the NT.

In terms of sheer mechanics, Stanley observed that the language of the quotation may be altered grammatically to make it fit the surrounding text. In addition, unclear grammar (e.g., antecedents noted but not included in the quotation) would be clarified, and "words, lines, or phrases felt to be redundant or irrelevant to the later author's purposes"[31] could be omitted. Such omissions, however, "give the impression of having been carefully crafted so as to produce a smooth-flowing literary unit able to stand on its own as an acceptable 'citation' within the later author's text."[32] These omissions also served to highlight the portions of the original text deemed most relevant by the author and avoid confusion or distraction on the part of the reader.

This is the extent of the omissions Stanley observed in citations; since he also notes that "clear instances of additions to the text for whatever reasons are almost entirely undocumented," this indicates an extremely high degree of faithfulness to the original text.[33] In other words, while ancient

---

30. John Barton, *Oracles of God: Perceptions of Ancient Prophecy in Israel after the Exile* (London: Darton, Longman and Todd, 1986), 170.

31. Christopher D. Stanley, "Paul and Homer: Greco-Roman Citation Practice in the First Century CE" *Novum Testamentum* XXXXII, 1 (1990): 48–78; 75.

32. Stanley, "Paul and Homer," 76.

33. Ibid. Altering the quotation simply to nuance the text toward the later author's interpretation was apparently not considered conventional practice, and may be found only in highly biased texts; Stanley names Heraclitus, Crates, Zeno, and Plutarch (only

conventions of citation may not reflect modern concerns regarding exact duplication, Stanley discovered that the representative authors he examined demonstrated a high regard for the original text, and this high regard translated into careful adherence to the original message and deliberate retention of links to the original context.

Another phenomenon may be seen in Hellenistic literature that is not necessarily identified as an alteration to the original text. Combined or conflated texts, while not as common as minor omissions, may also be found. Each single quotation unit within the combination or conflation follows the conventions established above for grammatical fit and omissions as well as faithfulness to the original wordings. In addition, after careful analysis of these unusual quotations, Stanley concludes that "far from pointing to occasional lapses in memory, the instances studied here seemed to reflect a high degree of literary artistry and to operate in direct subservience to the later author's literary purposes."[34] Thus an unusual use of quotation indicates a unique opportunity to see into the author's mind and discern the rhetorical import and trajectory of his text.

Finally, Stanley observed "a high degree of faithfulness to the original narrative context," indicating that these quotations of Homer were very rarely taken out of context.[35] In fact, the original context of these citations served as the rhetorical backdrop of the later text, providing an interpretive guide and reinforcing the rhetorical movement of the later work. In these instances, some functional aspects of the quotation were easily observable: most of these quotations illustrated the later author's point, while many served as an appeal to authority, adding to the rhetorical force of the argument. Symbolic readings of the original text, which were comparatively few, demonstrated an inductive inference of general principle from the specifics of the original text, extending the original judgment or argument to a new context, or resignifying the original text by placing it within a new context of "the later author's own literary agenda."[36]

These last observations edge into discussions of the purpose and function of quotation in Hellenistic literature, but provide an excellent

---

occasionally). In terms of which "original text" of Homer was used, Stanley discovered that "no unified picture emerges"; texts quoted included both accepted versions and marginal, "non-standard" texts (75). The wide range of texts observed here could have interesting implications for NT quotation of MT, LXX, Targums, and other, lesser-known texts.

34. Stanley, "Paul and Homer," 76. His discussion of these types of citations is especially intriguing in light of the montage found in Mark 1:2–3.

35. Ibid., 76.

36. Ibid.

demonstration of relationship between the mechanics of quotation and its function. In other words, an author's purpose in using quotation determines which citation technique he uses, and the citation technique used provides clues into the author's purpose. For this reason, studying one without considering the other provides an incomplete picture not just of what is happening within the text but also what is being communicated by the text. For this reason, a thorough grounding in the conventions of both the mechanics and functions of quotation is necessary to properly understand and interpret any given instance of quotation in the NT.

## *What was the purpose of quotation?*

In their use of quotation, Greco-Roman authors consistently—and unsurprisingly—remain within the bounds established by classical rhetoric. In other words, quotation, like any other rhetorical device, must clearly reinforce the rhetorical force of the text in a way the audience would recognize. In fact, the use of quotation is very similar to the use of figures of speech. Both may be used quite effectively in any of the species of rhetoric, both draw the attention of the audience and bring vividness to the speech or text, and both guide interpretation of the surrounding context. Beyond these functions, however, quotation carries not just the functions of figurative speech but also particular shades of meaning from the original text and the original author. It is precisely this interplay of functionality and shades of meaning that is the focus of Geoffrey Lloyd's study of quotation in the Hellenistic world.[37]

It should be noted from the outset that Lloyd makes little distinction between allusion and quotation, noting only that "when a Greek writer tells us what one of his predecessors 'says,' *phési*, this has often to be taken not as a record of what that predecessor wrote, let alone of words that he spoke, but rather in the sense of what he meant or could be represented as meaning."[38] This rather loose definition enables Lloyd to examine quotations of or allusions to works of which the originals are as yet unavailable. The texts he studies do, however, represent their quotations or allusions as direct quotations taken from speeches and literature.[39]

37. Geoffrey Lloyd, "Quotation in Greco-Roman Contexts," *Extrême-Orient, Extrême-Occident* 17 (1995): 141–153.

38. Lloyd, "Quotation in Greco-Roman Contexts," 143.

39. In his own words, "I shall concentrate on direct quotation in, broadly, philosophical and scientific writings, and leave to one side the play of literary allusion as Greek and Latin poets rework the tropes, themes, and images of earlier poetry" (Lloyd, "Quotation in Greco-Roman Contexts," 147).

Lloyd is thus able to limit his study to the phenomenon of the quotation in the later text, avoiding questions of the mechanics of quotation (comparisons between the original text and the quotation by the later author) in lieu of focusing on the functions of quotation and its rhetorical role in a text. In addition, the corpus he examines is comprised of scientific and philosophical texts and treatises, thereby also avoiding the wordplay and allusion so prevalent and highly valued in Greco-Roman poetry. His analysis of quotation in this body of literature, then, is especially pertinent to the NT texts, which are themselves more similar to philosophical works than to poetry.

Quotation in these texts may take one of three roles. First, the author uses quotation to reaffirm his own status as an expert, to remind the audience that here is one whose knowledge of the field is superb. Second, and in keeping with the first, quotation may "provide authority" on a given facet of an argument. Thus in both the first and second roles, quotation is used as a witness, to identify or reinforce authority: in the first case, to reinforce the authority of the author, and in the second, to reinforce the authority of the argument.[40]

The third role of quotation exists in tension with both of these in that quotation may also be used to demonstrate the superiority of the quoting author to the material or author being quoted.[41] This use of quotation is subversive, and the role of the text quoted is actually to turn back on itself, proving itself defunct in light of its new context. The means by which this is accomplished is by demonstrating its weaknesses and failures to the new audience,[42] setting itself up as the failed opposite to a new truth in a binary reality.

The issue at the heart of the use of quotation was authority: either the text cited affirmed the authority of the author (reinforcing *ethos*) and argument by agreeing with its context, or it de-authorized itself in its new context in order to prove the new authority of the author or argument. Thus, as Lloyd observes, quotation becomes a matter of rhetorical artillery in an agonistic culture, and that, from this perspective, the purpose of using quotation is not to fully represent each side of an argument but to tally up "as many points as one thought one could get away with."[43] In fact, Lloyd considers forensic debate to be the truest home of quotation:

---

40. This second case is fundamentally what is addressed by M.C. Albl, *"And Scripture Cannot Be Broken": The Form and Function of the Early Christian Testimonia*, NovTestSupp 96 (Leiden: Brill, 1999).

41. Lloyd, "Quotation in Greco-Roman Contexts," 147.

42. Ibid., 151.

43. Ibid., 152.

> You marshalled the best and most prestigious names on your side as you could. . . . You undermined your opponents, and their authorities, by selective quotations from them. Even the deployment of quotation to confirm your status as learned tallies with Greco-Roman rhetorical norms and goals, in this instance the need for any speaker to create as favourable an image of himself as he could to lend credibility to the case he argued.[44]

Thus the role of quotation in a text is always tied to the question of authority. In the agonistic context of forensic debate, this question of authority expresses itself as struggle between opponents to claim the sympathy of the audience via scoring the most points off of one another. The use of quotations in debate, then, becomes a quickly accelerating arms race in which wit garners the audience's delight and sympathy, while insight wins their persuasion. Thus authoritative quotation affirms the authority of the speaker and acts as proof both of an argument and of the rhetor's wit; from another perspective, quotation may be said to bear authoritative witness to both oration and orator.

## Texts as Witnesses in Greco-Roman Rhetoric

The role of quotation in establishing the authority—or at least the authoritative voice—of the speaker is, as noted above, well-attested. A slightly lesser-known but equally pertinent role for quotation is that of a witness. Text as a witness in support of an argument comes out clearly in Cicero's *De Inventione*. In the second part of his treatise, Cicero outlines appropriate ways to use quotation strategically in courtroom speeches (*De Inventione*, 2.40–49). What is key here is that the strategy is chosen based on its usefulness in supporting the argument. Again, the question at the heart of quotation was "how useful is this quotation, and what strategy may maximize its usefulness to the argument?"[45]

The usefulness of a text was entirely conceptualized within to the agonistic context of Greco-Roman society. From a textual perspective, this is what Margaret Mitchell terms the "agonistic paradigm of interpretation,"[46] in which speeches are envisioned within the framework of eliciting understanding and persuasion in the face of opposing viewpoints and the very real possibility of misunderstanding. Thus in the contest of words, "texts

---

44. Ibid.
45. Margaret Mitchell, *Paul the Corinthians and the Birth of Christian Hermeneutics* (Cambridge: Cambridge University, 2012), 26.
46. Ibid., 16.

are treated as evidence for or against one's own case, and employed as witnesses,"[47] just as today a lawyer may call witnesses to the stand or introduce evidence as a type of silent witness for his case. The strategic presentation of a quotation provides a ready-made hermeneutic for the text that enables it to slip neatly into the speaker's argument. Thus the authority of the source of the quotation combines with the rhetor's shrewd strategic presentation of the text, together shaping the quotation into an authoritative witness in favor of the speaker's argument.

## JESUS, MARK, AND QUOTATION IN MARK 12

While the Second Evangelist quotes the Hebrew Scriptures throughout his Gospel, the cluster of quotations in Mark 12 is especially intriguing. First, it is the most concentrated cluster of quotations in the Gospel. Second, quotations in the Gospel of Mark are predominantly placed in Jesus' mouth, yet here in Mark 12 there is an unusual back-and-forth movement as Jesus and his opponents quote Scripture at each other. In fact, the context of Mark 12 creates precisely the ambiance of forensic debate that Lloyd and Usher describe. Furthermore, as noted above in the discussion of Jewish rhetoric, Jesus uses these Hebrew texts as proofs confirming his legal interpretations. This use of text as proof echoes Cicero's appeals to texts as witnesses in favor of both argument and speaker.

Adding yet another rhetorical element to the narrative, Mark 11:27–33 introduces an overarching tension that heightens the atmosphere of competition inherent in Mark 12: the series of dialogues are prefaced by a blatant and critical challenge to Jesus' authority. Thus, in Mark 12 the concepts of both authority and witness coalesce in Jesus' use of quotation.

### Authority, Competition, and Debate

Mark begins building the atmosphere far ahead of the debates in 12:18–34. The challenge to Jesus' authority in 11:27–33 foreshadows the coming display.[48] The religious rulers of Judea—the chief priests, scribes, and elders—approach him to demand the source of his authority. Jesus confounds them by throwing their rejection of John the Baptizer in their faces, leaving them at an impasse: afraid of the crowds yet unwilling to compromise their posi-

---

47. Ibid.

48. Timothy C. Gray, *The Temple in the Gospel of Mark: A Study in Its Narrative Role* (Grand Rapids: Baker Academic, 2008), 77.

tion and honor,[49] they are unable to respond to Jesus' query with anything other than ignorance.

Jesus compounds their shame by telling a distinctly unflattering parable that is pointedly directed at them (12:1–17). There is no doubt that he identifies them with the rebellious tenants who kill the true heir to the vineyard. Capping the parable off with a quotation that simultaneously summarizes their rejection of him and implicitly judges them for their rejection of God's plan, Jesus has clearly won the encounter. The leaders are left to melt away in shame and plot to win back their authority and their honor.[50]

Jesus' use of a quotation here provides an excellent opportunity to briefly interact with the rhetorical conventions discussed above. The quotation is a word-for-word citation of Ps 117:22–23 in the LXX (118:22–23 MT) with no omissions or conflations. It clearly serves to reinforce Jesus' own authority by supporting his argument against his opponents. Applying these prophetic words to himself is itself an exercise of authority, thus providing an unwelcome answer to the leaders' original demand for the source of his authority: as the "stone," he is from the Lord just as was John the Baptizer. It is no wonder that between the parable and the quotation, the leaders left infuriated.[51] In a single quotation Jesus has offhandedly identified himself as both son and cornerstone, the authority of Scripture bearing witness not only to his own role and authority but also to the source of that authority: his father, the owner of the vineyard. In a very real sense, Jesus has drawn a line in the sand before his challengers—a line that, by his definition, places them on the wrong side.

## Forensic Debate

Having been bested in person, Jesus' opponents set out to try him by proxy. First they sent the Pharisees and Herodians, who tested him ostensibly with a question about paying taxes, but the crux of their challenge was an effort to force him into sanctioning political insurrection through economic

---

49. Joseph H. Hellerman, "Challenging the Authority of Jesus: Mark 11:27–33 and Mediterranean Notions of Honor and Shame," *JETS* 43/2 (June 2000): 213–228.

50. Robert Stein very briefly touches on the shame-honor dynamic at work here in his commentary. See Stein, *Mark*, 525–527.

51. In her commentary, Adela Yarbro Collins describes this pericope as a "battle of wits" that must have been especially enjoyable to Mark's audience. This description is particularly apt given the role of quotation within debate as a way to reinforce authority as well as demonstrate wit (and thus the sympathies of the audience, as Carneades demonstrates). See Collins, *Mark*, 541.

rebellion (12:13–17).[52] Jesus responds this time without a quotation, yet by the profound insight of his reply again emerges the victor.

Each time that Jesus' opponents are sent away defeated and shamed, the atmosphere chills and the sense of impending showdown grows. There is no doubt that this is a competition, and that engaging in this type of public, verbal battle translates immediately into forensic debate in the Greco-Roman rhetorical tradition. And within this tradition, quotation has the opportunity to play a very particular role.

The next two episodes (12:18–27, 28–34) follow the same pattern of controversy established above: a religious figure approaches Jesus with a question, and Jesus' response is so definitive that there is no room for rebuttal. In these two episodes, however, Jesus uses quotation in the place of *chreiai* to achieve the same sense of climactic response.

## Debate with the Sadducees

The Pharisees and Herodians having been soundly silenced, the Sadducees approach to try their hand. They immediately raise the stakes by invoking Scripture, yet in such a way that they are obviously mocking the popular belief in resurrection.[53] Their reference to Scripture may not technically be identified as a quotation, simply because it deviates so significantly from its source. Instead, they appear to be paraphrasing Deut 25:5, invoking the ancient tradition of levirate marriage (e.g., Gen 38:8).

Regardless, Jesus refuses to accept the defensive position they have forced on him and takes the offensive instead,[54] transforming the question into one of authority: who has the authority to properly interpret Scripture? His accusation of their inability to provide such a proper interpretation clearly deauthorizes the Sadducees, while the interpretation he offers is implicitly founded on the validity of his own authority.

Jesus caps this competition with a quotation of Exod 3:6. From a technical perspective, the quote is interesting because it demonstrates precisely the trends of omission observed by Stanley: there are no additions or changes to the wording, but the quotation omits the unnecessary copulative verb and the identification of God as "your" father.[55] In accordance with

---

52. See also Stein, *Mark*, 544.
53. Witherington, *Mark*, 327.
54. Marcus, *Mark 8–16*, 832.
55. The quotation in Mark 12:26 is ἐγὼ ὁ θεὸς Ἀβραὰμ καὶ [ὁ] θεὸς Ἰσαὰκ καὶ [ὁ] θεὸς Ἰακώβ, while the original text of Exod 3:6 reads Ἐγώ εἰμι ὁ θεὸς τοῦ πατρός σου, θεὸς Αβρααμ καὶ θεὸς Ισαακ καὶ θεὸς Ιακωβ. The omitted words are italicized for

the conventions Stanley describes, the quotation has eliminated extraneous detail in order to focus the audience's attention on the core issue highlighted within the quotation. After all, neither Jesus nor Mark have any desire to derail their audiences into questions of precisely of whom God is father.[56]

The quotation functions to support Jesus' argument, yet the use of this particular text is suggestive of the subversive role Lloyd describes. Jesus certainly avoids the mainstream interpretation which focuses on the insider language of the text, instead emphasizing the language of eternality implicit within the words. However, the subversion is only one of interpretation, and not of the text itself. In keeping with Stanley's observations, the quotation does remain well within the bounds of the original context.[57] In short, the interpretation Jesus derives is grammatically and contextually valid, although unexpected.[58]

The surprising use of this particular text to confound the Sadducees is calculated for maximum effect on both the Sadducees and the greater audience (both Jewish and Gentile). Jesus has taken a text from the only Scriptures the Sadducees recognized—the Torah[59]—and has turned it back onto them on the basis of his own authority and self-authorized interpretation. Jesus' repeated judgment of their failure to read Scripture insightfully is mortifying, although perhaps not as out of place in an agonistic culture as it seems to a modern Western reader.[60]

The combination of Jesus' unexpected use of the Exodus text and the fact that he used Sadducee-approved Scripture against Sadducee doctrine is clever and insightful, and certainly would have won the crowd in Jesus' context. Whether or not Mark's Hellenistic audience would have grasped the very Jewish irony is unknown; the fact that Mark felt the need to explain Jewish customs (7:3–4) suggests they may not have grasped the full wit of the encounter. However, there can be no doubt that the gist of the rhetorical *coup* would have been clear to both Jew and Gentile: both would have

---

ease of comparison.

56. Interestingly, though, the present tense verb has also been omitted; while grammatically unnecessary, its tense certainly supports Jesus' argument.

57. Marcus, *Mark 8–16*, 835.

58. Stein, *Mark*, 555.

59. E. Schweizer, *The Good News According to Mark* (Atlanta: John Knox, 1971), 246.

60. Joanna Dewey, "The Gospel of Mark as an Oral-Aural Event: Implications for Interpretation," pp. 145–163 in *The New Literary Criticism and the NT*, ed. Edgar V. McKnight and Elizabeth Struthers Malbon (Valley Forge, Penn.: Trinity Press International, 1994), 150–151.

recognized what Jesus did in his argument. In some things, it seems, the rhetoric is not so very different

## Debate with the Scribe

In this final debate, the Gospel presents Jesus as the final victor over his opponents. The chief priests, scribes, and elders faced defeat earlier in the Temple courts (11:27—12:12), the Pharisees and Herodians were silenced by Jesus' insight (12:13-17), and the Sadducees were routed by Jesus' clever interpretation of their Torah (12:18-27). Now Mark presents his audience with a representative scribe.

Surprisingly, this is Mark's most sympathetic portrayal of a scribe in the entire Gospel. Unlike the Synoptic parallels (Matt 22:34-40 // Luke 10:25-28), Mark depicts this man as a sincere seeker.[61] Given the agonistic context, however, even a sincere question is a challenge to debate when posed in a public forum. And few questions would engage Jews so deeply and even divisively as the question of which law is the most important.[62]

Jesus' response is immediate. There is no interpretation here; a straightforward quotation efficiently answers the scribe. The original text is found in Deut 6:4-5, and Jesus quotes the text nearly exactly. At first glance, there seems to be a shift from δύναμις (LXX) to διάνοια (Mark 12:30) and then the addition of the phrase καὶ ἐξ ὅλης τῆς ἰσχύος σου. Given Stanley's observations, however, an addition to a quotation as central to Judaism—in all its sects—as Deut 6:4-5 is highly unexpected. The reason for this surprising variation is found not in the Greek LXX, which seems to be Mark's text for the Hebrew Scriptures, but in the Hebrew. The final phrase in Hebrew reads וּבְכָל־מְאֹדֶךָ which is notoriously difficult to translate idiomatically. Literally, מְאֹד. means "much," making a substantival reading quite awkward: "muchness." The added phrase suggests a translation of the Hebrew that is concerned to retain the signification of the words at the expense of a one-to-one lexical translation.[63]

The second command Jesus quotes is a word-for-word reflection of part of Lev 19:18; material extraneous to Jesus' central point is again omitted for clarity and rhetorical force. The two quotations both serve the same

---

61. Marcus, *Mark 8-16*, 841.

62. See the parallels and variety of opinions evidenced in *Mak.* 23b-24, as well as Hillel's famous response in *Šabb.* 31A; see also Witherington, *Mark*, 330.

63. As Günther Bornkamm notes, this is a trend apparent in various books of the LXX as well. See Günther Bornkamm, "Das Doppelgebot der liebe," in *Neutestamentilche Studien für Rudolf Bultmann*, 2nd rev. ed., BZNW 21 (Berlin: Töpelmann, 1957), 88-89.

role, reinforcing the authority of Jesus' argument. Yet the reinforcement they offer is their own self-evident authority: like Jesus, these commands need claim no authority, for there is none who, when faced with their reality, can deny their place and their identity.

The decisiveness of Jesus' response further underscores the theme of Jesus' inherent authority; in fact, the scribe's response indicates recognition this quality of self-authorization in both Jesus and his quotations as he affirms Jesus' words (with some grammatical changes to suit the context[64]). Interestingly, the scribe adds εἷς ἐστιν καὶ οὐκ ἔστιν ἄλλος πλὴν αὐτοῦ to Jesus' words—a conflation of Deut 4:35 and 6:4 that orients the following quotations to the person of God. This change, combined with the scribe's confession that these commands even surpass the Temple cult, is intriguing in light of Jesus' own response to these agonistic episodes of debate in 12:35–37 (which will be addressed in the following section). Whether this is Mark's presentation and intended to highlight the role these quotations play in witnessing to Jesus or whether the grammatical changes are original to the Jewish context is difficult to determine.

With the conclusion of this episode, Jesus has routed his opponents. The chief priests, elders, and scribes were humiliated in 11:27—12:12; the Pharisees and Herodians were silenced in 12:13–17; the Sadducees were defeated on their own turf in 12:18–27; and Jesus' response to the sincere scribe established his authority—and their deauthorization—emphatically and definitively.[65] The Hebrew Scriptures have born witness to Jesus as the stone and as the authoritative interpreter, the one who holds the authority to pronounce one's status in or out of the kingdom of God. All those who Mark has established as Jesus' opponents have been silenced.[66] The contest has ended (12:24). The resolution, however, is still to come.

## The Response

Remaining within the geographic context of the Temple, Mark's arrangement offers a response to these debates. Having established his authority and gained the crowd's sympathies, Jesus takes the initiative—even the offensive—in his teaching.[67] He launches immediately into challenging the

---

64. Thus following the conventions ruling the mechanics of quotation set out by Stanley.

65. Marcus, *Mark 8–16*, 849.

66. Benoît Herman Marguerite Ghislain Marie Standaert, *L'Evangile Selon Marc: Composition et Genre Litteraire* (Nijmegen-Brugge: Sint-Andriesabdij, 1978), 328.

67. Marcus, *Mark 8–16*, 832. See also Stephen H. Smith, "The Literary Structure

popular conception of the messiah as David's son. He offers a quotation of Ps 110:1 (109:1 LXX) as a witness to his case. The quotation is nearly exact, differing only in one word, ὑποκάτω, for the LXX ὑποπόδιον. The change in meaning for the passage is nonexistent, and could simply represent another example of differing translations from the original Hebrew.

The quotation functions explicitly to support the authority of Jesus' argument, yet the content of the argument itself—that the messiah is "Lord"—combines with Mark's identification of Jesus as messiah to transform the quotation's function into witnessing to Jesus' own person and authority. Perhaps the best way to express this transformation is to consider the cultural differences between Jesus' audience and Mark's audience. In the original context, Jesus' Jewish audience would consider the quotation to support his case; on the level of the out-of-text world, the quotation supports Mark's argument for Jesus' identity. Yet one wonders if these arguments were so different. If these debates occurred in the time frame provided in the Gospel—the final few days in Jerusalem before the Passion—Jesus was, in fact, intent on finally unveiling his role and mission as Messiah.[68] A challenge to his authority (or, more specifically, to the source of his authority) would have provided just that opportunity. In Mark 12, Jesus wields the quotation as sword and evidence, decimating his opponents while the voice of the Scriptures calls out in witness of his person and mission (especially 12:10, 36). The formal similarities between Jesus' argumentation and that of the rabbis suggests a common source for their rhetoric.[69] The use of quotation described by Cicero and evidenced throughout classical literature provides just that common source.

Finally, given that a major chord in Mark is the gradual revelation of Jesus' identity,[70] Mark 12 is climactic for Jesus' public ministry. It is the clearest statement provided in a public venue witnessing to Jesus as both Messiah and Son of God ("Lord"). Unsurprisingly, the Gospel almost im-

---

of Mark 11:1—12:40" pp. 171–191 in *The Composition of Mark's Gospel*, ed. David E. Orton, Readers in Biblical Studies 3 (Leiden: Brill, 1999), 185.

68. Keener, *Historical Jesus*, 290–294.

69. It is highly doubtful that Jesus' rhetoric strongly influenced rabbinic rhetoric; given the antipathy of post-70 Jewish leaders toward Christianity, a deliberate distancing seems to have been that case rather than the reverse. Thus any parallels discovered in rabbinic literature would share rhetorical roots with Jesus, placing Jesus in the context of a developing rhetoric instead of functioning as the catalyst for rhetorical change (see Keener, *The Historical Jesus*, 189). Keener is here discussing parables, but if the rabbis were unlikely to follow Jesus' example in his more Jewish rhetoric, they would be even less inclined to follow rhetorical innovation based on Hellenistic strategies of argumentation.).

70. Witherington, *Mark*, 41, 53–4; see also Stein, *Mark*, 24–25.

mediately trips down the stairs into the Passion. Once Jesus reveals himself, the time for him to enact his role as ultimate ransom (10:45) comes quickly.

## The Message of Mark's Quotations

The Gospel of Mark deliberately sets up an atmosphere of debate that would be tremendously familiar to his Hellenistic audience. Jesus teaching in the Temple would sound very much like a philosopher teaching in the *agora*, and the frequent debates that took place there between philosophers would provide a context out of which a Gentile might understand the religious controversies of Jews. The arrangement of material from 11:27—12:37 highlights the debate factor, creating the rhetorical context within which Jesus' use of quotation could be given its greatest rhetorical force.

Quotation as an expression or invocation of authority is not a new idea, but it should be combined with the agonistic context in which debaters sought to score points off of one another to win sympathy from their audience. Wit, insight, and clever logic in the use of quotation were both entertaining and persuasive. Jesus' use of the Hebrew Scriptures to embarrass, correct, dumbfound, and enlighten his audience certainly fit the Hellenistic model of good, entertaining, and thought-provoking public debate.

In addition, the complete rout Jesus makes of his enemies is even more obvious and enjoyable when viewed from this Hellenistic perspective. For Mark's audience, Jesus achieves tremendous status through his absolute victory—a status that, as the Passion approaches, is seen more and more clearly to be ironic. The reversal of social position in the kingdom of God is made abundantly clear as Jesus turns his back on the popularity he had earned with the crowds in order to submit to God's plan and the revenge of his opponents. It would be a social dynamic completely foreign to the pervasive atmosphere of social climbing inherent in the patronage system, and an unforgettable object lesson for the Roman church.

However, the degree to which a reading based on Greco-Roman rhetoric fits Mark 12 should not overshadow the original Jewish context of the events and the fundamentally historical nature of the accounts. From this perspective, the appeal to the authority of Scripture coincides with its proof of Jesus' authority against that of his opposition. In fact, rabbinic parallels of quotation and strategies of argumentation indicate that Jesus and the rabbis drew from a common rhetorical source,[71] specifically in their use of quotation to prove their arguments, establish the authority of their interpretations, and thus bolster their own authority. In fact, Richard Hidary's analysis

---

71. Keener, *Historical Jesus*, 189.

of the Yerushalmi Berakhot reveals precisely the concept of text as proof or witness that Cicero describes in his *De Inventione* (2.45–49), placing Jesus and his use of quotation firmly within both classical rhetoric and rabbinical thought.[72] The concept of witness is, of course, by no means foreign to Judaism: Deut 19:15 famously requires the testimony of at least two witnesses in order to convict a defendant. Read in this light, Mark's Gospel records Jesus providing double the requirement in Mark 12.

Thus from both Greco-Roman and Jewish perspectives the quotations of Mark 12 witness not only to the truth of Jesus' legal interpretations but also to his authority as cornerstone and Lord. These episodes more than fully respond to the challenge to his authority in 11:28 and, by finally unveiling Jesus' identity as Son of David and Lord of the Kingdom, prepare Mark's audience for the imminent Passion.

## FINAL RHETORICAL CONSIDERATIONS

While Mark's presentation certainly highlights the Hellenistic rhetorical appeal of these episodes, the historical underlay remains, and remains thoroughly Jewish at the midpoint of developing Jewish rhetoric. That these events happened fundamentally as they are related suggests that what we see in Mark 12 is a distinctively Jewish twist, shaped by Jewish religious beliefs and a Palestinian Jewish vision of reality, within a Hellenistic rhetorical conceptual framework. It is significant, however, that this study has limited itself to considerations of quotation alone, leaving open the possibility that the Pharisees and rabbis deliberately chose to adopt some aspects of classical rhetoric for which the Scriptures offered no parallel.[73]

---

72. Hidary, "Classical Rhetorical Arrangement," 57–8.

73. Alternatively, Jewish rhetoric may have adopted classical rhetoric in a rather more holistic way, adapting the framework of the rhetorical system while investing it with uniquely Jewish content and reasoning. Fuller treatment of Jewish rhetoric, including plotting the trajectory of its development in the Second Temple period, will provide further insight into the relationship between classical and Jewish rhetoric.

# LUKE-ACTS

# 3

# The Exhortation to Monotheism in Acts 14:15–17

## Craig S. Keener

It is a privilege for me to be able to contribute this essay in honor of my friend, colleague and mentor, Ben Witherington. Soon after I had finished my PhD at Duke, Ben introduced me to publishers and scholars I would not have met on my own. He has continued to model for me both scholarship and kindness, looking out for me and treating me as a colleague well before I joined the faculty at his seminary. In honor of his excellent work on both Acts and rhetoric, I offer here an essay on a speech in Acts.

Given the word count allotted, I have focused on a particularly brief speech, the Lystra speech in Acts 14:15–17.[1] Because this is merely a speech summary, and because Barnabas and Paul address here a predominantly rural audience with less exposure to urban rhetoric than some audiences later in Acts, I focus less on specific rhetorical devices than on how the speech's content would resonate with and challenge religious thought in antiquity. The themes in this speech would likely appeal to Luke's ideal audience, knowledgeable of Gentile polytheism, rudimentary philosophic currents available in an urban setting, and the monotheism they as Jesus's followers

---

1. I adapt here material from the forthcoming vol. 2 in my Acts commentary, *Acts: An Exegetical Commentary*, 4 vols. (Grand Rapids: Baker Academic, 2012).

had inherited from Israel. The exhortation to monotheism here would strike chords familiar to many of Luke's contemporaries.

## THE LYSTRA SPEECH, LUKAN SPEECHES AND PAULINE PREACHING

Despite generally shared style and common theological interests, the speeches in Acts vary in many respects. They reflect, for example, a range of rhetorical levels, with speeches normally appropriate to the individual speakers and audiences in the narrative world. Likewise, readers may also find in the speeches' details a range in probability in terms of modern historiographic analysis. For example, many scholars believe that the speech of Gamaliel (Acts 5:36-37) and especially the conversation of Festus with Agrippa and Berenice (25:13-22) reflect Luke's reconstruction of what could have been said on such occasions for which available witnesses would be few.[2] At the opposite end of the spectrum, one speech in the we-material contains even some elements of Paul's own style when exhorting Christians (20:18-35).[3] Likewise, summaries of defense speeches (especially Acts 24-26) could reflect dependence on the sorts of court summaries normally available in forensic cases.[4] Nevertheless, speeches throughout Acts are normally appropriate to the audiences in the narrative world, fitting the expectations of rhetoric and of ancient historical composition.

The speech in Acts 14:15-17 suits its narrated audience. A comparison of Paul's[5] speeches in 13:16-47 (a synagogue audience), 14:15-17 (a rural community; see especially comment on 14:17) and 17:22-31 (urban philosophers) reveals Paul's adaptability to diverse audiences. Although such adaptability could be viewed negatively by critics,[6] the ability to adapt one's

---

2. Regarding Acts 25, see especially here Ben Witherington III, *The Acts of the Apostles: A Socio-rhetorical Commentary* (Grand Rapids: Eerdmans, 1998), 119-20; C. K. Barrett, *A Critical and Exegetical Commentary on the Acts of the Apostles*, 2 vols. (Edinburgh: T&T Clark, 1994-98), 1139.

3. See especially Steve Walton, *Leadership and Lifestyle: The Portrait of Paul in the Miletus Speech and 1 Thessalonians*, SNTSMS 108 (Cambridge: Cambridge University Press, 2000).

4. See especially Bruce W. Winter, "Official Proceedings and the Forensic Speeches in Acts 24-26," 305-36 in *The Book of Acts in Its Ancient Literary Setting*, ed. Bruce W. Winter and Andrew D. Clark, vol. 1 of *The Book of Acts in Its First Century Setting* (Grand Rapids: Eerdmans; Carlisle, U.K.: Paternoster, 1993).

5. Barnabas also speaks here (14:14), but Paul is the main speaker (14:12).

6. Clarence E. Glad, "Paul and Adaptability," pages 17-41 in *Paul in the Greco-Roman World: A Handbook*, ed. J. Paul Sampley (Harrisburg, Pa.: Trinity Press International, 2003), 20-21; Margaret M. Mitchell, *Paul and the Rhetoric of Reconciliation: An*

form to one's audience was essential for good rhetoricians (Quintilian *Inst.* 3.7.24).[7] Although the language is thoroughly biblical (see comments below), it omits direct quotations of Scripture, which would be irrelevant for this audience (in contrast to Acts 13:16-47).[8] Some elements of the speech may even contextualize Paul's message specifically for an audience in this region, suggesting authentic tradition that Luke has compressed here.[9]

The speech's setting fits a Lukan theme that has apologetic value. Ancients considered it virtuous for humans to reject divine honors.[10] Luke thus depicts positively the refusal of the apostles (here; Peter in 10:26; cf. 3:12), and contrasts the opposite behavior of a tyrannical persecutor (12:22-23, whose acceptance of divine honor is also noted by Josephus).[11]

Like all speeches in Acts, this speech is Lukan; yet, like the other Pauline speeches, it is also compatible with Pauline thought. Robert Grant could be right that the speech "may not be what Paul would have said," but rather, what Luke thinks "he should have said."[12] While the wording and choice of terse elements that survive Luke's editing are Luke's, however, the approach

---

*Exegetical Investigation of the Language and Composition of 1 Corinthians* (Louisville: Westminster/John Knox, 1991), 134; Duane Litfin, *St. Paul's Theology of Proclamation: 1 Corinthians 1-4 and Greco-Roman Rhetoric*, SNTSMS 83 (Cambridge: Cambridge University Press, 1994), 115-17; Peter Marshall, *Enmity in Corinth: Social Conventions in Paul's Relations with the Corinthians*, WUNT 2. Reihe, 23 (Tübingen: Mohr Siebeck, 1987), 71-73; Ps-Phocylides 49; cf. Dio Chrysostom *Or.* 4.123; Herodian 4.7.3-4; 4.8.1-3; 5.5.5. Whether the case of Alcibiades is more negative or positive may be debated (Plutarch *Alcibiades* 23.4-6; positive in Cornelius Nepos 7 [Alcibiades], 11.2-6).

7. For an example, see e.g., Albucius, adapting for both academic and popular audiences (Suetonius *Rhet.* 6); later, Libanius (Eunapius *Lives* 495-96). See further Litfin, *Theology*, 65, 104-6; cf. *Thebaid* frg. 8; Maximus of Tyre 1.2; Diogenes Laertius 2.66; *Exod Rab.* 47:5.

8. Cf. Nathalie Siffer, "L'annonce du vrai Dieu dans les discours missionnaires aux païens: Actes 14,15-17 et 17,22-31," *RevScRel* 81 (4, 2007): 523-44.

9. Stanley E. Porter, *Paul in Acts* (Peabody: Hendrickson, 2001); reprint of *The Paul of Acts: Essays in Literary Criticism, Rhetoric, and Theology*, WUNT 115 (Tübingen: Mohr Siebeck, 1999), 139, following especially Cilliers Breytenbach, "Zeus und der lebendige Gott: Anmerkungen zu Apostelgeschichte 14.11-17," *NTS* 39 (3, 1993): 396-413.

10. Scholars cite many examples (Aelian *Var. hist.* 8.15; Ps.-Callisthenes *Alex.* 2.22.12; Hans Conzelmann, *A Commentary on the Acts of the Apostles*, edited by Eldon Jay Epp with Christopher R. Matthews, translated by James Limburg, A. Thomas Kraabel, and Donald H. Juel, Hermeneia [Philadelphia: Fortress, 1987], 82, 110; Robert M. Grant, *Gods and the One God* [LEC 1; Philadelphia: Westminster, 1986], 26). Refusing any kind of honors sometimes led to greater praise in the long run (Valerius Maximus 4.1.6a); mortals failing to refuse divine honors was wicked (Josephus *Ant.* 19.345-46).

11. Josephus *Ant.* 19.345-46.

12. Robert M. Grant, *Paul in the Roman World: The Conflict at Corinth* (Louisville: Westminster John Knox, 2001), 9.

is more Pauline than scholars often recognize. In contrast to these Lukan speeches, most of Paul's letters address believers; substantial overlap appears, however, in their brief treatments of natural theology (Rom 1:19-22), idolatry (Rom 1:23-25; cf. 1 Cor 8:5-6; 10:20-21), and repentance from idolatry (1 Thess 1:9).

The hostility toward deity images here resembles 1 Thess 1:9, the Pauline passage offering the closest approximation of what Paul demanded for polytheists' conversion.[13] The natural theology in Luke's two Pauline speeches that address it is consistent with the natural theology expressed in Rom 1:19-25.[14] Both authors, however, qualify their brief examples of natural theology. In Romans, the revelation in nature makes humanity culpable for idolatry (Rom 1:18-23); but this revelation contrasts with the revelation in the gospel, which provides salvation (Rom 1:16-17).[15] In fact, Acts 14:15-17 and Rom 1:19-25 might even echo the same source in Wisdom 13-15,[16] although the connection is much clearer in the somewhat longer Romans passage.[17] Wisdom of Solomon used God's revelation in nature to make idolatry morally indefensible,[18] and apparently drew from Stoic models.[19]

---

13. With David Wenham, "The Paulinism of Acts Again," *Themelios* 13 (1988): 53-55; Witherington, *Acts*, 426; Grant, *Paul*, 9.

14. With e.g., Porter, *Paul in Acts*, 145. Philo and many other monotheistic thinkers challenged pagan natural philosophy (Isaac Miller, "Idolatry and the Polemics of World-Formation from Philo to Augustine," *JRH* 28 [2, 2004]: 126-45).

15. C. E. B. Cranfield, "Romans 1.18," *SJT* 21 (3, 1968): 330-35, predicates both "revelations" on the gospel, but this argument depends too heavily on the connective force of the γάρ.

16. Klaus Haacker, *The Theology of Paul's Letter to the Romans* (Cambridge: Cambridge University Press, 2003), 103-4.

17. In Rom 1, see e.g., William Sanday and Arthur Headlam, *A Critical and Exegetical Commentary on the Epistle to the Romans*, 5th ed., ICC (Edinburgh: T&T Clark, 1902), 52; W. D. Davies, *Paul and Rabbinic Judaism: Some Rabbinic Elements in Pauline Theology*, 4th ed. (Philadelphia: Fortress, 1980), 28; David A. deSilva, "Wisdom of Solomon," *Dictionary of NT Background*, ed. Craig A. Evans and Stanley E. Porter (Downers Grove, Ill.: InterVarsity, 2000), 1268-76 (here 1274); Morna D. Hooker, "Adam in Romans I," *NTS* 6 (4, 1960): 297-306 (here 299, noting differences as well); James D. G. Dunn, *The Theology of Paul the Apostle* (Grand Rapids: Eerdmans, 1998), 91; Charles H. Talbert, *Romans*, SHBC (Macon, Ga.: Smyth & Helwys, 2002), 63. Günther Bornkamm, *Early Christian Experience*, trans. Paul L. Hammer (New York: Harper & Row; London: SCM, 1969), 53, deems the parallels well-known.

18. Cf. deSilva, "Wisdom of Solomon," 1272.

19. H. A. A. Kennedy, *The Theology of the Epistles* (New York: Scribner's, 1920), 26; Bogdan Poniży, "Recognition of God according to the Book of Wisdom 13:1-9," *PJBR* 1 (2, 2001): 201-6; cf. John J. Collins: "Natural Theology and Biblical Tradition: The Case of Hellenistic Judaism," *CBQ* 60 (1, 1998): 1-15; Evangelia G. Dafni, "Natürliche

As with the speech in Acts 17:22–31, in 14:15 Paul begins by establishing common ground with his audience (mentioning shared nature in 14:15; cf. also the agricultural imagery of 14:17). The approach here resembles the apologetic in Josephus and many Diaspora Jewish writers, and Luke's presentation of it would appeal to many philosophic currents in his day.[20] The similarities with 17:22–31 might suggest that both reflect a pattern of Hellenistic Jewish apologetic as found in Wisdom of Solomon or Philo,[21] though Paul's more directly confrontational summons to repentance (14:15; 17:30; cf. 19:26; 1 Thess 1:9) goes beyond the approach of most of his contemporaries.

## CHALLENGING IDOLATRY

Themes in the Lystra speech would resonate with Jewish people and some Gentiles. Nevertheless, Barnabas and Paul speak more boldly than most Diaspora Jews and more strictly than even the vast majority of ancient philosophers. The wording at points appears diplomatic (especially in 14:16–17), but the speech summary's beginning suggests that the apostles' ultimate goal was not simply to make a successful oration by rhetorical standards. Rhetoricians advised securing hearers' favor by praising their ancestors,[22] which 14:16 does not do. Identifying their common humanity might help build rapport at the beginning of a speech, as rhetoricians advised,[23] but the opening verse nevertheless challenges some of ancient Gentiles' most deeply held beliefs.

### Jewish views

This concise speech summary confronts idolatry more bluntly than apologists often did. Although Jewish critiques of idolatry circulated more among themselves than in public preaching to polytheists, the critique here would

---

Theologie im Lichte des hebräischen und griechischen Alten Testaments," *TZ* 57 (3, 2001): 295–310.

20. See F. Gerald Downing, "Common Ground with Paganism in Luke and Josephus," *NTS* 28 (4, 1982): 546–59. Of course it would be inadequate to view Paul and Barnabas as philosophers here (see C. Kavin Rowe, *World Upside Down: Reading Acts in the Graeco-Roman Age* [New York: Oxford University Press, 2009], 21–22).

21. Grant, *Paul*, 9.

22. Socratics *Ep.* 28.

23. See e.g., Cicero *Inv.* 1.15.20; *De or.* 1.31.143; Quintilian *Inst.* 4.1.5.

sound familiar. Jewish literature often mocked paganism,[24] following the lead of some biblical prophets (1 Kgs 18:27; Is 44:12–17; 46:6–7; Jer 10:3–5; Ps 115:4–8).[25] Luke's antiidolatry polemic develops ideas already found in Isaiah.[26]

From a Jewish perspective, idolatry was one of the worst sins[27]—possibly the worst.[28] Later rabbis envisioned it as one of the great sins before the flood.[29] Jewish tradition depicted Abraham's[30] hostility toward idolatry;[31] after destroying household idols,[32] he faced conflict with his family.[33] Later rabbis declared that Abraham was the first person to leave idolatry.[34]

Jewish polemic emphasized that false gods, far from being creators, were created by humans (*Sipre Deut* 43.6.9). Later Christian writers echoed this approach. Far from being innate, for example, an emperor's "divinity" was dependent on mortals' decision and support (Tert. *Apol.* 5.2). Not surprisingly, Gentiles thought that converts to Judaism hated Gentiles' deities (e.g., Josephus *Ant.* 20.77) and that converts to the Christian movement denied them (Lucian *Passing of Peregrinus* 13).

Many Jewish people would have affirmed this speech's teaching that nature revealed God's unity and character (cf. 14:17). Nevertheless, Jewish apologetic rarely confronted Gentiles directly, publicly demanding that they

---

24. E.g., Wisd 13:10—14:7; Bel and Dragon; Ep Jer; *Let. Aris.* 134–38. For other polemic, see e.g., *Sib. Or.* 3.8–35; 4.4–23; among later Christians, *Sib. Or.* 8.359–428.

25. Many texts use *reductio ad absurdum* to ridicule paganism.

26. David W. Pao, *Acts and the Isaianic New Exodus*, WUNT 2. Reihe, 130 (Tübingen: Mohr Siebeck, 2000; repr., Grand Rapids: Baker, 2002), 181–216.

27. *Jub.* 36:5; Ep Jer passim; *tos. Sanh.* 13:8; *Peah* 1:2; *Sipra VDDeho.* par. 1.34.1.3; *ARN* 40A; *b. Git.* 57b; *Shab.* 145b–146a; *p. Sanh.* 3:5, §2; 6:7, §2; 8:8, §1; 10:1, §2; 10:3, §2; *Lev. Rab.* 37:1; *Tg. Ps.-Jon.* on Num 35:25. The evil inclination encouraged this activity (e.g., *Sipre Deut* 43.4.1; *Song Rab.* 2:4, §1; 7:8, §1).

28. Wisd 14:27; *Mek. Pisha* 5.40–41; *p. Ned.* 3:9, §3. Idolatry was equivalent to repudiating all of God's law (*tos. Bek.* 3:12; *Sipre Deut* 54.3.2; *b. Kid.* 40a), and could result from such repudiation (*Sipre Deut* 43.4.1).

29. E.g., *3 En.* 5:6–11. Idolatry made them susceptible to demons (*Gen. Rab.* 23:6; 24:6).

30. Similar traditions were applied to Job in *Test. Job* 2–5.

31. E.g., *Jub.* 21:3 (summarizing his righteousness); *Apoc. Ab.* 1–8. Cf. further Abraham's fight against idolatry in David Flusser, "Abraham and the Upanishads," *Imm* 20 (1986): 53–61 (citing e.g., *Jub.* 11:16–18; 12:1–6, 12–14; Josephus *Ant.* 1.155–56).

32. *Jub.* 11:12–14. Cf. Judg 6:25–27.

33. *Jub.* 11:16–17; 12:1–8.

34. *Pesiq. Rab.* 33:3. In *Gen. Rab.* 39:1 (attributed to a Tanna), he questioned and God revealed himself to him.

turn from false gods.³⁵ Most Jewish sources denouncing idolaters apparently directly (e.g., Is 44:11; 46:12; *Sib. Or.* 3.547–48) were not designed to be read by the statue venerators themselves.³⁶ Paul and Barnabas here escalate the rhetoric of OT prophets by confronting the worshipers directly.

## Gentile concerns about traditional polytheism

Yet even some Gentiles ridiculed features of mythology they considered incongruous with moral reason.³⁷ Such criticisms applied most widely to the worship of animals, since northern Mediterranean peoples associated this practice with Egyptians, whom Greeks and Romans often looked down on in their own day. God specifically warned Israel to reject images of animals (Deut 4:17–18),³⁸ and it is not surprising that Jewish people criticized these practices.³⁹ Nevertheless, not only Jews but also many Greeks and Romans mocked this behavior as superstition.⁴⁰ This was especially the case "after they heard of a Roman emissary who accidentally killed a cat and apparently was murdered by an Egyptian mob in 59 B.C."⁴¹ Pliny complains about

---

35. James D. G. Dunn, *The Acts of the Apostles* (Valley Forge, Pa.: Trinity Press International, 1996), 191.

36. Third-person denunciations are also prominent in the context of some of these references, e.g., Is 44:9–20; 46:6–7.

37. E.g., Dio Chrysostom *Or.* 11, passim (e.g., 154, mocking the changing of Hecuba into a dog). For other critics of Greek religion, see e.g., Grant, *Gods*, 20.

38. Huub van de Sandt, "Why Is Amos 5, 25–27 Quoted in Acts 7, 42f.?" *ZNW* 82 (1–2, 1991): 67–87, thinks that Luke in Acts 7 read the calf story (Exod 32) intertextually in relation to Deut 4:1–28.

39. E.g., *Let. Aris.* 138; Wisdom 13:13–14 (but also mocking Greeks' human images); Josephus *Ag. Ap.* 2.81, 85, 128–29, 139 (gladly taking to task Apion on a point where Josephus's Hellenized audience will agree; he contrasts Moses in *Ag. Ap.* 2.75–76). The Jewish belief was well-known (so Strabo 16.2.35; Tacitus *Hist.* 5.5).

40. E.g., Plutarch *Isis and Osiris* 71, *Mor.* 379DE; Lucian *Parliament of the Gods* 10–11; *Astrology* 7 (if genuine); Maximus of Tyre 2.5 (but cf. 2.10); see further Brook W. R. Pearson, "Idolatry, Jewish Conception of," *Dictionary of Background*, 526–29 (here 526–28). Paul may mock them in Rom 1:23 (Grant, *Gods*, 47; Brook W. R. Pearson, "Polytheism," 815–18 in *Dictionary of Background*, 818). Apollodorus *Bib.* 1.6.3 claims that the gods disguised themselves as animals in Egypt (ultimately leading Egyptians astray; cf. apparently Egyptian claims in Lucian *Sacrifices* 14). Even where Greek and Egyptian culture interpenetrated in Egypt, of course, Egyptian practices remained (see Sylvain Dhennin, "An Egyptian Animal Necropolis in a Greek Town," *Egyptian Archaeology* 33 [Fall, 2008]: 12–14).

41. Grant, *Paul*, 67 (citing Diodorus Siculus 1.83.6–9). Egyptians lavished care on their sacred animals (Diodorus Siculus 1.84.1–8).

those who worship animals, especially "loathsome ones."[42] Philostratus's *Apollonius* attacks Egyptian worship of animal shapes, arguing that by contrast Greek portrayal of the gods as humans honors the gods.[43] (One who wished to mock Greek myths might similarly point out Zeus' transformation into a bull and other animals.)[44]

Criticisms of polytheism and statue veneration were not, however, limited to Egyptian practices. More than most, the second-century satirist Lucian ridiculed popular notions about the gods and fate,[45] contending that the myths' gods are, like mortals, slaves to Fate.[46] The gods of myths, far from being blissful immortals, can be wounded, imprisoned, and tortured.[47] Thus, for example, Diomedes, backed by Athena, could wound the deities Aphrodite or Ares.[48] For Lucian, those who took the myths seriously were like children or the deranged.[49] Apollonius, too, was said to have dismissed

---

42. Pliny *Nat.* 2.5.16.

43. Philost. *Vit. Appoll.* 6.18-19. Max. Tyre 2.3 concurs that human images are nobler for deities than animal images are.

44. E.g., Lucian *Dialogueues of Sea-Gods* 305-306 (11/7, *South Wind and West Wind* 1); 325-326 (15, *West Wind and South Wind* 2); 327, ¶3; *Dialogueues of the Gods* 206 (6/2, *Eros and Zeus* 1); *Dialogueues of the Gods* 207-8 (7/3, *Zeus and Hermes* 1); *Dialogueues of the Gods* 269-271 (2/22, *Pan and Hermes* 1-2); Byzantine polemic in Ps.-Lucian *The Patriot* 4.

45. See Lucian *Zeus Catechized* 2-5; cf. Pliny *Nat.* 2.5.22; Lucian *Double Indictment* 2; Josephus *Ag. Ap.* 2.245.

46. Lucian *Zeus Catechized* 7-8.

47. Lucian *Zeus Catechized* 8; also in *Sacrifices* 5-6; cf. *Zeus Rants* 40. For such susceptibility of deities to harm, see e.g., Homer *Il.* Apollonius Rhodius 3.853; Apollodorus *Epitome* 4.2; Apollodorus *Bib.* 1.7.1; Libanius *Encomium* 1.10; cf. the similar demise of the bronze giant Talos, when he died from loss of his ichor (Apollonius Rhodius 4.1679-80; Apollodorus *Bib.* 1.9.26); or Chiron relinquishing immortality to evade the pain of his wound (Apollodorus *Bib.* 2.5.4); and perhaps Polyphemus in Euripides *Cycl.* 231, 321 (David Kovacs, "Introduction" to *Cyclops*, pages 53-58 in Euripides, *Cyclops, Alcestes, Medea*, edited by David Kovacs, LCL [Cambridge: Harvard University Press, 1994], 55); in ancient Near Eastern accounts, see e.g., *Ancient Near Eastern Texts Relating to the OT*, ed. James B. Pritchard, 2nd ed. (Princeton: Princeton University Press, 1955; hereafter *ANET*), 139-40; William F. Albright, *Yahweh and the Gods of Canaan* (Garden City, N.Y.: Doubleday, 1968), 125-27; Cyrus H. Gordon, "History of Religion in Psalm 82," pages 129-31 in *Biblical and Near Eastern Studies: Essays in Honor of William Sanford LaSor*, edited by Gary A. Tuttle (Grand Rapids: Eerdmans, 1978), 130-31. Such "divine" mortality was rejected by Stoics (e.g., Seneca *Ep. Lucil.* 95.49-50), and writers evaded such wounded deities by allegorization (Heraclitus *Homeric Problems* 30.1, 4; 31.1, 11; 52.5-6; 53.1).

48. Homer *Il.* 5.339-42, 855-59, 870, 881-87; cf. 5.130-32, 335-39, 829-30.

49. Lucian *Lover of Lies* 2-5. Lucian is harsher in *Amber* 3, 5-6; cf. also the criticism in Valerius Maximus 4.7.4.

stories of divine immorality as senseless fictions fit only for children or old women.[50]

Some other Gentiles complained about deities proliferated so as to correspond to all human characteristics or needs.[51] Since anything and everything could be personified and deified, why worship any deities in particular?[52] Some asked why particular immortals in the myths remained old while others remained young;[53] others mocked their conflicts with fellow deities.[54] Many ridiculed mythical deities' extramarital affairs;[55] in one satire, for example, Zeus requested that Helios the sun god take a break for three days, allowing Zeus an extended time to commit adultery.[56] In another satire Zeus must defend lust.[57]

Others challenged mythical deities' weaknesses. How could a woman elude a divine pursuer, given that even a man could normally overpower a woman?[58] How could deities prove unable to rescue mortals they loved?[59]

---

50. Philostratus *Vit. Apoll.* 5.14.

51. E.g., Pliny *Nat.* 2.5.14–16, 19.

52. Lucian *Icaromenippus* 9; *Philosophies for Sale* 4.

53. E.g., Pliny *Nat.* 2.5.17; Lucian *Sacrifices* 11.

54. E.g., Pliny *Nat.* 2.5.17; Lucian *Dialogueues of the Gods* 240 (16/14, *Hermes and Apollo* 2). Although angry at the negligence of Helios for nearly destroying the earth, Zeus allows him to evade discipline in Lucian *Dialogueues of the Gods* 278–280 (24/25, *Zeus and Helios* 1–2). Heraclitus evades this charge by allegory (*Homeric Problems* 52, esp. 52.4).

55. E.g., Pliny *Nat.* 2.5.17; Lucian *Prometheus* 17; *Parliament of the Gods* 7; *Lover of Lies* 2; *Dialogueues of the Gods* 206 (6/2, *Eros and Zeus* 1); 231 (19/11, *Aphrodite and Selene* 1); 233–234 (20/12, *Aphrodite and Eros* 1); 243 (17/15, *Hermes and Apollo* 3); 245–46 (21/17, *Apollo and Hermes* ¶¶1–2); 269–271 (2/22, *Pan and Hermes* 1–2); 272, ¶4; *Dialogueues of Sea-Gods* 305–6 (11/7, *South Wind and West Wind* 1); 325–327 (15, *West Wind and South Wind* 2–3); Philostratus the Elder *Imagines* 1.8. Some deemed it wrong for a deity to engage in sexual intercourse with a human (Hermogenes *Progymn.* 5.On Refutation and Confirmation, 11; cf. Philostratus *Vit. Apoll.* 6.40). Zeus does withhold intercourse if the offspring of the union could overthrow him; see Lucian *Dialogueues of the Gods* 205 (5/1, *Prometheus and Zeus* 2).

56. Lucian *Dialogueues of the Gods* 229 (14/10, *Hermes and Helios* 1), mocking (for a more serious version, see e.g., Apollodorus *Bib.* 2.4.8).

57. Lucian *Dialogueues of the Gods* 214–219 (9/6, *Hera and Zeus* ¶1–5). Zeus was angrier in the more serious version of the same myth (Apollodorus *Epitome* 1.20).

58. Aphth. *Progymn.* 5. On Refutation, 29S, 13R; cf. Lucian *Dialogueues of the Gods* 242, *Hermes and Apollo* 2. Most mortal objects of Apollo's affection seem to have spurned him (e.g., Apollodorus *Bib.* 3.12.5; Ovid *Metam.* 2.603–11; Lucian *Dialogueues of the Gods* 242 (17/15, *Hermes and Apollo* 2); 244 [18/16, *Hera and Leto* 1]).

59. Lucian *Dialogueues of the Gods* 239–240 (16/14, *Hermes and Apollo* 1–2); Philostratus the Elder *Imag.* 1.24; Philostratus the Younger *Imag.* 14; also Josephus *Ag. Ap.* 2.245. For deities' inability to protect beloved mortals, see e.g., Euripides *El.* 1298–1300;

Some noted Zeus' weakness, when Hera put him to sleep so the Greeks could win a battle.[60] Other inconsistencies elicited criticism. How could gods sleep with Helios spending the night with them?[61] How could Hephaistos remain perpetually disabled?[62] Some thinkers also saw little sense in carrying deities on one's fingers (i.e., rings)[63] and many noticed that oracles often hedged their responses to prevent being mistaken.[64] Many mocked Cretans' claims to possess Zeus' tomb.[65] Few philosophers took the ancient myths literally;[66] some charged with slander the poets who depicted deities as immoral.[67]

Mythical portrayals of deities played into such criticisms by moralists. Newly-born Hermes stole people's property[68] and killed someone likely to

---

Apollodorus *Bib.* 3.10.3; cf. Apollodorus *Bib.* 1.5.1.

60. Heracl. *Homeric Problems* 39.1 (on Homer *Il.* 14.347–53). Cf. 1 Kgs 18:27; contrast Ps 121:3–4.

61. Lucian *Icaromenippus* 28 (mythographers would have probably replied that Helios was moving back eastward beneath the earth; but he would have trouble making the banquets without reliable assistants).

62. Lucian *Dialogueues of the Gods* 241 (17/15, *Hermes and Apollo* 1); 243 (18/16, *Hera and Leto* 1).

63. E.g., Pliny *Nat.* 2.5.21.

64. Lucian *Dialogueues of the Gods* 244 (18/16, *Hera and Leto* 1).

65. Callimachus *Hymn* 1 (to Zeus), lines 8–9; Lucian *Sacrifices* 10; *Parliament of the Gods* 6; *Timon* 4; *Zeus Rants* 45; *Lover of Lies* 3; Ps.-Lucian *The Patriot* 10 (Byzantine); cf. Euhemerus *Sacred History* 6 (in Frederick C. Grant, *Hellenistic Religions: The Age of Syncretism* [Indianapolis: Bobbs-Merrill; New York: Liberal Arts, 1953], 76); Philostratus *Vit. Soph.* 2.4.569; *Sib. Or.* 8.45–49; Martin Dibelius and Hans Conzelmann, *The Pastoral Epistles: A Commentary on the Pastoral Epistles*, edited by Helmut Koester, trans. Philip Buttolph and Adela Yarbro (Philadelphia: Fortress, 1972), 136.

66. Grant, *Paul*, 4–5; beyond philosophers, e.g., Libanius *Invect.* 7.2. Allegorizing allowed them to develop acceptable morals (Cicero *Nat. d.* 2.28.70; cf. Josephus *Ag. Ap.* 2.255; Gilbert Murray, *Five Stages of Greek Religion* [New York: Columbia University Press, 1925], 202; Everett Ferguson, *Backgrounds of Early Christianity* [Grand Rapids: Eerdmans, 1987], 98); some simply rewrote stories (e.g., *Recantation of Stesichorus*; Pindar *Olympian Odes* 1.52–53).

67. Dio Chrysostom *Or.* 37.32 (Favorinus). Dio Chrysostom *Or.* 11.19, protests Homer's depiction of the gods, going on even to charge him with lying (11.23). (This was not Dio's approach always; 12.23 favors Hesiod, and 18.8 regards Homer as the greatest poet).

68. E.g., Ovid *Metam.* 2.685–86; Lucian *Dialogueues of the Gods* 220 (11/7, *Hephaistos and Apollo* 1); Philostratus the Elder *Imag.* 1.26; cf. Lucian *Prometheus* 5. He also stole Apollo's property in Apollodorus *Bib.* 3.10.2; in 2.1.3, Zeus ordered him to steal a cow. For earlier deities' covetousness, see e.g., Cyrus H. Gordon, *The Ancient Near East* (New York: W. W. Norton, 1965), 100; Walter C. Kaiser, Jr., "The Ugaritic Pantheon" (PhD diss., Brandeis University, 1973), 63.

betray him.⁶⁹ Divinities could become animals to mate with each other.⁷⁰ Likewise deities—whether single or married—seduced and raped various women⁷¹ and sometimes boys;⁷² yet they might slay mortals who proved unfaithful.⁷³ (Jewish and Christian critics often focused on these features of immorality.)⁷⁴ Jealous about Zeus's affairs, Hera sought vengeance on

---

69. Ovid *Metam.* 2.687-707 (esp. 705-7; cf. Mercury killing by turning to stone in 2.830-32).

70. Zeus became a bull to mate with Hera when she was a cow (Aeschylus *Suppliant Women* 299-301; cf. Poseidon's behavior in *Thebaid* frg. 11, from scholiast D on *Iliad*, 23.346). Earlier, Baal apparently turned into a bull to mate with his sister Anath when she became a heifer; see *ANET* 139; Gordon, *Near East*, 99; Albright, *Yahweh*, 128-29; James C. Moyer, "Hittite and Israelite Cultic Practices: A Selected Comparison," 19-38 in *Scripture in Context II: More Essays on the Comparative Method*, ed. William F. Hallo, James C. Moyer, and Leo G. Perdue (Winona Lake, Ind.: Eisenbrauns, 1983), 25; Kaiser, "Pantheon," 9, 58, 60, 155-56; cf. perhaps divine bestiality in *ANET* 84; that of Helios' daughter Pasiphae in Apollodorus *Bibl.* 3.1.2-4; 3.15.8; Ovid *Metam.* 8.131-37, 155-56; Libanius *Narration* 21; 22.

71. E.g., Sophocles *Searchers* 212-15; Euripides *Antiope* 69-71, frg. 223.72-77; *Pirithous* 22-24; *Alope* frg. 107; *Archelaus* frg. 228a.15-16; *Danae* frg. 1132.26-34; *Andromeda* frg. 136; Menander *Heros* frg. 2; Apollodorus *Bib.* 1.5.1; 1.7.8-9; 1.9.3; 3.2.1 (bringing about her death); 3.1.1; 3.4.3; 3.5.5; 3.7.6; 3.8.2; 3.10.1, 3; 3.12.2, 5-6; 3.15.2, 4; *Epitome* 1.9, 22; *Thebaid* frg. 11 (from scholiast D on *Iliad*, 23.346); *Cypria* frg. 10 (from Athenaeus *Deipn.* 334b); frg. 11 (from Philodemus *Piety* B 7369); Varro *Latin Language* 5.5.31; Ovid *Metam.* 2.714-47; 3.1-2, 260-61; 4.234-44; 5.391-408; 14.765-71; Silius Italicus 13.615; Lucian *Dialogueues of the Gods* 250 (23/19, *Aphrodite and Eros* 1); Pausanias 8.25.7-8; Parthenius *Love Romance* 15.3 (leading to another's death); Achilles Tatius 1.5.5-7; Apuleius *Metam.* 6.22; Libanius *Speech in Character* 27.3; *Narration* 1; 4.1-2; 17; 31; 32; 39; 41 (cf. *Narration* 3). Once in a while a human escaped, whether by outwitting a deity (Apollonius Rhodius 2.946-54) or by running faster (Libanius *Speech in Character* 27.4; cf. *Narration* 17).

72. For the boy Ganymede (raped by Zeus), see e.g., Callimachus *Epig.* 53; Apollodorus *Bib.* 3.12.2; Virgil *Aen.* 1.28; Ovid *Metam.* 10.155-61; Lucian *Parliament of the Gods* 8-9; *Dialogueues of the Gods* 208-12 (10/4, *Zeus and Ganymede* ¶¶1-5), especially 208, ¶1; 213 (8/5, *Zeus and Hera* ¶2); 214, ¶¶2-3; Ps.-Lucian *Affairs* 14; *Charidemus* 7; Alciphron *Parasites* 23 (Limenterus to Amasetus), 3.59, ¶2; Philostratus *Letters* 8 (46); Philostratus the Younger *Imag.* 8. For Apollo's love for Hyacinthus, see e.g., Apollodorus *Bib.* 3.10.3; Ovid *Metam.* 10.162-219; Lucian *Dialogueues of the Gods* 239-240 (16/14, *Hermes and Apollo* 1-2); 242, *Hermes and Apollo* 2; 244 (18/16, *Hera and Leto* 1); Philostratus the Elder *Imag.* 1.24; Libanius *Narration* 2. Occasionally goddesses or nymphs acted similarly (e.g., Lucian *Sacr.* 7; Apollonius Rhodius 1.1226-39; Ovid *Metam.* 4.368-79; Silius Italicus 5.15-21; Apollodorus *Bib.* 3.12.4).

73. E.g., Ovid *Metam.* 2.603-11 (despite his subsequent remorse, 2.612-13). Cf. Libanius *Narration* 2; 4.2; 32.

74. E.g., Josephus *Ag. Ap.* 2.244-46, 275; Athenagoras 20-22; Theophilus 1.9; Ps.-Clem. *Hom.* 4.15.1—4.19.3.

his paramours.[75] Angry at humans' neglect[76] or disrespect,[77] divinities also sought their deaths.[78] Gods could deceive with divine effectiveness.[79]

Mortals also sometimes questioned the justice of deities (although not the purer, idealized deities of many philosophers).[80] They could even threaten to disbelieve in deities if they failed to act![81] Polytheists could also pit some deities against others;[82] the most prominent literary example, known to virtually all Greeks, was the Trojan War.[83] Different deities could have competing agendas.[84] To become ruler, Zeus had overthrown his own father.[85] Such depictions of divine morality, probably reflecting what their human creators would do if they had divine power, in turn offered models for human behavior.[86] Recognizing the connection, Jewish and Christian

---

75. E.g., Aechylus *Aetna*, frg.; Euripides *Bacchanals* 94–98; Sophocles *Searchers* 212–15; Callimachus *Hymn* 4 (to Delos), lines 55–58; Apollodorus *Bib.* 1.4.1, 3; 3.4.3; Ovid *Metam.* 2.477–88; 3.261–72, 280–309; 4.416–530; Appian *Hist. rom.* 12.15.101; Lucian *Dialogueues of the Gods* 207 (7/3, *Zeus and Hermes* 1); 213 (8/5, *Zeus and Hera* ¶¶1–2) (of Ganymede); 228 (12/9, *Poseidon and Hermes* 2; Lucian *Dial. S.-G.* 315 (9/10, *Iris and Poseidon*, ¶1); Seneca *Hercules* 1–29; Libanius *Narration* 12.

76. E.g., Euripides *Hippolytus* 1–28, 1400–3 (because deities desire honor, 8); Apollonius Rhodius 3.64–65; nonlethally in Pindar *Hymns* frg. 37; Apollodorus *Bib.* 1.9.15. A mortal woman who preferred another to a divine lover might be killed (Apollodorus *Bib.* 3.10.3).

77. Ovid *Metam.* 4.543–62; 5.409–37. A mortal who challenged Apollo was skinned to make a wine-bottle (Apollodorus *Bib.* 1.4.2; Philostratus the Younger *Imag.* 2); Athena flayed Pallas alive (Apollodorus *Bib.* 1.6.2). A deity could also seek the destruction of the object of his jealousy (Apollodorus *Bib.* 2.4.3; 3.14.1; one view in 3.4.4).

78. Often they inspired them with folly that destroyed them (Homer *Il.* 18.311–13; but cf. also 1 Sam 2:25; 2 Sam 17:14).

79. Statius *Ach.* 1.364.

80. E.g., Euripides *Orest.* 417–18, 595–96. This seems to exceed sentiments such as those in 2 Sam 6:8; Ps 89:38–49.

81 Odysseus in Euripides *Cycl.* 606–7. Polytheists often reminded a deity of favors owed, soliciting aid on contractual grounds (see e.g., Homer *Il.* 1.39–41; 10.291–94; *Od.* 1.61–62, 66–67; 4.762–64; 17.240–42; Apollonius Rhodius 1.417–19; Virgil *Aen.* 12.778).

82. E.g., in Silius Italicus 9.438–39; Apollodorus *Bib.* 3.14.1; Libanius *Narration* 7.1–3; 17; cf. Hephaistos opposing Ares's adultery with Hephaistos's wife (Homer *Od.* 8.266–366; Libanius *Narration* 26.1–2).

83. E.g., Ovid *Tristia* 1.2.4–5.

84. E.g., Aeschylus *Eum.* 179–84, 299–300; Ovid *Tristia* 1.2.4–5; Silius Italicus 9.438–39.

85. E.g., Aeschylus *Eum.* 640–51.

86. E.g., Philostratus *Vit. Soph.* 2.1.554; Achilles Tatius 1.5.5–7; cf. Pindar frg. 199 (from Strabo 17.1.19); Diodorus Siculus 1.27.1; Philostratus *Love Letters* 30 (58); Harold Mattingly, *Christianity in the Roman Empire* (New York: W. W. Norton, 1967), 23. Cf. Jewish and Christian critiques on this point (Josephus *Ag. Ap.* 2.244–46; *Ps.-Clem.*

apologists announced the superiority of their God partly by condemning the morality of pagan deities.[87] Early Christian apologists, denounced especially for their monotheism, sought to differentiate their foundational stories from the tales of polytheistic deities.[88]

Eager to evade the negative model, many intellectuals allegorized the myths or even attributed the worst divine acts to lesser beings merely named after the higher deities who were their leaders.[89] Thus Heraclitus salvages the story of Hera putting Zeus to sleep by allegorizing it,[90] and allegorizes deities' extramarital affairs[91] and Hephaistos's continuing disability.[92] The Neoplatonist Proclus notes that the poets were wrong to depict heroes and deities like mortals;[93] such beings should rather be praised as wholly pure.[94] Thus it is bad to depict their "thievery... rapes, wanderings, adulteries, wars, plotting...,"[95] or "crimes against fathers and tying them up and castrating them."[96] Such scenes prove problematic for the schooling of young hearers.[97] Yet Proclus claims to defend the true meaning of the myths against impious people who ignorantly criticize the gods' immorality.[98] His criticism may have applied to Epicureans;[99] some scholars think it directed at least in part against Christian critics.[100]

---

Hom. 4.15.1—4.19.3). Gentile admonitions to imitate deities naturally did not appeal to these models (e.g., Xenophon *Cyr.* 6.2.29; Cicero *Tusc.* 5.25.70; Seneca *Dial.* 1.1.5; 7.8.4; Musonius Rufus 8, p. 64.14; Epictetus *Disc.* 2.14.12–13; Dio Chrysostom *Or.* 3.82; Plutarch *That we ought not to borrow* 7, *Mor.* 830B; Heraclitus *Ep.* 5; Maximus of Tyre *Or.* 35.2; *Sentences of Sextus* 44–45; Libanius *Thesis* 1.3).

87. E.g., Josephus *Ag. Ap.* 2.232–49, 275; Athenagoras 20–22; Theophilus 1.9; Tatian 33–34.

88. See Jaroslav Pelikan, *Acts* (Grand Rapids: Brazos, 2005), 163, noting especially Origen's *Contra Celsum* (e.g., *Cels.* 4.5).

89. For the latter approach, see Proclus *Poet.* K147.7–10, 21–25.

90. *Homeric Problems* 39.2–17; cf. Proclus *Poet.* K135.19–22.

91. *Homeric Problems* 68–69, esp. 68.8–9; 69.8–16.

92. *Homeric Problems* 26.1, 7–8.

93. Proclus *Poet.* K44.7–16; K96.11.

94. K65.19–23; K72.24–26; K96.9–10; K99.18–19. If they fabricate stories about the gods, they must retain their genuine character (K65.29–30).

95. K45.18–21; quotation from K45.20–21, trans. p. 9.

96. K72.20–26 (quotation lines 21–22; trans. p. 65).

97. K82.2–7; K83.8.

98. K74.15–16; K74.25–31.

99. As in K119.2–3.

100. Robert Lamberton, in *Proclus the Successor on Poetics and the Homeric Poems: Essays 5 and 6 of his Commentary on the Republic of Plato* (trans. introduction, and notes by Robert Lamberton; SBL Writings from the Greco-Roman World 34; Atlanta:

Granted, Homer's myths do not inculcate virtue in the young,[101] Proclus notes, but mature hearers can catch the stories' "mystical" significance.[102] Thus the fall of Hephaistos from heaven merely depicts the movement of the divine from high to low; binding Kronos depicts creation's unity with its origin; Ouranos's castration reflects degeneration from the original order, and the like.[103] War among deities simply signifies the original united creation versus fragmentation and ultimately matter.[104] Both Ares and Hephaistos having Aphrodite in some manner signifies the presence of beauty in each of their spheres;[105] even the intercourse of Zeus and Hera is symbolic.[106] The immorality of deities in Greek myths, then, constituted a problem for moral instruction noticed by others besides monotheistic critics.

Jews and early Christians resisted not only polytheism, but also the attachment of images to the divine. In reality, cult statues were not the dominant feature of Greco-Roman religious practice[107] the way they had been in the ancient Near Eastern milieu against which OT prophets polemicized[108]—though, as we shall note below, they did remain significant.[109] Most intellectuals recognized a difference between a divinity and its image;[110] the statues merely symbolized the deity, a reminder to worshipers.[111] Although cult statues ideally should depict a deity's character appropriately,[112] mere statues could only illustrate, not communicate the essence of, deities.[113]

---

Society of Biblical Literature, 2012), 69n90.

101. K80.5–6.

102. K80.10–12; K83.9–10; cf. the symbolic approach of some in K131.5–9. Thus the poets "disguised" truth (K90.92–93) with "symbolic" teaching (K134.3; K135.18–19).

103. K82.10–17.

104. K90.8–14.

105. K141.16–21. Similarly, the pursuit of and wars for Helen merely teach the value of invisible beauty (K153.25–29).

106. K132.16; signifying this generative dyad as an origin of the universe in K134.10–15.

107. James B. Rives, *Religion in the Roman Empire* (Oxford: Blackwell, 2007), 32–34.

108. Rives, *Religion*, 34.

109. Rives, *Religion*, 34–36.

110. Lucian *Portr. D.* 23; cf. Hans-Josef Klauck, *The Religious Context of Early Christianity: A Guide to Graeco-Roman Religions*, trans. Brian McNeil (Minneapolis: Fortress, 2003), 27; still harsher critiques by Cynics, in F. Gerald Downing, *Cynics, Paul and the Pauline Churches: Cynics and Christian Origins II* (London: Routledge, 1998), 213.

111. Grant, *Paul*, 4.

112. Dio Chrysostom *Or.* 12.74–75, 77.

113. Dio Chrysostom *Or.* 12.52, 54, 59. Against images made by people, see Iamblichus *Letter* 18.1–3 (Stobaeus *Anth.* 3.11.35).

Still, even those who recognized these distinctions often felt that images helped humans to appreciate their gods concretely.[114] Some Platonists tried to reconcile their emphasis on the supreme good (an emphasis that later Christian Platonists used to promote monotheism) with deity images. Though northern Mediterranean peoples often ridiculed Egyptians' veneration of animal figures (see comments above), some Platonists argued that deities sanctified lower (material) forms by using these forms to represent themselves.[115] Maximus of Tyre, for example, thought even animal images acceptable if they turned people's thoughts toward God.[116] Some writers later appealed to this understanding against Christians, contending that the supreme deity allowed the worship of additional deities.[117] Christians' strict monotheism and total aversion to deity images would alienate Christians from public life in their communities.[118]

## TURNING FROM FALSE DEITIES

In Acts 14:15, the apostles emphasize that they share a common humanity with those who wish to venerate them; their language evokes and challenges the crowd's claim in 14:11 that the apostles have become merely "like" people.[119] Greek-speaking Jews already employed this term to designate shared humanity (4 Macc 12:13) or createdness (Wisd 7:3). A rhetorical connection within the same sentence is also possible, although the frequency of the verb ποιέω (156 times in Luke-Acts) reduces the certainty of this connection.

114. Dio Chrysostom *Or.* 12.60 (though preferring human figures, 12.61). For Celsus's defense of venerating images, opposing Christian criticisms, see John Granger Cook, *The Interpretation of the NT in Greco-Roman Paganism* (Tübingen: J. C. B. Mohr, 2000; Peabody, Mass.: Hendrickson, 2002), 91–94.

115. Iamblichus *Myst.* 7.1; cf. Maximus of Tyre 2.2, 10. Later Christian Platonists were able to adapt this approach to defend the incarnation (and ultimately the use of icons) while retaining Platonic notions. For the early Christian Platonists, cf. e.g., Frend, *Rise of Christianity*, 369–79, 660, 664, 719.

116. Maximus of Tyre 2.10. Such a position is ridiculed in Lucian *Parliament of the Gods* 11.

117. *Apocritica* 4.20–23 (in *Porphyry's Against the Christians: The Literary Remains*, ed., trans. R. Joseph Hoffmann [Amherst, N.Y.: Prometheus, 1994], 83–88). Cults stressing a supreme God but allowing intermediary grew in popularity in late antiquity (Kirsopp Lake, "Proselytes and God-Fearers," 5:74–96 in *The Beginnings of Christianity: The Acts of the Apostles*, 5 vols., ed. F. J. Foakes-Jackson and Kirsopp Lake [London: Macmillan, 1933], 94).

118. See David A. deSilva, *Honor, Patronage, Kinship, and Purity: Unlocking NT Culture* (Downers Grove, Ill.: InterVarsity, 2000), 47.

119. Marianne Fournier, *The Episode at Lystra: A Rhetorical and Semiotic Analysis of Acts 14:7–20a*, AUSt 7.197 (New York: Lang, 1997), 84.

Paul and Barnabas may contrast what the crowd is "doing" with what God "did" in creating heaven, earth, the sea and all that is in them. In this case, the wording underlines that the crowd's action is sacrilegious, responding to God's benevolence with betrayal rather than the appropriate gratitude. Because gratitude was a necessary response to benefaction in antiquity,[120] such betrayal appeared heinous.

In view of Luke's general usage (Luke 1:16-17; 22:32; Acts 9:35; 11:21; 15:19; 26:18; 28:27), the speech's summons to "turn" is functionally equivalent to a call to "repent" (see e.g., 2:38); note the essential equivalence of the language in 3:19 and 26:20.[121] Other Diaspora Jewish sources also depict "repentance" as a necessary response to idolatry (e.g., *Jos. Asen.* 9:2), even for Egyptian priests (*Sib. Or.* 5.497).[122] Although historians usually summarized (as presumably here) or, more often, elaborated speeches in their own words, the language also fits what we know of the historical Paul. He describes Gentiles' conversion in terms of "turning from idols" to a "living God" (1 Thess 1:9).

"Living God" in this context emphasizes God's active concern for people.[123] Although the title "living God" was frequent in early Judaism,[124] Jewish sources sometimes contrasted the "living God" (as here) with the lifeless deities of polytheism (e.g., Jer 10:10 [cf. 10:8-10];[125] *Jos. Asen.* 8:5).

---

120. E.g., Xenophon *Mem.* 2.2.13; Cicero *Fam.* 13.22.2; Seneca *Controv.* 9.1.intro; 9.1.9; Valerius Maximus 5.2; Pliny *Ep.* 3.2.6; 4.13.10; 7.15.3; 7.31.7; Fronto *Ad Ant. Pium* 9.1; Peter Garnsey and Richard Saller, *The Roman Empire: Economy, Society, and Culture* (Berkeley: University of California Press, 1987), 148; deSilva, *Honor*, 109-10, 116, 142; idem, "Patronage," 768; James R. Harrison, *Paul's Language of Grace in Its Graeco-Roman Context*, WUNT 2.172 (Tübingen: J. C. B. Mohr, 2003), 40-43; deSilva, "Patronage," 766-71 in *Dictionary of Background*, 768. People also viewed gratitude toward deities as obligatory (e.g., Aelius Aristides *Panath.* 21, 161-62D; Menander Rhetor 2.17, 437.7-9, 13-15; Diogenes Laertius 8.1.24; cf. Porphyry *To Marcella* 35.534-35).

121. Cf. Lk 17:4. Jewish sources normally invite turning to God, with Christians adding turning to Jesus (Acts 11:20-21; Jacques Dupont, *The Salvation of the Gentiles: Essays on the Acts of the Apostles*, trans. John R. Keating [New York: Paulist, 1979], 71); yet even for Christians, polytheists' conversion required turning to monotheism (cf. 1 Thess 1:9).

122. Cf. perhaps also Philo *On Virtues* 175-82 (as understood by Per Jarl Bekken, *The Word Is Near You: A Study of Deuteronomy 30:12-14 in Paul's Letter to the Romans in a Jewish Context*, BZNWK 144 [Berlin: de Gruyter, 2007], 85-90); cf. also later in Islam (Qur'an 39.17).

123. Cf. Christian Dionne, "La figure narrative de Dieu dans le discours à Lystre (Ac 14,15-17)," *ScEs* 57 (2, 2005): 101-24.

124. E.g., *Jub.* 1:25; 21:4; *Sib. Or.* 3.763; 4Q504 frg. 1-2Rv.9; frg. 8R.12; 5Q10 frg. 1.4; pervasive in Philo (over 100, perhaps close to 150, times); later, cf. *b. Shab.* 137; *Erub.* 13b; *Pesah.* 87b; *Yoma* 35b; *Hag.* 12b; *Ned.* 65a; *Git.* 6b; *Qid.* 36a.

125. Although the LXX omits Jer 10:10. Cf. the usage in Josh 3:10; 1 Sam 17:26, 36;

In denouncing the worship of these false deities as "vain" (μάταιος), Barnabas and Paul evoke biblical language[126] also echoed in other Diaspora Jewish sources.[127] Paul employs a cognate verb with reference to idolatry in one of his letters (ματαιόω, Rom 1:21).[128]

## Heaven, Earth and Sea

The speech's "maker of heaven, earth, and sea" (Acts 14:15) fits Luke's style (see 4:24; cf. "Lord of heaven and earth" in 17:24; Luke 10:21) and is not unexpected in a Lukan speech summary. Because speakers typically gestured toward visible objects they mentioned,[129] Luke's audience may envision Paul and/or Barnabas instinctively gesturing toward heaven and earth when mentioning these locations. Where the same formula appears earlier, in Acts 4:24, its setting in prayer would probably reinforce for Luke's audience the allusion to the words' original setting in Ps 146:6 (cf. also allusions in Rev 5:13; 10:6; 14:7; 21:1). Luke's use here might evoke the psalm's context: God has healed in Acts 14:10, and Ps 146:8 praises God as the healer; that the Septuagint is less clear on this point, however, may weaken the argument. Although Paul nowhere uses this full formula from the psalm, the idea would not be foreign to him (cf. 1 Cor 8:5; 10:26; Eph 3:15; Col 1:16, 20; especially Phil 2:10). Certainly he argues about God from creation (Rom 1:20),[130] with moral implications concerning idolatry (Rom 1:25).

The Lystra speech's formula may echo Scripture, but Gentiles would not find the language unfamiliar. Already in the Augustan era, for example, Roman poets spoke of the supreme God ruling heaven, earth and the sea.[131]

---

2 Kgs 19:4, 16; Is 37:4, 17; Dan 6:20, 26; cf. also 2 Cor 6:16.

126. Lev 17:7 (LXX only); 1 Kgs 16:2 (LXX only), 13, 26; 2 Kgs 17:15; 2 Chron 11:15 (LXX); Is 2:20 (LXX); 44:9; Jer 2:5; 8:19 (LXX); 10:3, 15; 51:18 (LXX 28:18); Ezek 8:10 (LXX); Jon 2:8; Wisd 13:1; 15:8; 3 Macc 6:11; using a different term, Wisd 14:14. The language applied to any kind of deception in which people trusted (e.g., Ezek 13:6–9, 19; 21:29; 22:28; Sir 34[31]:5). Cf. also J. N. D. Kelly, *A Commentary on the Epistles of Peter and Jude* (Grand Rapids: Baker, 1981), 74, on LXX background for 1 Pet 1:18.

127. E.g., the probably pre-Christian oracles in *Sib. Or.* 3.29, 547–48; cf. the euhemeristic application to the human "gods" in 3.551–54 (esp. 554).

128. Cf. *Sib. Or.* 3.555: idols lead to thinking vain things.

129. See William David Shiell, *Reading Acts: The Lector and the Early Christian Audience*, BIS 70 (Boston: Brill Academic, 2004), 57–62, esp. 57. See Walter E. Pilgrim, "Luke-Acts and a Theology of Creation," *Word and World* 12 (1, 1992): 51–58, for God as creator in Luke-Acts.

130. Also Porter, *Paul in Acts*, 147 (mentioning the Stoic description there).

131. Virgil *Georg.* 4.221–22 (Virgil also links these three parts of creation in *Aen.* 1.58, 280); Ovid *Metam.* 1.180; Horace *Ode* 1.12.13–18 (cf. 3.45–48).

Later orators could speak of Apollo's glory filling these same three spheres at his birth.[132] Typical Gentile conceptions diverged from those articulated by the apostles here, however: in polytheism, heaven, earth and the sea were actual deities themselves.[133] Although the originating issue may have been appeal to Zeus and Hermes (Acts 14:12), Paul would have known the wider polytheistic system of belief to which that appeal belonged.

Most striking to the hearers in the narrative world may be the challenge to local Phrygian beliefs, beliefs that others also widely associated with Phrygia. Many ancient sources portray the earth as mother,[134] or mention the earth mother or mother earth,[135] "Great Mother,"[136] "Mother of the gods,"[137] "Mother of all,"[138] the Idaean Mother,[139] or "Mother Cybele."[140] Yet it was Phrygia in particular that was especially known for the worship of Earth as a mother goddess.[141] Technically, Lystra was in Lycaonia rather than Phrygia; the Phrygian language was spoken in nearby Iconium (cf. Acts 13:51—14:1), but not in Lystra.[142] Nevertheless, Lystra was close enough to the shifting border that it could be influenced by and associated

---

132. Menander Rhetor 2.17, 439.18–19 (the linking of these spheres also appears in 439.20–21).

133. Rives, *Religion*, 16.

134. Aeschylus *Seven against Thebes* 16; Pindar *Nemean Odes* 6.1-2; *Ol.* 7.38; Ovid *Metam.* 1.393; *Fasti* 2.713–19; Valerius Maximus 7.3.2; Pliny *Nat.* 2.63.154; Suetonius *Jul.* 7.2; Philostratus *Vit. Apoll.* 1.15; 4 *Ezra* 10:9–14 (in the context of Zion as mother, 9:41—10:24); as nurse, Pausanias 1.22.3; Athenaeus *Deipn.* 10.451E; for Nature as mother, Pliny *Nat.* 24.1.1; 37.78.205.

135. E.g., Aeschylus *Suppliant Women* 890; *Libation-Bearers* 44; Lucretius *Nat.* 2.581–99.

136. E.g., Virgil *Aen.* 10.220 (cf. 10.234); Pliny *Ep.* 10.49.1; *Greek Anth.* 6.220. In iconography she is identified with Cybele (Giovanni Uggeri, "Mater Magna," *Brill's New Pauly: Encyclopaedia of the Ancient World*, ed. Hubert Cancik, Helmuth Schneider, and Christine F. Salazar [Leiden: Brill, 2002–2010], 8:458–59, here 459).

137. E.g., Apollonius Rhodius 3.716; Sextus Empiricus *Pyr.* 3.217; Valerius Maximus 8.15.3; Pliny *Nat.* 2.6.37; Diogenes Laertius 6.1.1. Prometheus as a Titan was a child of earth (Lucian *Zeus Rants* 1; *Prometheus* 3).

138. Homeric Hymn 30, to Earth, line 1; Virgil *Aen.* 6.595; *Greek Anth.* 7.461; cf. Philo *Creation* 133.

139. Valerius Maximus 7.5.2; Grattius lines 19–20.

140. Seneca *Troj.* 72; cf. Catullus 63.9.

141. For specifically Phrygian associations, see e.g., Euripides *Bacch.* 58–59, 79; Lucretius *Nat.* 2.611; *Rhet. Her.* 4.59.62; Valerius Maximus 7.5.2; Seneca *Ep. Lucil.* 108.7; Lucian *Gout* 30–32; Ps.-Lucian *Affairs* 42. Cf. Richard L. Gordon, "Ma," 8:49–51 in *Brill's New Pauly*, on the traditional Anatolian mother goddess "Ma" (i.e., "mother"), though she was not centered specifically in Phrygia.

142. *MAMA* 7, p. xliv; see also Stephen Mitchell, *Anatolia: Land, Men, and Gods in Asia Minor*, 2 vols. (Oxford: Clarendon, 1993), 2:155.

with Phrygia. Euripides already associated "Mother Rhea" (Zeus's mother) with Phrygia,[143] and some spoke of the "mother of the gods" as Phrygian.[144] Even in the Egyptian Isis cult, later syncretism recognized Phrygians as the first to honor the mother of the gods.[145] The mother goddess Cybele's music was distinctly Phrygian.[146] Although Cybele was by this period more hellenized, she remained "mother."[147]

Of course, the worship of neither mother goddesses in general nor Cybele in particular was limited to Phrygia.[148] By this period, even Romans honored the mother goddess;[149] being fairly ecumenical, they had brought her cult to Rome itself,[150] though Roman citizens were initially barred from participating in it. (The associated rites of Attis found welcome only during the reign of Claudius—the period Luke's narrative here depicts—though they became popular thereafter.)[151]

The apostles' biblical preaching would naturally challenge more than local worship of the earth mother. The crowds equated Barnabas with Zeus (Acts 14:12), mythically deemed ruler of heaven. According to the tradition myth, Zeus received the rule of heaven, Hades of the underworld, and Poseidon of the sea.[152] The apostles proclaim instead a single god as both ruler and creator of the entire cosmos.

---

143. Euripides *Bacch.* 58–59 (Rhea being Zeus' mother). For Cybele as Zeus's mother (Rhea in Greek myth), see e.g., Martial *Epig.* 9.39.

144. Diogenes Laertius 6.1.1; cf. *Orphic Hymns* 27.12.

145. Apuleius *Metam.* 11.4–5.

146. E.g., Lucretius *Nat.* 2.618–20; cf. Apuleius *Metam.* 8.30.

147. Lynn E. Roller, "The Great Mother at Gordion: The Hellenization of an Anatolian Cult," *Journal of Hellenic Studies* 111 (1991): 128–43.

148. Note Cybele in e.g., Samothrace (Katherine Welch, "A Statue Head of the 'Great Mother' from Samothrace," *Hesperia* 65 [4, 1996]: 467–73) and Crete (Ian F. Sanders, *Roman Crete: An Archaeological Survey and Gazetteer of Late Hellenistic, Roman, and Early Byzantine Crete* [Warminster, Wilts., U.K.: Aris & Phillips, 1982], 37; Strabo 10.3.11, 13), though mother goddess veneration appears already in Minoan Crete (Sarah B. Pomeroy, *Goddesses, Whores, Wives, and Slaves: Women in Classical Antiquity* [New York: Schocken, 1975], 13–14). For other mother goddesses, see e.g., Tacitus *Germ.* 40, 45; cf. Jer 7:18; 44:17.

149. See Valerius Maximus 1.1.1.

150. Valerius Maximus 7.5.2; 8.15.3; Silius Italicus 17.1–4 (line 8 calls her Cybele); cf. the temple in Tacitus *Ann.* 4.64; Tiberius's interest in Pliny *Nat.* 35.36.70. See also discussion in Uggeri, "Mater Magna," 458.

151. See discussion in Grant, *Gods*, 33; Klauck, *Context*, 124.

152. E.g., Lucian *The Dance* 37. Cf. some heavenly, earthly and chthonic deities in Homer *Il.* 3.276–78; *PGM* 1.315–16; 17a.2–3 (cf. the three tiers in *Pr. Jos.* 11); heavenly, terrestrial and marine (*PDM Suppl.* 131–34); heavenly, marine and chthonic (Josephus *Ag. Ap.* 2.240); deities above and below in Livy 31.31.3; *PGM* 1.264.

## God testified through nature (Acts 14:16-17)

Given the article's focus on polytheism and statue veneration, it should suffice to merely summarize points in the rest of the Lystra speech. God, though merciful, disapproved of their idolatry. Claiming that God permitted past eras of wrong behavior (14:16) probably means that he "overlooked ignorance" (17:30), unhappily putting up with it. This passage, 17:30 and Rom 3:25 might all echo Wisdom 11:23, where God mercifully overlooks people's sins "for repentance," probably meaning that he spares them destruction to allow them to repent.

Despite God's patience, he had revealed himself benevolently all along through the gifts of nature. Rhetorically prudent speakers would appeal to what their hearers valued (Arist. *Rhet.* 1.9.30, 1367b), as here. Although much of Lycaonia was inhospitable to agriculture (Strabo 12.6.1), in contrast to nearby Phrygia (Horace *Ode* 2.12.22), Lystra was primarily a rural community, for whom more urban rhetoric might have been alienating.[153] Stephen Mitchell emphasizes the radical contrast between urban life and that of rural villages in Asia Minor, including in matters of "[l]anguage and nomenclature, diet and lifestyle, cults and patterns of authority."[154]

Although mostly polytheists, ancient hearers would have readily associated talk of fertility with deities. Greeks invoked Demeter before sowing (e.g., Epictetus *Diatr.* 3.21.12), for example, and temples included rituals to ensure fertility.[155] Phrygians looked to their goddess of justice for fertility,[156]

---

153. For tensions between urban and rural populations in the early Empire, see Keener, *Acts*, 1:589-96; Ramsay MacMullen, *Roman Social Relations: 50 B.C. to A.D. 284* (New Haven: Yale University Press, 1974), 15, 30, 32; Clarence L. Lee, "Social Unrest and Primitive Christianity," 121-38 in *The Catacombs and the Colosseum: The Roman Empire as the Setting of Primitive Christianity*, ed. Stephen Benko and John J. O'Rourke (Valley Forge, Pa.: Judson, 1971), 128. Emphasis on rural stereotypes has sometimes been overplayed here, however, since for Luke the Lystrans' behavior is not stereotypically rural, but stereotypically *Gentile* (see Keener, *Acts*, 2:2169).

154. Mitchell, *Anatolia*, 1:195.

155. E.g., in Egypt (Frankfurter, *Religion in Egypt*, 37-46).

156. Mitchell, *Anatolia*, 2:18. Other peoples also had fertility deities; see e.g., Epictetus *Diatr.* 3.21.12; in Roman Egypt, David Frankfurter, *Religion in Roman Egypt: Assimilation and Resistance* (Princeton: Princeton University Press, 1998), 37-46; cf. Françoise Dunand, *Religion populaire en Égypte romaine*, ÉPROER 77 [Leiden: Brill, 1979], 77-78); on older fertility emphases and practices in agrarian societies, see e.g., *ANET*, 126-128, 129-42; Walter Harrelson, *From Fertility Cult to Worship* (Garden City, N.Y.: Doubleday, 1969), 12-13; John Bright, *A History of Israel*, 3rd ed. (Philadelphia: Westminster, 1981), 118-19; James C. Moyer, "The Concept of Ritual Purity among the Hittites" (PhD diss., Brandeis University, 1969), 59.

but especially to Zeus.¹⁵⁷ Ancient speakers could go further: at least in a later era, some sycophantic rhetors credited rains and harvests (Menander Rhetor 2.1–2, 377.22–24) and all prosperity (377.20–22) to the emperor. Neither Luke's audience nor, likely, Luke himself, would have been aware how relevant the apostles' reported words were to hearers in southern Asia Minor: Phrygian and Pisidian inscriptions honor Zeus Kalakagathios, giver of good benefits and fruitfulness.¹⁵⁸ By contrast, Luke's biblically informed ideal audience understood the one God as provider of fruitfulness (Gen 1:12, 29–31) and as sovereign over seasons and fruitfulness (*1 En.* 2:1—5:3, especially 5:2). It was he who bestowed agricultural productivity (e.g., Deut 28:3–12; *Test. Iss.* 5:4).

What was true of fertility in general was also true of the specific sorts of blessings noted in this speech—rain and fruitful seasons. In attempts to secure rain, people employed a variety of religious rituals,¹⁵⁹ including some rituals commonly perceived as magic.¹⁶⁰ Although Zeus and local surrogates were the chief storm deities,¹⁶¹ people also could attribute rains to various other deities.¹⁶² (More "secular" explanations also existed, although they were less pervasive.)¹⁶³

Monotheists naturally reserved this activity for the one God. Scripture already emphasized his benevolence in sending rain and sustaining creatures (Lev 26:4; Ps 145:15; 147:8–9; rain in its [rainy] seasons, Jer 5:24).¹⁶⁴

---

157. Mitchell, *Anatolia*, 2:23.

158. Eckhard J. Schnabel, *Paul the Missionary: Realities, Strategies and Methods* (Downers Grove, Ill.: InterVarsity; Leicester, U.K.: Apollos, 2008), 167, also highlighting the regional prominence of Zeus Bronton as patron deity of agriculture, and this deity's connections with Hermes.

159. Note rituals (cf. Iambl. *V.P.* 10.51) and propitiatory sacrifices to counter drought (Pausanias 2.29.8; Alciphron *Farmers* 33 [Thalliscus to Petraeus], 3.35, ¶¶1–2; rejected by Seneca *Nat. Q.* 4.7.3).

160. E.g., Ovid *Am.* 1.8.9–10; Iambl. *Bab. St.* 10 (Photius *Bibl.* 94.75b); cf. Frankfurter, *Religion in Egypt*, 226.

161. On Zeus as a weather deity, see Lucian *Icaromenippus* 25–26; W. K. C. Guthrie, *The Greeks and Their Gods* (Boston: Beacon, 1950), 37ff, 125–26; particularly in Anatolia, Rives, *Religion*, 60. Cf. the emphasis on Zeus's local function here in Cilliers Breytenbach, "Zeus und der lebendige Gott: Anmerkungen zu Apostelgeschichte 14.11–17," *NTS* 39 (3, 1993): 396–413.

162. Cf. Parthenius *Love Romance* 6.6; heroes in Diogenes Laertius 8.2.59; Pausanias 2.29.8; Philostratus *Hrk.* 15.6.

163. Pliny *Nat.* 2.39.105–6; 2.43.112 (giving a much more accurate perspective in 2.42.111). Against incantations affecting rain, see Seneca *Nat. Q.* 4.7.3.

164. Albert Kaumba Mufwata, *Jusqu'aux Extrémités de la Terre: La référence aux prophètes comme fondement de l'ouverture universaliste aux chapitres 2 et 13 des Actes des Apôtres*, CahRB 67 (Paris: Gabalda, 2006), 16; Luke Timothy Johnson, *The Acts of*

In early Jewish sources, God alone sent rain (*1 En.* 2:3), despite the proliferation of subordinate angels in Jewish tradition.[165] God sent rain in response to prayers (whether public[166] or those of holy persons),[167] obedience to the Torah,[168] festivals[169] (including prayers at the festival of tabernacles,[170] and possibly the water-drawing ceremony at that festival),[171] the temple service,[172] sacrifices,[173] and other acts.[174] God benevolently created people so that he could care for them (*Sipre Deut* 38.1.3).

Seasons governed the work cycle for the vast majority of the Empire's people, and naturally invited religious consideration. Thus, for example, seasons figured heavily in myths about rising deities.[175] Luke's informed

---

the Apostles, SP 5 (Collegeville, Minn.: Liturgical Press, 1992), 249; Dunn, *Acts*, 191.

165. Cf. e.g., God not delegating the keys of rain, in *b. Sanh.* 113a; *Taan.* 2a; *Gen. Rab.* 73:4; *Pesiq. Rab.* 42:7; *Tg. Neof.* 1 on Gen 30:22; *Tg. Ps.-Jon.* to Deut 28:12; cf. Josephus *Ant.* 18.285; *Sipre Deut* 38.1.4.

166. E.g., *b. B.M.* 28a.

167. E.g., 1 Sam 12:17-18; Jdt 8:31; Josephus *Ant.* 13.343-46; 14.22; *m. Taan.* 3:8; *tos. Taan.* 2:13; *Ab. R. Nat.* 6A; *b. Taan.* 8a; 19b-20a; 23ab; 24a-26a; *p. Taan.* 1:4, §1; 3:9, §§6-8; 3:10, §1; 3:11, §4; cf. 1 Kgs 17:1; 18:41-46; James 5:17-18; Craig A. Evans, "Holy Men, Jewish," 505-7 in *Dictionary of Background*; Geza Vermes, *Jesus the Jew: A Historian's Reading of the Gospels* (Philadelphia: Fortress, 1973), 70, 76.

168. Lev 26:3-4; Deut 11:13-14; *Sipre Deut* 41.6.4; *Num. Rab.* 3:12. God could withhold rain to punish sins (Deut 28:48; *1 En.* 101:2; *Ps. Sol.* 17:18; Josephus *Ant.* 8.318-19; *b. Taan.* 7b; *Lev. Rab.* 35:10) or (apparently) in mourning the temple's destruction (*b. Taan.* 19b).

169. *Tos. Suk.* 3:18; *Eccl. Rab.* 7:14, §3; *Song Rab.* 7:2, §2.

170. See prayers for rain then in *m. Taan.* 1:1; *b. B.M.* 28a; *p. Taan.* 1:1, §§1-10. Later tradition associates God's decisions about rain with this festival (e.g., *tos. Ros Has.* 1:13; *Pesiq. Rab Kah. Sup.* 7:2; *p. Ros Has.* 1:3, §43; perhaps also *m. Ros Has.* 1:2; but cf. *m. Taan.* 1:1), though cf. instead the New Year (soon after) in *Sipre Deut* 40.4.2; *p. Ros Has.* 1:3, §§45-46.

171 So George Foot Moore, *Judaism in the First Centuries of the Christian Era*, 3 vols. (Cambridge: Harvard University Press, 1927-30; repr., 3 vols. in 2. New York: Schocken, 1971), 2:44-45 (comparing the functions of libations among pagans); Helmer Ringgren, *Israelite Religion*, trans. David E. Green (Philadelphia: Fortress, 1966), 190; Harrelson, *Cult*, 69; Beth Uval, "Streams of Living Water: The Feast of Tabernacles and the Holy Spirit," *JerPersp* 49 (1995): 22-23, 37. See esp. *b. Taan.* 25b; cf. Zech 14:16-19.

172. *Ab. R Nat.* 4A; *b. Taan.* 19b, bar.; *Pesiq. Rab.* 52:3.

173. *Pesiq. Rab.* 52:3; cf. *Gen. Rab.* 13:5.

174. Repentance (*Gen. Rab.* 13:14); tithes (*Pesiq. Rab Kah.* 1:4); and almsgiving (*Lev. Rab.* 34:14).

175. Cf. Apollodorus *Bib.* 1.5.3; 3.14.4; Ovid *Metam.* 5.564-71; Giulia Sfameni Gasparro, *Soteriology and Mystic Aspects in the Cult of Cybele and Attis*, ÉPROER 103 (Leiden: Brill, 1985), 29, 43-49; W. K. C. Guthrie, *Orpheus and Greek Religion: A Study of the Orphic Movement*, 2nd ed. (New York: W. W. Norton, 1966), 55-56. By now it ought to go without saying that such seasonal revivification differs starkly from the

audience, however, understood that God governed the seasons (Gen 8:22; Ps 74:17; Philo *Creation* 59).[176]

Although God also "testified" more specifically to his salvific message through signs, as in 14:3,[177] his long-term testimony to humanity here comes through his generous benefactions to humanity through creation. The litotes "not without witness" is typically Lukan (Acts 12:18; 19:23, 24; 21:39; 27:20),[178] but Luke presumably condenses a more comprehensive early monotheistic apologetic here. Divine testimony in creation (cf. Ps 19:1–6) ensured humanity's moral responsibility (Wisdom 13:1). This is true also in Pauline theology (Rom 1:20), where, as here, God's kindness should encourage repentance (Rom 2:4).

This Jewish apologetic approach was able to exploit some similar ideas found among a number of philosophers, especially Stoics. Stoics saw in both the order of the universe and tokens of divine benevolence an indication of the divine mind.[179] One may also compare one of the Cynic epistles, in which night and day and the fruit-bearing earth attest God's character (Heraclitus *Ep.* 4). Presumably the Lystran crowd, many of whom spoke the local Lycaonian dialect as their first language, lacked much direct acquaintance with Stoic philosophy. Nevertheless, this basic idea informed a traditional Diaspora Jewish apologetic bridge with which both Paul and Luke were presumably familiar. Indeed, for ancient hearers in general, agricultural blessings naturally raised the issue of divine benevolence. Locals who came to the market may have even heard extemporaneous speeches by traveling

---

Jewish notion of resurrection behind the Christian teaching (see at greater length Craig Keener, *The Historical Jesus of the Gospels* [Grand Rapids: Eerdmans, 2009], 334–39; idem, *The Gospel of John: A Commentary*, 2 vols. [Grand Rapids: Baker Academic, 2003], 1172–77; N. T. Wright, *The Resurrection of the Son of God* [Minneapolis: Fortress, 2003], 80–81; Michael R. Licona, *The Resurrection of Jesus: A New Historiographical Approach* [Downers Grove, Ill.: InterVarsity; Nottingham, U.K.: Apollos, 2010], 536–37).

176. Cf. also *Let. Aris.* 190 (trans. M. Hadas, p. 175): God gives humanity "health and food and all other things in due season."

177. For one discussion of miracles as they relate both to historiography and to philosophic theology, see Craig Keener, *Miracles: The Credibility of the NT Accounts* (Grand Rapids: Baker Academic, 2011); in Acts, for miracle reports see idem, *Acts*, 1:320–82; for signs theologically, see ibid., 537–49.

178. On litotes, see e.g., Galen O. Rowe, "Style," 121–57 in *Handbook of Classical Rhetoric in the Hellenistic Period, 330 B.C.–A.D. 400*, ed. Stanley E. Porter (Leiden: Brill, 1997), 128; cf. *Rhet. Her.* 4.38.50.

179. See Keener, *John*, 341–42, 371–72, 376–77; cf. Diogenes Laertius 7.1.134, 147. Howard Clark Kee, *Miracle in the Early Christian World: A Study in Sociohistorical Method* (New Haven: Yale University Press, 1983), 199, applies this concept to Acts 14:17.

speakers before on a related concept; one practice topic in declamation schools was "Whether the gods exercise providential care for the cosmos."[180]

## CONCLUSION

Many intellectuals expressed concerns about traditional mythology and sometimes polytheism and the worship of statues; Jewish people repeated Isaiah's denunciations of idolatry, but not normally in public proclamation to Gentiles themselves. Luke's depiction of the monotheistic proclamation of Paul and Barnabas therefore strikes chords that would be familiar to much of his audience, but the apostles' direct and public appeal to Gentiles to turn from idolatry goes beyond what was usual. It is consistent with Paul's description of some Gentiles' response to his early ministry—"the way that you turned to God from idols to serve the living and genuine God" (1 Thess 1:9).

---

180. Grant, *Gods*, 49–50. Among philosophers, Stoics and Epicureans (Acts 17:18) would diverge radically on this point.

# 4

# Luke, Paul, and the Law

**ROBERT BRIAN KIDWELL**

IT HAS BEEN ARGUED now for a number of years, especially by German scholars, that the Paul of the epistles and the Paul of Acts are irreconcilable. For example, Ernst Haenchen contends that Paul is portrayed in Acts as a miracle worker, while 2 Cor 12:12 depicts Paul defending himself against his Corinthian opponents' critique of his lack of miracle working power. In Acts, Paul is portrayed as quite eloquent, while 2 Cor 10:10 provides evidence that the real Paul has a delivery that is "feeble, unimpressive." Moreover, while Paul frequently refers to his own apostleship (e.g., Rom 1:1), Luke grants apostleship only to the Twelve. Finally, Luke portrays the division between Paul and the Jews as largely due to a rejection of the resurrection, while the letters portray the real issues as those related to the Mosaic Law.[1]

Exegetes since Haenchen's time have endeavored to reply to these and other proposed differences. For example, Ben Witherington has responded to the disparity in the way Paul speaks in Acts versus the way he speaks in his epistles by contending that the distinctive audiences play a large role in forming these variations:

---

1. Ernst Haenchen, *The Acts of the Apostles: A Commentary*, trans. Bernard Noble and Gerald Shinn (Philadelphia: Westminster, 1971).

> One of the mistakes that must not be made is fretting too much over the fact that the speeches of Peter and Paul in Acts seldom sound like the Peter and Paul of their letters. The lone exception to this is of course the speech to the Ephesian elders in Acts 20. There is a reason for this exception—this is the only speech addressed to Christians by either Paul or Peter, and of course the letters are *all* addressed to Christians. The rhetoric is different because the audience is quite different in Acts and in the letters.[2]

In other words, the speeches in Acts are primarily directed towards evangelism and winning the lost to Christ, while the epistles are addressed to those already a part of the church body. Therefore, we should not expect Paul to speak in the same way or to discuss the same subjects.

My own interest in this dialogue revolves around the dissimilar perspectives regarding the Law. Jacob Jervell asserts that Luke's stance towards the Law is "the most conservative outlook within the NT."[3] We see, for example, that Luke focuses a great deal on the moral teachings of the Law. From the beginning of his Gospel the characters who are involved in the infancy narratives are noted for their devout observance of the commandments (Zacharias and Elizabeth, 1:6; Joseph and Mary, 2:22–24, 27, 39, 41–42; Simeon, 2:25; Anna, 2:36–37). Such concern for the Law does not end with the beginning of Jesus ministry or even with his crucifixion. For instance, while preparing his body for burial, Jesus' followers are careful to observe the Sabbath day before completing their task (Luke 23:56). In fact, this concern for keeping the Law extends on into Acts. When Stephen is accused of speaking blasphemous words against Moses and of speaking against the Law, Luke is quick to defend him by noting that his accusers are "false witnesses" (Acts 6:11–14).[4] During Paul's trial, the apostle is also repeatedly accused of breaking the Law (Acts 18:13; 21:28) but Luke records his defense against this charge when Paul declares that he has strictly observed the commandments from his youth (Acts 22:3; 24:14; 25:8).

Craig Blomberg tries to diminish the value of the above evidence from the birth narratives by placing these characters in the old era:

> Yet despite these repeated references to the faithfulness to the Law of these humble Jewish people, the emphasis of Luke 1 and 2 falls much more on the coming dawn of a new day, the

---

2. Ben Witherington III, *NT Rhetoric: An Introductory Guide to the Art of Persuasion in and of the NT* (Eugene, OR: Cascade, 2009), 47.

3. Jacob Jervell, *Luke and the People of God: A New Look at Luke-Acts* (Minneapolis: Augsburg, 1972), 141.

4. All scripture quotations are taken from the *New American Standard Bible*.

fulfillment of the promises of redemption long awaited, and the inauguration of a new relationship between God and his people.... Thus while Luke 1 and 2 offer no positive proof for any coming changes in the Law and even portray pious folk obeying the Law as the appropriate way of serving God at that time, these chapters nevertheless point forward to the advent of a new age. Should changes in the Law be forthcoming, therefore, the reader should not be unprepared for them.[5]

Blomberg then tries to extend this argument into Acts by arguing that for NT Christians "the implications of the new covenant dawned on them only over time."[6] Unfortunately, while this assessment might be valid for someone like Stephen who appears early in the story of Acts, it seems highly unlikely that Blomberg's argument can extend to someone like Paul, who by the time of his arrest has written the epistle to the Galatians and has passed through the debate of the Jerusalem council in Acts 15. In other words, Paul has had quite a bit of time to reflect on the validity of the Law and still responds as he does at his trial. Consequently, Luke's attitude toward the Law cannot entirely be explained away by the novelty of the Christian faith. Luke still stresses the continuing value of keeping the Law, at least for his Jewish Christian listeners.

Luke's support for the continuing observance of Mosaic Law is also evidenced in his positive attitude toward the Pharisees. Greg Witte notes that Jesus is invited to dinner by Pharisees three times in Luke's account (Luke 7:36; 11:37; 14:1) implying a friendly relationship between the two. Furthermore, in Luke 13:31 the Pharisees warn Jesus of Herod's plan to kill him. The book of Acts speaks of Christian Pharisees (15:5) and twice reports that Pharisees defended Paul and the disciples (5:33–42; 23:6–10).[7] Moreover, in analyzing Luke's perspective regarding Jesus' conflict with the Pharisees, S. G. Wilson points out that it was not the Pharisees position regarding the Law of Moses or their own innovations which prompted Jesus' criticism of them. Rather Wilson concludes: "Luke apparently saw nothing objectionable in a Pharisaic lifestyle *per se*, including the commitment to an expanded legal system; he objects only to the neglect of central commands, whose centrality they themselves recognized (Luke 10:25f)."[8] Luke's depiction of the Pharisees as friendly toward Jesus and other Christians,

---

5. Craig L. Blomberg, "The Law in Luke-Acts," *JSNT* 22 (1984), 57.

6. Blomberg, "The Law in Luke-Acts," 70.

7. Greg Edward Witte, "Salvation and the Law in Luke-Acts" (PhD diss., Union Theological Seminary, 1985), 10.

8. S. G. Wilson, *Luke and the Law* (New York: Cambridge University Press, 1983), 19.

his minimizing of the differences between them, and Paul's declaration in Acts 26 that he has been careful to observe the Law from his youth would certainly seem to support Jervell's contention that Luke has a quite positive view toward the Law.

However, in sharp contrast to this positive view of Luke, the Paul of the epistles takes a very strong position against the observance of the Law and notes his many battles with those who try to impose Law on his converts. For example, in Gal 3:10 he argues that those trying to live by "the works of the Law are under a curse" and in the next verse says that "no one is justified by the Law." In Rom 6:14 he contrasts those who are "under law" with those who are "under grace." In Rom 7 he contends that the Law has been the instrument of sin in bringing about humanity's death and that the Law serves to incite sin rather than being a tool to overcome the desires of the flesh. In Rom 7 Paul also uses the illustration of a woman who is freed from the law pertaining to adultery by the death of her husband in order to contend that Christians have been freed from the Law through our participation in the death of Christ (7:1–6). In this way, Christ becomes the "end of the law for righteousness to everyone who believes" (Rom 10:4).

If we were to focus only on the above carefully selected statements from Luke and Paul, it would be easy to argue that the two are indeed irreconcilable regarding this subject of the Law and that the Lukan picture of Paul cannot be conformed to the apostle we know from the epistles. Luke envisions the continuing validity of the Law while Paul sees its time as fulfilled. However, one finds that Luke's position on the Law, as well as that of Paul, is not as one-sided as these statements would make it appear. While the texts we have examined reveal, as Jervell claims, that Luke tends to be very conservative in his stance toward the Law, he, too, has many things to say about the Law which are more in line with what we often think of as Paul's typically negative attitude. Indeed, Richard Pervo cites texts which cause him to arrive at a conclusion quite contrary to what Jervell claims. Pervo writes: "Insofar as Acts is concerned the Law of Moses cannot make one right with God (13:38–39), is an intolerable burden (15:10), and, insofar as it deals with dietary laws and regulations for purity, is opposed to the manifest will of God (10:10–16)."[9]

A similarly negative attitude may be arrived at through examination of texts from Luke's Gospel. For example, Jesus announces that the Law was declared up until the time of John the Baptist but that now the message of the kingdom is being proclaimed (Luke 16:16), indicating much like Paul in

---

9. Richard I. Pervo, *Acts A Commentary*, ed. Harold W. Attridge (Minneapolis: Fortress, 2009), 544.

Rom 8, that a higher law, the law of the Spirit is replacing the old letter of the Law. Furthermore, while it may be argued that Jesus does not criticize the observance of the Law by the Pharisees nor try to replace their minutia with summary love commands, there are places where the Pharisees and Jesus do disagree and these instances occur when the Pharisees do not believe that Jesus is adequately living up to the requirements of the Law. This occurs especially in Jesus' failure to observe the Pharisees' Sabbath expectations. Luke shows Jesus not only healing on the Sabbath but also permitting his disciples to "thresh" grain (Luke 6:1–11). Jesus' response is not to argue that the disciples were really doing something which was perfectly lawful to do on the Sabbath, but rather to refer to a similar incident in the life of David in which David did that which was "not lawful" (6:4). He then continues in v. 5 to say that "The Son of Man is Lord of the Sabbath." Speaking of Jesus, Seifrid thus remarks that "at crucial points, Luke gives evidence that he maintains an ethic which transcends Torah (and hence *may* overturn it)."[10] Jesus' reference to David may enable us to infer that there are times when it is proper not only for Jesus but also his followers (it was the disciples who were "threshing" grain and not Jesus.) to disobey the Law in preference to a higher law. And, thus, while Luke does not place the summary commands of love on the lips of Jesus, we may deduce that such an understanding was there even if Luke prefers to leave it unsaid.

Furthermore, Wilson argues that Jesus may not only ignore, or overturn, the Law, but he may also add to it as in the case of the young ruler in Luke 18:18–27. The ruler asks Jesus what he must do to "inherit eternal life." Jesus then quotes various commandments from the Decalogue and the ruler responds that he has observed these from his youth. Jesus then responds that he still lacks one thing and tells him to sell all his possessions and follow Christ. Wilson argues that the implication of this is "that obedience to the commands of the Law alone is no guarantee of eternal life. . . . It is conceivable that the distribution of wealth fulfills the command to love one's neighbour, but it is not the most natural thing to identify the call to follow Jesus with the command to love God."[11] Jesus thus sees the Law both as something which may be set aside when the higher law of love demands it and also as something which is insufficient when defining what discipleship is all about.

Paul, too, sometimes reflects a more Lukan attitude toward Law than what the above evidence from his letters would demonstrate. While in Rom 7:11–12 Paul does contend that the Law has been used by sin to bring

---

10. M. A. Seifrid, "Jesus and the Law in Acts," *JSNT* 30 (1987), 40.
11. Wilson, *Luke and the Law*, 29.

about death, he still affirms in this same passage that the Law is "holy and righteous and good." Moreover, we see that Paul bases much of his ethical teaching on OT Law (e.g., Rom 12:20 from Prov 25:21-22).[12] While Paul wants to summarize the Law as we find Jesus doing in Matt 22:37-40 under the two great commandments (Rom 13: 8-10), it should be recalled that these very summation statements are drawn directly from the Law itself (Deut 6:5; Lev 19:18). And, while Paul may concede that it is a sign of a weak conscience to be bound by things such as Sabbath and scruples regarding the eating of meat and drinking of wine, he still notes that those who feel bound by such things, whether from the fourth commandment or merely an overly sensitive conscience, still need to follow their scruples, for to not do so would be sin (Rom 14:23). Moreover, stronger Christians need to show love towards their weaker fellow Christians and abstain from these things if not doing so would cause them to stumble and fall. Thus for Paul, harmony among Christians and the welfare of believers is more important than one's own personal freedom from the Law's commands. Finally, Paul makes it clear that his own observance of the Law is situational (1 Cor 9). He thus may be accused of living two different lives, one among the more Law conscious Jews and another among those Gentiles who feel free in relation to the Law. Therefore, we may conclude from Paul's own statements that his attitude toward Law is multidimensional, sometimes very negative but at times positive as well.

Philipp Vielhauer has written one of the most commented upon comparisons between the Lukan Paul and the Paul of the epistles.[13] However, after analyzing all the data regarding the two perspectives on the Law, Vielhauer himself concludes that he finds only two places where these two views of the apostle cannot be reconciled. One incident is the circumcision of Timothy (Acts 16:3). Vilhauer comments: "Circumcision is never a matter of indifference, but rather is confession and acknowledgement of the saving significance of the law, is a denial of baptism, and therefore splits the church."[14] The other occasion is the incident in Jerusalem where Paul is asked by James to participate in a Jewish rite in the Temple (Acts 21:15-26). Vielhauer writes that the motivation given to Paul by James is "highly suspect" and comments:

---

12. Note that Paul does not restrict the Law to the Mosaic legislation in the Pentateuch but often uses the term "law" to refer to other passages in the OT (e.g., the Psalms in Rom 3:10-19).

13. Philipp Vielhauer, "On the 'Paulinism' of Acts," in *Studies in Luke-Acts*, ed. Leander E. Keck and J. Louis Martyn (Philadelphia: Fortress, 1966), 33-50.

14. Ibid., 40-41.

True enough, the Jewish accusations are formulated as biased distortions of Paul's teachings; but it was Pauline doctrine that the Mosaic law was not the way of salvation, that circumcision was not a condition of salvation, and that Jewish 'customs' were without significance with regard to salvation. To this extent the charge of 'apostasy from Moses' was entirely appropriate. To convince the Jew that the charge was unjust would have been extremely difficult for the pioneer of the Gentile church and the author of Galatians and II Corinthians.[15]

Most scholars who endeavor to resolve this tension have referred to Paul's statement in 1 Cor 9 that when he is among the Jews he is willing to observe Jewish Law for the sake of the gospel. However, like Vielhauer, C. K. Barrett finds this solution problematic and comments:

[T]he real question here is not whether on occasion Paul would do what Jews did: 1 Corinthians 9 proves conclusively that he was prepared to do this. The question is whether Paul was prepared to use a special occasion such as the one described in order to suggest something that was not true, namely that he too (καί αὐτός, he just like the ardent Jews who suspected his loyalty) was regularly observant of the Law as understood within Judaism. Readiness to do this is not covered by 1 Corinthians 9. The issue is not only a moral one. Paul, one would think, must have observed that a single action such as that suggested to him could not prove the point, and that if his motives were suspected this would enrage the Jews even more than simple apostasy. Undoubtedly the plan, as described in Acts, misfired.[16]

Barrett's point appears to be supported by Paul's statements in 1 Cor 10:27-28. When Paul discusses eating meat as a guest in a home, he declares that one should go ahead and eat, and not worry about whether it has been offered to an idol. However, if someone makes an issue of the meat being offered to an idol, then one needs to refuse to eat. What was a matter of indifference then becomes a matter of principle. The same principle would then seem to apply when it comes to Law. If one is among a group of legalists and one is asked to observe some law, in order not to offend them and promote the gospel, one could observe that law as a matter of indifference. However, if that observance is presented as a matter of necessity, one would then have to reject that observance in order to disprove their claim. We

---

15. Ibid., 39-40.
16. C. K. Barrett, *A Critical and Exegetical Commentary on the Acts of the Apostles*, 2 vols. (Edinburgh: T & T Clark, 1998), 1013.

must ask ourselves then if James' request and Paul's acquiescence to that request intimates that the Lukan Paul, as Vielhauer suggests, believes that observance of the Law is a necessity for salvation, at least in regard to the Jews. This, as Vielhauer notes, would be irreconcilable with the Paul of the epistles.

Other scholars have found difficulty with Acts 21 and have noted difficulties in reconciling its statements with the Paul of the letters. Indeed, Samuel Brandon contends that something insidious is occurring and writes that the suggestion by James may be a deliberate attempt to discredit Paul in the eyes of his Gentile companions and deliberately expose Paul to danger.

> When it is recalled that Paul is described as being accompanied on his journey to Jerusalem by representatives of his Gentile converts, it is obvious that the spectacle of his submission to this test, imposed upon him by the Jerusalem Church, must have been peculiarly harmful to his prestige in their eyes and disturbing to their understanding of his teaching about the unique essentiality of faith in Christ. . . . The sequel of Paul's detection and molestation by the Jewish mob in the Temple might reasonably have been expected, and the question naturally arises whether James and the elders might not also have anticipated the danger to which they were exposing the champion of Gentile Christianity in requiring him thus publicly to prove his orthodoxy. Moreover, it is not without significance that Luke tells us nothing of the reaction of the Jerusalem Christians to Paul's arrest and imprisonment, which fact contrasts strangely with what he tells earlier in his narrative of their concern for the safety of Peter when arrested and imprisoned by Agrippa I.[17]

William Furneaux comments as well on the callousness of the Jerusalem church towards Paul:

> The whole tone of the narrative implies that Paul was coldly received. We are not told of any expression of gratitude for the splendid offering from the Gentile brethren. It looks as though his misgiving as to its reception (Rom. xv. 31) was confirmed. Nor do we hear that the Christians of Jerusalem later put in so much as a word on his behalf with either the Jewish or the Roman authorities, or expressed any sympathy with him during his long imprisonment at Caesarea. And this conclusion is borne out by the Epistles, which say so much of the collecting of

---

17. S. G. F. Brandon, *The Fall of Jerusalem and the Christian Church: A Study of the Effects of the Jewish Overthrow of A.D. 70 on Christianity* (London: SPCK, 1951), 135.

the contribution, but are silent about the reception with which it met.[18]

Yet, while it is difficult to explain the questions Brandon and Furneaux raise, the text at the same time does tell us that James and the elders praised God concerning Paul's mission to the Gentiles both here and in Acts 15. This would indicate that James and the elders were not endeavoring to trap Paul, as Brandon suggests, but were truly rejoicing in his accomplishments. At the same time, however, it does appear that they were also trying to clear up a misunderstanding on the part of the Jerusalem Jewish Christians. But whatever the attitude of James and the Jerusalem church may have been, these questions do nothing to explain Paul's own acquiescence to James' request. Why does Paul give in to their demands?

James Boice, thus, places the largest blame for the occurrences in Act 21 not on James but rather on Paul. He believes that Paul was in fact rebelling against the leading of God in even going to Jerusalem and believes that Paul's acceptance of James' proposal would compromise the gospel:

> This was what we would call realistic politics. Quite simply, it was a compromise. On an earlier occasion, if something like this had been suggested to Paul, we would have expected Paul to have reacted indignantly, as he did in Antioch when Peter moved away from the Gentiles in order to sit with the Jews and eat kosher food. Paul had been right to oppose Peter. Yet this was far worse than anything Peter had been guilty of. Peter was caught in a hypocritical position. But Paul's error was worse than mere hypocrisy, though it was that too. It was a compromise of the gospel. The same apostle who had written so many NT books, the man who had argued so forcefully that we are saved by Jesus Christ alone was about to go to the Jewish temple and in the presence of the very priests who had crucified the Lord, there participate with others in a sacrifice of an animal that was meant to be an atonement for his sin. That is, he was about to turn his back on the only sufficient sacrifice of Christ.[19]

There are several rejoinders to be made regarding Boice's critique. First, Luke notes that Paul had already performed a Jewish rite in the keeping of a vow in Acts 18:18 in which there would have been no pressure from the Jerusalem church which would have led to this compromise. Secondly,

---

18. William Mordaunt Furneaux, *The Acts of the Apostles: A Commentary for English Readers* (Oxford: Clarendon, 1912), 342.

19. James Montgomery Boice, *Acts: An Expositional Commentary* (Grand Rapids: Baker, 1997), 360–61.

if Paul did compromise in Acts 21, there is no remorse in any of his later reports of this incident. Finally, there is no real suggestion in the text that what Paul was doing should be viewed as in any way a negative statement regarding Christ's atonement, nor a replacement for it.

A number of other scholars also suggest a compromise but not nearly of the magnitude which Boice suggests. For example, John Phillips writes:

> To comply with their request might cause his Gentile friends to stumble; to refuse to do so would confirm his Jewish brethren in their already low opinion of him. Of the two evils, he chose the lesser, judging that the conscience of his Gentile friends, enlightened by his own teaching (Rom. 14:1—15:7), was far stronger than that of these Jewish elders, bound as they were by traditions and shackles that kept them imprisoned to obsolete forms and ceremonies.[20]

James Dunn contends that Paul was compromising but that his compromise was only a temporary one. "Obviously this was not the time to engage in theological debate on the role of the law for believers; passions needed to be cooled first (if at all). We may presume that it was such considerations which secured Paul's agreement."[21] We do here need to remember that Jerusalem at this time was becoming a powder keg that would soon explode in a war between the Jews and Romans and result in the destruction of the city. Certainly one can appreciate with Dunn that Paul was cognizant of the circumstances and would want to do something to alleviate the tense situation.

Foakes-Jackson also suggests a compromise but without the excellent motivation suggested by Dunn.

> According to Acts Paul accepted the compromise. Did he really accept it? His epistles are logically inconsistent with it, and before long Christian practice recognized this fact and followed the epistles. Yet human nature is so inconsistent, and especially in religious matters we cling to customs so long after we can justify them or wish to enforce them on others, and are so loath to break with a church of which we have inherited the traditions, that I am not sure that Paul may not have been much nearer

---

20. John Phillips, *Exploring Acts: An Expository Commentary* (Grand Rapids: Kregel, 1986), 420.

21. James D. G. Dunn, *The Acts of the Apostles* (Valley Forge: Trinity Press, 1996), 287.

the standard of custom implied by Acts than his own writings would indicate.²²

A few pages later the same conjecture is made with a little bit different argument:

> The question has often been raised whether Paul could have acted thus consistently with his own principles. Strict logic would probably have forbidden him to do so; and Acts certainly represents him as much more observant of the Jewish Law than the Epistles would have suggested. But two considerations prevent the conclusion that the Epistles must be followed. (i.) The sentimental power of tradition always affects men's conduct in the practice of religion, and frequently overpowers logic. (ii.) After all it was Paul himself who said that he had been 'all things to all men'—in what way was he 'a Jew to the Jews' if not by observing the Law when he was with them?²³

Thus, this proposal posits both the idea that Paul compromised as a result of the limitations of his human nature but also the suggestion that he did not compromise a great deal since he probably normally lived a life very compatible with Jewish Law.

Furneaux' solution is similar to Foakes-Jackson without the reference to Paul's human nature and inconsistency. He suggests that Paul did indeed keep the Law and that acceding to James' request was not out of character for him.

> He spoke as strongly as possible against the Law as a means of salvation. He taught that Gentiles might become Christians without first becoming Jews. But he had never taught the Jew to throw aside the Law. 'Was any man called being circumcised,' he wrote, 'let him not become uncircumcised' (1 Cor. vii. 18). He himself must have kept up his Jewish habits or he would not have been tolerated at all among the Jews. His intercourse with them during such periods as his first three months at Ephesus would have been impossible, if he had not been living in general compliance with the ceremonial law. But these things were to him external matters, in no way essential to the religious life.²⁴

---

22. F. J. Foakes-Jackson, *The Beginnings of Christianity: Part 1 The Acts of the Apostles* (London: MacMillan and Co., 1933), 271.

23. Foakes-Jackson, *The Beginnings of Christianity*, 273.

24. Furneaux, *The Acts of the Apostles*, 343–44.

Furneaux' solution certainly is in line with Luke's later statements about Paul in Acts 26, and the citation from 1 Cor 7 is an interesting suggestion in support of Paul's own affirmation of keeping the Law. Otto Bauernfeind agrees with Furneaux' assessment and says there is no evidence in Paul's epistles that he ever sought to be freed from his Jewish heritage. "Aber das alles bedeutete nun eben doch nicht, dass Paulus die Christen, die ins Judentum hineingeboren waren, von der dem Judentum gegebenen Beschneidung und dem Gesetz loslosen wollte. Wenn er das wirklich gewollt hatte, dann musste man in der immerhin ganz umfangreichen Briefsammlung, die wir von ihm besitzen, irgendwo doch einmal eine Spur davon finden!"[25]

Thus, Foakes-Jackson, Furneaux, and Bauernfeind all suggest that Paul's normal practice was to live as a Jew. James, therefore, would be merely suggesting that Paul demonstrate something that was true and would not be a violation of any principle that might be suggested based on 1 Cor 10:27–28. This would certainly harmonize Luke's assessment of Paul with his epistles. The passage in 1 Cor 9 does suggest that Paul lived among the Jews as a Jew and the text cited by Furneaux in 1 Cor 7 gives further support that Paul continued to live a Jewish lifestyle.

That Paul normally desired to live as a Jew is in fact supported by the context of Acts 21 itself. "After all," Darrell Bock asks, "why is he so anxious to reach Jerusalem by Pentecost? It is because he keeps the feasts."[26] Such a desire is not merely the invention of Luke and the contention of Acts (20:16), but is supported by Paul's own statement in 1 Cor 16:8. Paul had left Ephesus and made his way to Jerusalem at this time, at least in part, in order to keep the Jewish feast of Pentecost. Why should this desire be surprising to anyone? We all have those traditions and customs that have become such a part of us that we cannot imagine laying them aside. Paul had observed the feasts for years and there was no real reason to stop doing so. They were a part of his Jewish heritage and they reflected on his Christian one as well. We may recall in this regard that Jesus himself used various symbols from his Jewish heritage to point to truths regarding himself and the Gospel (e.g., John 7:37–39; 8:12).

Moreover, while Vielhauer is correct that the Paul of the letters often takes a strong stance against circumcision, it may be noted that this strong stance is in the context of letters primarily addressed to Gentiles who did not normally practice circumcision. Thus, for Paul not to take a strong

---

25. Otto Bauernfeind, *Kommentar und Studien zur Apostelgeschichte* (Tübingen: Mohr Siebeck, 1980), 246.

26. Darrell L. Bock, *Acts* (Grand Rapids: Baker Academic, 2007), 644.

stance against it in these Gentile letters would also intimate that circumcision was essential for salvation. On the other hand, for a Jew to continue to practice circumcision need not imply such a requirement. It might rather simply be practiced as a part of one's heritage and as a reminder of one's physical ancestor, Abraham. While Paul does indicate that physical circumcision without a change of heart accomplishes nothing (Rom 2:25–29), the procedure itself, if properly understood, is not inimical to salvation by faith. After all, circumcision is practiced today among a whole host of people for a variety of reasons with no thought of any spiritual ramification. Certainly this proper perspective would be a difficult one for Jewish Christians who associated the rite so much with the OT covenant but it is not impossible. One could argue in this regard that many Christians hold an erroneous view of baptism as well, placing too great an emphasis on the physical action without a corresponding change of heart.

Note, too, that James challenges Paul not only regarding his stance on Jews continuing to observe the practice of circumcision but also on his views regarding their "customs" (21:21). Luke employs this word more than any NT writer (10 of the 12 total occurrences). Wilson points out that Luke sometimes uses the two ideas of law (νόμος) and custom (ἔθος) almost interchangeably.[27] A clear example of this is Acts 6:14 where, after Stephen has been accused of speaking against the Law in the previous verse, it says: "for we have heard him say that this Nazarene, Jesus, will destroy this place and alter the customs which Moses handed down to us." Wilson goes on to note, however, that in rabbinic literature, custom is what results from observing the Law and that "custom was never confused with legislation."[28] That custom is not equivalent to law in Luke can clearly be seen from Luke 22:39 where we are told it was Jesus' custom to go to the Mount of Olives. Certainly this habit was not a legal requirement.

Yet while custom does not bear the same legal stricture as law, the observance of custom was still viewed as very important in the Roman world. Frank Thielman writes: "Luke wants to show furthermore that Christians do not despise their Jewish roots, nor do they advocate that Jews abandon the essential elements of their ancestral customs. Where they have parted ways with Jewish custom, they have been driven to do so against their own instincts and by the overpowering authority of God himself (Acts 10:1—11:18; 15:6–11)."[29] Thus, Thielman is suggesting that Luke continues

---

27. Wilson, *Luke and the Law*, 4.

28. Ibid., 5.

29. Frank Thielman, *The Law and the NT: The Question of Continuity* (New York: Crossroad Publishing, 1999), 139–40.

to have Jewish Christians observe the Law, not primarily because of seeing it as a legal requirement, but rather as a part of their heritage which they should not easily abandon. He continues, however, by saying: "Luke's frequent characterization of the Mosaic law as a body of ethnic customs subtly identifies the law itself with the Jewish people. Customs are, by definition, the laws of a certain group and are therefore neither universal nor eternal."[30] Gerald Downing says: "It was a commonplace of contemporary thinking about religion and society that ancestral custom should be observed. It was almost as much a commonplace that such observance aims at human flourishing *(eudaimonia)* and an explicit corollary was adduced, that no such observance should threaten human flourishing."[31] Downing quotes Cicero in support of this position and we know from a study of the Jews living in Roman society that certain exceptions were granted them in order to maintain their historic religious traditions. Similar latitude was granted to Christians until it was determined that they were to be seen as separate from Judaism and thus were a new, distinct religion and not under the protections of a *licit* religion.

If such regard for customs and national laws was so important to the culture of this time that the Romans would include exceptions for subjugated peoples, then Paul may have acceded to James' request not only because it was in line with his own personal preference but also as a means to show that he was not seeking to overthrow ingrained Jewish practices. As Luke wants to make clear, Paul was not a ringleader of Jewish dissension for which he was being accused (Acts 24:5). Again, at a time when the Jewish people were especially sensitive to their own culture, Paul's acquiescence may have been very appropriate. I conclude then that Paul did set aside the Law at times, but it is likely that he did so only when he viewed it as a hindrance to the Gospel, as for example when it hindered table fellowship among the members of the body of Christ (Gal 2:11–14).

Consequently, as in our earlier point regarding circumcision, we need to take into account the fact that Paul was writing his letters primarily to Gentile Christians. They certainly did not need to adopt Jewish principles in order to become, or remain, Christians. For them to embrace the Law was to embrace it not on the terms of their ethnicity and culture but rather to embrace it as a need for meriting salvation. Paul's rhetoric, therefore, may reflect a more negative view towards the Law in these situations than his own life normally reflected. On the other hand, the situations in Acts usually reflect Paul in a Jewish context where he would normally follow his

---

30. Ibid., 142.

31. F. Gerald Downing, "Freedom from the Law in Luke-Acts," *JSNT* 26 (1986), 49.

Jewish pattern. As an ethnic Jew, raised in a culture steeped in the Mosaic Law, keeping the Law would be something that came naturally to him and may indeed have been something difficult to lay aside. This would be quite in contrast to a Gentile who would see the Law as foreign and difficult to embrace.

If so, then perhaps Luke's rather conservative position regarding the Mosaic Law is not so distinct as some scholars have argued. Perhaps the NT does picture a church in which Jewish Christians continue to maintain their heritage, not as a matter of salvation but rather because they have come to see it as a valuable part of their heritage. It can certainly be argued, too, as Blomberg suggested earlier, that their understanding regarding the nature of salvation was yet in development. Paul himself in Rom 14 recognizes that some still have a weak conscience in regard to certain commands that they have held dear. Paul himself affirms that in such a situation to fail to respect one's conscience is sin. However, if Thielman is correct that many of these laws are tied to Jewish ethnicity, then it may also be argued that these may gradually slip away as not being eternally valid. Consequently, Jewish Christians may eventually decide that the burden in keeping the Law's minutia is not worth maintaining their heritage. Furthermore, if such distinctions cause division in the body, then such divisive matters of indifference should be laid aside.

On the other hand, for Jewish and also Gentile Christians, Jesus' statements in Luke 16:16–18 indicate that the Law continues to retain its validity in a way which is defined and even heightened in its requirements by Jesus and his own kingdom principles. Certainly in examining the ethics of Paul in his epistles one can see that a high standard is raised up by the apostle for his churches. This is again not to say that either Luke or Paul see Law as a means of attaining or retaining salvation. Salvation for both is through faith in Jesus Christ. However, both, I would argue, would strongly disagree with the antinomian spirit of our age. For both Luke and Paul, law remains a vital part of the Christian life. There is thus no reason to doubt the veracity of Luke's depiction of Paul. When one takes into account Paul's own positive statements regarding the Law in his letters, when one notes that Paul is in the midst of a Jewish setting where he himself claims to live like a Jew, and when one considers the importance of one's heritage in the culture of Luke's time, then we need not doubt that Paul often lived as a law observant Jew and should not be troubled by James' request in Acts 21.

# JOHANNINE LITERATURE

# 5

# Reconsidering the Puzzle of "Earthly Things" in John 3:12

**Joseph R. Dongell**

If I told you earthly things, and you do not believe,
how will you believe if I tell you heavenly things?[1]

JOHN 3:12

IT WILL SURPRISE THE casual reader of the Nicodemus story to learn that John 3:12 has proven to be "tantalizingly mysterious and vague," something "not easy to fathom."[2] It has stood as perennial "puzzle" creating "perplexity" in the minds of serious commentators on the Fourth Gospel.[3] Interpreters of 3:12 often seem to announce their conclusions with resignation,

---

1. All Bible translations are the author's, unless otherwise indicated.

2. D. Moody Smith, Jr., *John*, Abingdon NT Commentaries (Nashville: Abingdon, 1999), 97; D. A. Carson, *The Gospel according to John* (Grand Rapids: Eerdmans, 1991), 199.

3. Barnabas Lindars, *The Gospel of John*, New Century Bible Commentary (Grand Rapids: Eerdmans, 1981), 155; John Ashton, *Understanding the Fourth Gospel* (Oxford: Clarendon Press, 1991), 349.

as if to say, "I offer this view unenthusiastically, seeing it only as the least problematic solution."

## A SIMPLE SAYING

But the interpretive problem lies not with basic content of 3:12 itself, at least not as universally translated. Were we to meet it as an isolated saying, we should have little reason to stumble over it. As it stands, it asserts the common and sensible notion that elementary matters must be mastered before complex ones can be entertained. Medical students must master simple surgeries before progressing to complex and delicate ones. Basic dance steps must be learned before elaborate variations should be tried. Those violating this required sequence are not only doomed to failure, but will be judged as somewhat morally defective.

Such advice makes good sense even if applied more restrictively to the teachings of Jesus. It suggests a division in his teaching between what is elementary (earthly) and what is advanced (heavenly),[4] without requiring us to determine precisely which teachings constitute either element. It is enough that we grasp the general idea it seeks to establish: that disciples (or aspiring disciples) should accept the necessity of graduated religious instruction, and that reaching prematurely for what is esoteric will violate the ethic required among humble learners.

So reasonable is this idea, and so easily aligned with normal human intuition, that we should not be surprised at finding many near parallels throughout both the Jewish and Greco-Roman contexts.[5] Often cited in this regard is Wisdom of Solomon 9:16, "We can hardly guess at what is on earth, and what is at hand we find with labor; but who has traced out what is in the heavens?" Meeks goes so far as to classify 3:12 as a cliché, a counter-punch routinely used to elevate a master teacher by embarrassing the ignorant questioner.[6] All of this suggests that in 3:12 Jesus has ventured not far at all from well-worn patterns of speech and thought deployed by other sages of his day.

---

4. Henceforth we will use "earthly" or "earthly things" to translate τὰ ἐπίγεια, and "heavenly" or heavenly things" to translate τὰ ἐπουράνια in 3:12.

5. Craig S. Keener, *The Gospel of John: A Commentary*, Vol. 1 (Peabody, MA: Hendrickson, 2003), 559–60; Bruce J. Malina and Richard L. Rohrbaugh, *Social-Science Commentary on the Gospel of John* (Minneapolis: fortress, 1998), 84.

6. Wayne A. Meeks, "The Man from Heaven in Johannine Sectarianism," *Journal of Biblical Literature* 91 (1972): 53.

## THE PUZZLE OF CONTEXTUAL CONNECTION

But if 3:12 makes perfectly good sense as it stands, why has an interpretive cloud descended upon it? The trouble begins the moment we try connecting 3:12 to the thought-flow of the Nicodemus story within which it stands (3:1–21). Readers quite naturally expect to find a logic governing the movement from one utterance to the next in the exchange between Jesus and Nicodemus. Specifically, if in 3:12 Jesus upbraids Nicodemus for failing to believe *earthly* things and warns him that *heavenly* things now lie beyond his grasp, we readers expect to be able to identify just what part of Jesus' teaching to Nicodemus was earthly and what was heavenly. But as the history of interpretation shows, these identifications have proven problematic. Before proposing a fresh solution to the problem, it will be helpful to review the interpretive options presently on the table.

## SOLUTIONS ON THE TABLE

1) Most readers, we suppose, would quickly surmise that the heavenly things in view must be Jesus' teaching about the New Birth. The New Birth, after all, comes from above, appears to the primary focus of Jesus' teaching in this passage, and is brought about by the Spirit of God (certainly a heavenly agent). Accordingly, the rebuke Jesus delivers in 3:12 should be read as explaining to Nicodemus just why the New Birth remains an impenetrable mystery to his mind. To paraphrase: "You cannot understand the heavenly truth of the New Birth, because you have refused to believe certain (earthly) truths I have just offered to you."

But readers will be hard pressed to identify exactly what earthly teachings Nicodemus has already refused to believe. Of course Jesus has just appealed to natural (earthly) phenomena (such as the blowing wind and physical birth) to coax Nicodemus toward new spiritual insight. But it makes little sense to imagine that Nicodemus has refused to believe that these natural phenomena occur within normal human experience as Jesus has intimated.[7] Surely Nicodemus and Jesus agree that the blowing wind cannot itself be seen, and that babies come from their mothers' wombs.

Sensing the force of this objection, many have concluded that the earthly things already rejected by Nicodemus must be these same natural phenomena *taken in an enriched sense*, in a sense approaching the New Birth, but not quite identical with it. Accordingly, Barrett suggests that the

---

7. C. K. Barrett, *The Gospel according to St. John: An Introduction with Commentary and Notes on the Greek Text* (Philadelphia: Westminster, 1978), 177.

earthly realities of wind and human birth already point *parabolically* to Christ and to God's activity in him, having been designed by the Creator to engender true faith.[8] Similarly Sanders and Mastin see earthly things as consisting of Jesus' *teaching* about the New Birth, while the heavenly things must refer to the *actual experience* of the New Birth itself.[9] Close to this is R. H. Lightfoot, who claims that Nicodemus had balked at accepting the *necessity* of New Birth, a hesitation rendering him unable to welcome the *work* of the New Birth.[10]

Each of these suggestions does succeed at preserving the New Birth itself as the supreme heavenly reality lying at the center of this nighttime conversation. Furthermore, the disbelief of Nicodemus regarding earthly things is now made more psychologically understandable if earthly things are judged as representing some form (even if a lower grade) of spiritual truth. But this resolution is earned at the cost of creating such heavy overlap between the senses of the "earthly" and the "heavenly" that the two become only slightly different angles from which to view a single entity, the New Birth. Accordingly, the overall meaning of 3:12 would rest upon a fairly subtle distinction not readily discernable from the text, and would manage to deliver a now rather timid claim. To paraphrase: "If you do not believe certain dimensions of the New-Birth truth, you cannot believe/experience other dimensions of New-Birth truth."

2) Since it has proven difficult to demonstrate just what earthly things Nicodemus could have refused to believe *prior* to Jesus' teaching about the New Birth, the majority of exegetes appear to have shifted the New Birth backward in the earthly-heavenly sequence, so that the New Birth itself is now judged to be that earthly teaching rejected by Nicodemus.[11] According to this view, 3:12 now forms a ridge dividing the entire story into two parts.[12] The verb moods within the conditional clauses of 3:12 itself are said to support such a division of the passage: Jesus apparently *looks back* upon the unbelief of Nicodemus regarding the earthly New Birth (in 3:1–10), and

---

8. Ibid.

9. J. N. Sanders and B. A. Mastin, *A Commentary on the Gospel according to St. John* (Peabody, MA: Hendrickson, 1968), 126.

10. R. H. Lightfoot, *St. John's Gospel: A Commentary* (London: Oxford, 1956), 117.

11. A great many follow this pathway: Raymond E. Brown, *The Gospel according to John*, Vol. 1, Anchor Bible (Garden City, NY: Doubleday, 1966), 132; Ben Witherington III, *John's Wisdom: A Commentary on the Fourth Gospel* (Louisville: Westminster John Knox, 1995), 98; Andreas J. Köstenberger, *John*, Baker Exegetical Commentary on the NT (Grand Rapids: Baker, 2004), 126–27.

12. Brown, *The Gospel according to John*, 132.

then *forward* (to 3:13–21) towards heavenly teaching not yet offered.[13] To paraphrase accordingly: "Because you have already refused to believe the earthly truth of the New Birth, it will be impossible for you to believe any of the more advanced heavenly truths I might yet deliver." But such a move requires careful justification for viewing the New Birth as an earthly matter.

For Haenchen and others, the New Birth can be considered an earthly phenomenon because of its *location*. It takes place upon the earth, and among human beings (whose horizon is the earth). It stands to reason, then, that heavenly things would be any events transpiring exclusively in heaven.[14] For Tasker and others, the key is found in the mode of the New Birth's *explanation*. Because it can be explained (at least partially) in terms of natural phenomena, we can appropriately classify it as an earthly thing. Conversely, heavenly matters share no features common with natural experience, and must therefore be explained without the aid of natural analogies.[15] A variation of this view is espoused by Hoskyns, who judges that the New Birth can be grasped by human observation and reasoning, unlike heavenly truths requiring divine revelation for understanding.[16] For Thüsing the issue is one of *salvation history*. Whereas earthly things were taught by Jesus during the earthly phase of his ministry, heavenly things will be taught by the Risen Christ to the church through the Holy Spirit.[17]

But identifying the New Birth with earthly things fails to satisfy us for several reasons. First, the *prima facie* thrust of the whole story is that the New Birth itself is the heavenly teaching of Jesus offered by Jesus. The New Birth is from above, is effected by the Spirit of God (surely a heavenly agent), and should most naturally be judged to be that supremely elevated truth which Nicodemus hopelessly aspires to grasp.[18] The fact that New Birth stands as a prerequisite for 'seeing the Kingdom of God' does not, on that account, make it an elementary truth largely pointing beyond itself to matters more glorious and elevated. As the story unfolds, the tragedy stalk-

---

13. The aorist indicative (εἶπον) in the first conditional clause ("if I told you") points to the past (i.e., 3:1–10), while the aorist subjunctive (εἴπω) in the second clause ("if I tell you") can easily be read as pointing to the future beyond 3:12 (i.e., 3:13ff).

14. Ernst Haenchen, *John*, Vol. 1, Hermeneia: A Critical and Historical Commentary on the Bible (Philadelphia: Fortress, 1984), 204.

15. R. V. G. Tasker, *The Gospel according to St. John: An Introduction and Commentary* (Grand Rapids: Eerdmans, 1960), 71.

16. Edwyn Hoskyns and Francis Noel Davies, *The Fourth Gospel* (London: Faber and Faber, 1947), 216–17.

17. Wilhelm Thüsing, *Die Erhöhung und Verherrlichung Jesu im Johannesevangelium*, Neutestamentliche Abhandlungen 21 (Münster: W. Aschendorff, 1979), 257.

18. Here Barrett's instinct is surely right, "[W]e cannot call new birth an earthly thing: it is 'from above.'" Barrett, *Gospel according to St. John*, 177.

ing Nicodemus is surely not that he might fail to achieve access to distant esoterica, but that he might fail to receive the Spirit's gift immediately under discussion: New Birth. The very diversity of approaches attempting to explain how the New Birth can legitimately be considered an earthly phenomenon underscores, in our judgment, the fundamental unlikelihood of that characterization. Only when it is judged unworkable to identify the New Birth as heavenly, do interpreters feel compelled (it seems) to develop support for the counter-intuitive alternative that Jesus must have spoken of the New Birth as an earthly matter.

Second, it should be noted that verb moods in 3:12 only permit us, but do not require us, to divide the whole story fore and aft of this verse. We agree that the aorist indicative verb ("If I *told* you earthly things") indeed looks back upon earthly teaching as having occurred somewhere before the rebuke we find in 3:12. But the subjunctive found in the balance of 3:12 ("If I *tell* (εἴπω) you heavenly things") does not require us to conclude that Jesus has not yet spoken heavenly things mentioned here. We acknowledge that this (second) conditional clause in 3:12 appears to match the form of a third class condition, which by the stricter expection of Classical Greek usually points ahead to something in the future not yet having occurred.[19] But in the shifting sands of Koine Greek, the third and fifth classes of conditional clauses have become intermingled in form, allowing conditions that look toward a specific future fulfillment (third class) to share appearances with conditions that apply more generally, having no specific temporal anchoring (fifth class).[20] In other words, the form of 3:12b does not require a reader to look to the future (as with a third class conditional), but allows the reader to view the claim more as a general truth that may have multiple instantiations across time. In fact the shift within the Nicodemus story from the 2nd person singular ("you, Nicodemus") to the 2nd person plural ("you, Nicodemus, and those like you") already moves 3:11-12 into a more gen-

---

19. Wallace actually cites 3:12 as an example of a third class condition, and offers a paraphrase to communicate the future sense that would be involved: "If I should tell you heavenly things—and it is likely that I will—how is it possible for you to believe?" Daniel B. Wallace, *Greek Grammar Beyond the Basics: An Exegetical Syntax of the NT* (Grand Rapids: Zondervan, 1996), 698.

20. The fifth class conditions speak to generic situations, to matters considered to be true across a broad time frame, to matters that are not necessarily tied to one specific event. The muddied relationship between "form and content" of third and fifth class conditional clauses requires, then, that interpretation of them must take its primary clues from the sense of the context. When Wallace classifies 3:12 as a third class as opposed to a fifth class condition, he appeals primarily to his reading of the internal logic of 3:12 and to its context, not to its form. Wallace, *Greek beyond the Basics*, 698. We will argue below for a new treatment of 3:12 and its context that will pull the second conditional clause more towards the fifth class, that of a present general condition.

eralized perspective, less focused on the exact temporal movement of Jesus' conversation with Nicodemus himself.[21] To paraphrase 3:12 as a fifth class conditional: "If I tell you heavenly things (whether in the past, present, or future), you will (at that time) not believe." Such an interpretation would allow Nicodemus to have heard and disbelieved heavenly things *long before* the rebuke he received in 3:12. In other words, Jesus' heavenly teaching may still be reasonably identified with the New Birth taught before 3:12, specifically in 3:1–10.

3) But if neither option above will survive the objections raised against them, perhaps Bultmann's treatment of the issue might prove attractive. In his judgment, the puzzle can be resolved only by recognizing that 3:12 has originated outside the Fourth Gospel itself, in Gnostic circles. According to Gnostic doctrine, "man . . . is called on to see the earthly world as alien to himself . . . [and that] whoever refuses to accept the understanding of the world and man contained within [Gnostic] cosmology will also refuse to believe in the Gnostic doctrine of redemption."[22] While Bultmann admits that the Evangelist has not embraced the whole network of Gnostic teaching, he is convinced the Evangelist has preserved in 3:12 a major portion of Gnostic teaching regarding the human condition. Bultmann, then, wishes to identify Jesus' earthly teaching with the Gnostic perspective on the meaningless situation of man. "Only by seeing himself [as hopelessly alienated in his earthly condition] can man gain the prior understanding which is necessary in order to understand the [fuller, heavenly] revelation."[23]

Bultmann has not created a following for himself regarding his treatment of 3:12.[24] Surely the charge against Bultmann's larger program, that he has anachronistically reconstructed an early Gnosticism from later Gnostic sources, should be a telling mark against his proposal here.[25] We only add

---

21. In 3:11 the 2nd person plural is carried by the verb λαμβάνετε ("you do not receive our witness"). In 3:12 the 2nd person plural is carried by twice-repeated 2nd personal pronoun functioning as indirect object ὑμῖν ("to you folks"), along with the verb πιστεύσατε ("you folks will not believe"). It may also be that the generalizing movement to the 2nd person plural introduces the kind of uncertainty (regarding both the time and the exact identity of the hearers of Jesus' heavenly teaching) that could trigger the use of the subjunctive εἴπω ("if I tell") in the second conditional clause. See Wallace for the possibility of such an accounting of the subjunctive. Wallace, *Greek Grammar beyond the Basics*, 697.

22. Rudolf Bultmann, *John: A Commentary*, translated by G. R. Beasley-Murray, R. W. H. Hoare, and J. K. Riches (Philadephia: Westminster, 1971), 148.

23. Ibid., 149.

24. As Ashton puts it, "Bultmann's exegetical bravura at this point is quite dazzling, but not altogether persuasive." Ashton, *Understanding the Fourth Gospel*, 349.

25. A fine survey of the Gnostic issue with conclusions pointing in this direction

that his explanation of 3:12 more or less abandons the effort to discern from within the dynamics of the Nicodemus story itself any fruitful clues identifying the earthly and heavenly components of Jesus' teaching.

4) A more recent proposal sharing Bultmann's pessimism of following contextual clues appeals to the putative rhetorical nature of 3:12. Recognizing that many echoes to it have been found throughout Jewish and Greco-Roman sources, Meeks sees 3:12 as a cliché, a standard rhetorical weapon in the arsenal of those engaged in verbal jousting.[26] As such, 3:12 rides above the particularity of the conversation between Jesus and Nicodemus, serving only to deliver the proverbial slap in the face. The earthly and heavenly language of 3:12, then, functions only within the internal logic of the put-down itself, and invites no particular connection with elements found in the Nicodemus story. A paraphrase conveying the force of such a rejoinder could be something like, "You just don't get it, do you!" Readers sensitive to the rhetorical nature of 3:12 as cliché (as characterized by Meeks) will not be drawn into the hopeless quest of determining which parts of the Nicodemus dialogue correspond to earthly things, and which correspond to the heavenly.

Aside from the obvious strengths of this approach, we hesitate to embrace it for two reasons, both of which relate to ways in which 3:12 does not fit (as precisely as one might hope) the form of a stock expression. First, the use of an aorist indicative ("If I *told* you") has the effect of lowering our eyes from the higher plane of generalization, to the particulars of this conversation itself, to what lies (in the relative past) before 3:12. "If I *told* you" draws us into considering the textual antecedents of 3:12, and raises our expectations of finding some particular identification of earthly things (whether there in 3:1–10 or earlier).

Second, it is often overlooked that 3:12 is not addressing a required sequence in acquiring *knowledge*, but a required sequence in developing *belief*.[27] This critical feature distinguishes 3:12 from the focus of nearly all parallels that have been identified for it, and reveals that 3:12 represents a significant modification of the cliché (as generally deployed) towards the specialized interests of Johannine theology. This observation also leads us to conclude that if the cliché lying behind 3:12 has already been cracked open and reshaped to participate in the theme of *belief* running through the larger Nicodemus story (see 3:15, 16, 18 [3x]), then it is entirely reasonable

---

can be found in Keener, *The Gospel of John*, 161–69.

26. Meeks, "Man from Heaven," 53. Meeks is followed by Smith, *John*, 97; and Malina and Rohrbaugh, *Social-Science Commentary*, 84.

27. Actually Meeks himself is keen to accentuate this distinctive feature of 3:12. Meeks, "Man from Heaven," 53.

to expect that its other elements (i.e. earthly and heavenly things) should likewise participate meaningfully in the conceptual flow of the story. The cliché-like appearance of 3:12, then, may not ultimately relieve us of the need to identify (with particularity) those earthly and heavenly matters disbelieved by Nicodemus.

## A FRESH PROPOSAL

We now turn to a fresh proposal for resolving the puzzle at hand. It is an exceedingly simple solution, but one requiring morphological, grammatical, stylistic, and theological defense. It is anchored in that awareness every professor of exegesis seeks to create in the minds of students for reading texts well. More specifically, it involves the necessity of preserving (and testing out) every possible parsing option when encountering ambiguous morphological forms.

In 3:12, we notice that the aorist active indicative verb (εἶπον), though nearly universally parsed and translated as a *first person singular*, may just as easily be parsed and translated as a *third person plural*. Laying out the whole of 3:12 translated in these two ways shows the shift in sense that would be involved (with italics marking the distinction):

> *Traditional translation*: If *I* told you earthly things and you do not believe, how will you believe if I tell you heavenly things?
>
> *Proposed translation*: If *they* told you earthly things and you do not believe, how will you believe if I tell you heavenly things?

We may say, by way of provisional explanation, that the proposed translation allows a new approach in identifying the earthly and heavenly teachings referenced in 3:12. First, it allows Jesus' teaching of the New Birth (as set forth in 3:1–10) to be his heavenly teaching, surely the *prima facie* drift of the dialogue. Second, it suggests that the earthly teaching over which Nicodemus (first) stumbled *had already been delivered to him by others*. Thus we are relieved of the task that has proven most challenging, that of finding something within 3:1–10 that can convincingly pass for earthly teaching supposedly from Jesus.

## FULLER EXPLANATION

1) In terms of morphology, the parsing ambiguity of εἶπον is known to every beginning Greek student. In the second aorist active indicative, the

first person singular ("I spoke") and the third person plural ("they spoke") share the same form. When finding no explicit nominative subject present in the sentence to settle the matter, readers must decide how to interpret the form by observing the contextual flow of thought. In 3:12 no explicit subject (either noun or pronoun) is supplied for εἶπον, opening the door for us to consider just how the context might shape our decision about its accurate parsing.[28]

2) But our proposal has more to commend it than a technical parsing possibility. In our judgment, features of the Johannine theological vision (especially regarding Christology and the problem of Jewish unbelief) *strongly support* our reading of 3:12.

First, as noted above, 3:12 exhibits a distinctive interest in the matter of *belief*, or more precisely, that of *unbelief*. It is crucial, then, to locate the logic of 3:12 within the larger Johannine analysis of Jewish unbelief. As it turns out, the Fourth Gospel is deeply invested in explaining Jewish unbelief in the face of Jesus' ministry. Chapter 5 contains some of Jesus' most blistering accusations, not so much against any *intellectual* shortcomings of his opponents, but against their deficiencies in *moral and spiritual character*. To the point, Jesus claims, in 5:37–38, that their rejection of him stems from the fact that they have had no relationship with God at all! "His voice you have never heard, his form you have never seen; and you do not have his word abiding in you." Their vacuous spiritual lives were judged as having guaranteed that they would reject Jesus and his teaching *even before meeting him in person*.

As the accusations continue, Jesus diagnoses a complete lack of love for God on their part (5:42). As he sees it, such a deficiency explains why they crave the giving and receiving of glory among themselves. Because vertically oriented love for God has collapsed, they have become consumed with the horizontal quest of establishing value in and for each other. It is this perverse passion for glory, well entrenched *before they ever encountered Jesus*, that renders them unable now to embrace him: "How can you believe,

---

28. It is true that in Koine Greek second aorist indicative verbs are more and more attracting to themselves first aorist endings. Wallace, *Greek Grammar beyond the Basics*, 19. One might wonder just what the Johannine practice is with reference to the aorist active indicative form εἶπον. When wishing to express the 3rd plural, has John shifted exclusively to using a first aorist ending (i.e., to εἶπαν for the 3rd plural), so that the εἶπον in 3:12 must be treated as a 1st singular (as it now almost universally is)? But on at least eleven occasions in the Fourth Gospel we find εἶπον used to express the 3rd plural, as established unambiguously by the context: 6:25, 6:28, 6:30, 6:34, 7:3, 7:35, 7:45, 8:13, 18:25, 18:31, 18:34. It is clear that in the Fourth Gospel εἶπον frequently enough is used as a 3rd plural, and therefore must be resolved each time (either into a 1st singular or a 3rd plural) by appealing to its context.

who receive glory from another and do not seek the glory that comes from the only God?" (5:44)

As this flourish comes to a close, Jesus offers a third explanation of unbelief following along this same line, one touching even more directly on the interpretive puzzle of 3:12. In 5:44–6 Jesus claims that Moses, their highly esteemed hero, will not be for, but against them in the final judgment. Surely this was shocking and offensive to their sensibilities given the exalted position of Moses in the outlook of Judaism.[29] But despite their regard for Moses, Jesus claimed that they had not *believed* him. Furthermore, it was precisely this unbelief toward Moses that lay as the underlying cause for their rejection of Jesus. The accusation insists that Moses and Jesus stand in such close continuity with each other that the rejection of one implies (and even necessitates) the rejection of the other.

One might even say that the Fourth Gospel envisions that no Jew of Jesus' day, particularly one with the status and learning of Nicodemus, could meet Jesus apart from having already established a track record of embracing or rejecting the stream of messengers God had previously sent to Israel. The dividing line between those Jews who would follow Jesus (as did the first disciples) and those who would reject him is the same line (in the vision of the Fourth Gospel) dividing those who had already believed Moses and the prophets, and those who had not. Unbelief in Jesus, according to the Fourth Gospel, should be viewed almost as a later emerging symptom growing out of the *previously established* disease of unbelief.

If this understanding of unbelief is brought to bear on the interpretation of 3:12, we are invited to understand that the difficulty Nicodemus was having with faith in what Jesus would teach resulted from a "pre-existing condition," a bearing of unbelief existing antecedently to his encounter with Jesus. Such unbelief would have been directed at earlier agents (perhaps John the Baptist, or the prophets, or Moses) who had addressed Israel in God's behalf. If this conceptual background for 3:12 is in play, the *earthly* and *heavenly* bodies of teaching would correspond nicely with the two phases of revelation set forth in 5:46–47: the *earlier* revelation delivered through Moses (or others in his prophetic lineage), and the *final* revelation being now offered by Jesus. When 3:12 is set beside 5:46–47 and read according to our proposal, these two passages echo each other closely both in form and content, enabling us to discern a common analysis of Jewish unbelief beneath them.[30]

---

29. A good survey of material pointing to the high stature of Moses in Jewish estimation at this time is found in Keener, *Gospel of John*, 660–62.

30. Blank draws much attention to the close (formal) parallel between 3:12 and 5:47, but does not pull them as closely together conceptually. He, of course, is working

> If they told you earthly things and you do not believe,
> how will you believe if I tell you heavenly things? (3:12)
>
> If you believed Moses, you would believe me.
> But if you do not believe his writings, how will you believe my words?
> If you do not believe Moses,
> how will you believe me? (5:46-7)

Our proposal for reading 3:12 also makes good sense from the standpoint of Johannine Christology. In 3:31 the status of Jesus as the heavenly revealer is celebrated by distinguishing him from all other voices: "He who comes from above is above all; he who is of the earth belongs to the earth, and of the earth he speaks." Were this verse interpreted apart from its immediate context, we might conclude that the contrast between the heavenly and the earthly should be viewed as the contrast between *Jesus* and *the whole of humanity* (understood either under the bondage of sin or under the realities of weakness and limitation).[31]

But in the final form of the Fourth Gospel, the immediately preceding context (3:22-30) clearly focuses upon John the Baptist as standing in both continuity and discontinuity with Jesus.[32] Regarding continuity, the Baptist is lauded as the forerunner who has been sent to prepare the way (3:28b). He also experiences great joy when hearing the voice of Christ, no doubt having longed for his arrival (3:29). But regarding discontinuity, there is a separation between them as between a groom and his best man. It is the bridegroom who will be the star of the approaching event, while the friend will rightly be eclipsed; "He must increase, but I must decrease" (3:30). It is immediately on the heels of this contrast (3:22-30) that we read of a contrast between one "who comes from above" and one "who belongs to the earth and speaks of the earth" in 3:31. This juxtaposition (of 3:22-30 with 3:31ff) leads us to conclude that John the Baptist (and by extension all other messengers, agents and prophets of God) can be said to be "of the earth" and

---

under the assumption that εἶπον in 3:12 is to be read as a 1st singular. Josef Blank, *Krisis: Untersuchungen zur johanneischen Christologie und Eschatologie* (Freiburg: Lambertus, 1964), 60.

31. Schnackenburg is among those arguing to reorganize the text, so that 3:31ff follow directly upon 3:13. Under this arrangement, the references to John the Baptist (3:22-30) no longer lead up to 3:31ff, and the one who "speaks from the earth" (in 3:31) looks back, perhaps, upon Nicodemus as a representative of humanity in general. Rudolf Schnackenburg, *The Gospel according to St. John*, Vol. 1, Introduction and Commentary on Chapters 1-4, translated by Kevin Smyth, Herder's Theological Commentary on the NT (London: Burns and Oates, 1968), 380-81.

32. Smith, *John*, 106-7.

can be characterized (even when functioning in an authoritative, revelatory role) as "speaking of the earth."

But the language of 3:31ff appears aimed at establishing more than a *relative* difference between Jesus and the Baptist (and all earlier prophets). The distinction between the One who comes from above and the one who belongs to the earth is surely proposed as *ontological* in nature.[33] Jesus (no matter where he is or what he is saying) simply *is* "from above," while John the Baptist (and all other prophets, etc.) simply *are* "of the earth" (whatever they might be saying). While all these earth-bound prophets do indeed speak for God, revelation from Jesus' lips is qualitatively different from that of all his predecessors. Everything taught by Jesus bears the stamp of fullness and finality, having been uttered by one experiencing unsurpassable intimacy with the Father (see 1:11 and 18).

While it is frequently concluded from this high Christology that *only Jesus* can speak from this unique perspective as the Heavenly Revealer, we suspect that this passage is driving at an even stronger conclusion: that Jesus *speaks only* from this heavenly perspective. In other words, even if Jesus were to speak in parables or in dark ambiguities,[34] he would nonetheless be speaking from within his unparalleled status of being the only Son of the Father. Jesus does not alternate between speaking "from the earth" and "from above" according to the needs and abilities of a given audience. He doesn't merely *have* heavenly teaching to share when it might seem appropriate, or *have* heavenly teaching to offer when an audience seems receptive. Since he *is* a being from heaven, he can speak from no other perspective. *In other words, everything he declares is heavenly, and nothing he declares is earthly.*

If this assessment of the Fourth Gospel's Christology is valid and brought to bear on 3:12, the deeper strength of our proposal emerges. Since Jesus teaches only heavenly things, then the earthly teachings that Nicodemus had not believed cannot have been anything Jesus either had taught or would yet teach. Rather, these earthly things were delivered to him through the mouths of earlier servants of God, those who spoke "from the earth." From the larger Johannine critique of Jewish unbelief we gather that these earlier servants must be identified, essentially, with the whole prophetic lineage, including Moses, Isaiah, Elijah, and John the Baptist in particular.[35] In that light our proposed paraphrase of 3:12 is a follows:

33. Andreas J. Köstenberger, *A Theology of John's Gospel and Letters*, Biblical Theology of the NT (Grand Rapids: Zondervan, 2009), 287–88.

34. See, for example, John 16:29: His disciples said, "Now you are speaking plainly, and not in any figure."

35. "Rather the discourse draws to its climax with declarations of the supremacy of the revelation through Christ over all other prophets and prophecies." G. R.

> If [the prophets] told you earthly things and you did not believe, how will you believe if I tell you heavenly things?

## HISTORICAL INTERLUDE

Before addressing objections that would likely arise to this proposal, some comments about the history of interpretation are in order. We admit at the outset that no modern interpreter known to us has discussed, mentioned, or even noticed the translational (and interpretive) option of reading εἶπον as a 3rd plural ("they told"). This raises the specter of the scholarly dilemma noted by A. R. Burn, that in a desire to approach interpretive challenges with freshness and creativity, we might indeed succeed at producing novel solutions. But the problem with novel solutions, opines Burn, is that "a truly original theory has a high probability of being a perverse theory."[36] A theory that has never been entertained before, or has never been embraced by anyone but its originator, is likely one that can safely be left to the side. We can add some merit to our proposal, then, if it can be shown to have even a glimmer of precedent.

On the boundary between modern and pre-modern biblical commentators stands Frederic Louis Godet, a Swiss Protestant who wrote (in French) a number of scholarly works that attracted international attention. One of these works, a commentary on the Fourth Gospel, was taken up by American scholar Timothy Dwight and translated in English. In Godet's treatment of the interpretive challenge of 3:12, he mentions the very proposal we are advancing here (of reading εἶπον as a 3rd plural). For reasons we will pass over for the moment, Godet did not endorse such a reading, but identified Heinrich Ewald as its originator.[37]

Students of the history of biblical criticism may remember the name but forget the larger story of Heinrich Ewald. His fame is linked mostly with the OT, more particularly with early attempts at developing a documentary hypothesis regarding the Pentateuch, and with having the distinction of being Julius Wellhausen's teacher. Brilliant and cantankerous at once, Ewald lived in a day when biblical scholars were not so forcefully relegated, as they usually are now, to working in one Testament or the other. He ranged beyond the boundaries we might have assigned to him as "an OT scholar" by

---

Beasley-Murray, *John*, Word Biblical Commentary (Waco, TX: Word, 1987), 53.

36. *Herodotus: The Histories*, translated by Aubrey de Selincourt, with an Introduction and Notes by A. R. Burn (New York: Penguin, 1954), 23.

37. Frederic Louis Godet, *Commentary on the Gospel of John*, translated by Timothy Dwight (Grand Rapids: Kregel, 1978), 387–88.

devoting some of his energies to writing not only a biblical theology (covering both Testaments) but also a commentary on the Fourth Gospel.[38]

In his commentary on John's Gospel Ewald supplies a translation of 3:12a that clearly treats εἶπον as a 3rd plural: "Wenn *sie* das irdische euch *sagten* und ihr nichts glaubtet" (If *they* spoke earthly things to you and you do not believe [emphasis added]).[39] In the subsequent notes he identifies the *sie* ("they") as Israel's prophets who so often were rejected by God's people. Unfortunately Ewald neither develops his thoughts much further theologically, nor addresses the grammatical and stylistic objections he certainly could have anticipated. We are left to wonder if his proposal might have gained a stronger foothold had he undertaken to support it more thoroughly.

Godet, in assessing Ewald's proposal regarding 3:12, sets it aside as unworkable for two reasons: 1) There is no clear antecedent to "they" in the text prior to 3:12. How could a reader be expected to conjure εἶπον as a 3rd plural without clearer contextual guidance? 2) If we were to read εἶπον in the first conditional clause of 3:12 as a 3rd plural ("If *they* told you earthly things"), should we not find the emphatic pronoun ἐγώ standing in the second conditional clause ("if *I* tell you heavenly things") marking this contrastive shift from "they" to "I"? In Godet's view, the habits of Johannine expression would have demanded such a presence for ἐγώ.[40]

## RESPONSE TO OBJECTIONS

Our examination of Godet and Ewald not only identifies noteworthy support for our proposal (Ewald himself), but specifies the two principle objections against it (as detailed by Godet). Each objection is serious, but can be countered effectively, in our view, by a fuller assessment of the grammatical and stylistic dynamics involved.

### 1) A 'missing' antecedent for "they"

How should readers of 3:12 be expected to decode εἶπον as a 3rd plural if there is no prior identification of who "they" are? We begin by returning to

---

38. A helpful review of Ewald and his significance is found in John Rogerson, *OT Criticism in the nineteenth Century: England and Germany* (Philadelphia: Fortress, 1985), 91–103.

39. Heinrich Ewald, *Die johanneischen Schriften, übersetzt und erklärt*, Vol. 1 (Göttingen: Dieterich, 1861), 64.

40. Godet, *Commentary on the Gospel of John*, 387–88.

our analysis of Johannine Christology laid out above. It was our contention that (from the perspective of the Fourth Gospel) a sharp distinction was understood between the "one coming from above," and all prior spokespersons for God. In our judgment, their ontological difference (one from above, the others from the earth) requires that their teaching be recognized as *fundamentally different in character* (i.e. the one from above teaches *exclusively* heavenly things, those of the earth teach *exclusively* earthly things). From this analysis we now conclude that the writer sensed no obligation, in 3:12, to supply an explicit subject for εἶπον. So clearly in the writer's mind (we surmise) were "earthly things" associated with the rejected teachings of God's prophets (who spoke from the earth) that the writer would not have imagined a need to add signposts in the text explicitly pointing in such a direction.

We may add to this a grammatical consideration that, while not supplying proof to our claim, eases its abruptness somewhat. Grammarians have noticed several kinds of circumstances in which NT writers employ a 3rd plural verb without explicitly "setting the table" by supplying a prior (grammatical) antecedent.[41] The kind of circumstance we have in mind for 3:12 involves appealing to the larger context for an *inferred* identification of a "they." We can imagine saying, "If you arrive late at the First Baptist Church, *they* will seat you in the balcony." Here our minds easily take the clue from "church," and discern that, among the many groups in attendance, "they" must be the *ushers*, perhaps under the direction of the pastor. In other words, an appeal to the larger context, combined with some awareness of the realities under consideration, will often allow us to identify ambiguous references without great difficulty.

While nothing in the context surrounding 3:12 so neatly resolves the identity of "they" as in the example we created above, we suggest that the drift of the whole story points to a full awareness (on the part of Nicodemus) of God's prior revelation through the prophets, and that such a reality underlies the logic of the entire encounter.

Specifically we find that only two verses earlier in 3:10 Jesus chides Nicodemus for being Israel's teacher while not understanding the matter of New Birth. By characterizing him as Israel's teacher Jesus is surely not

---

41. Edwin A. Abbott, *Johannine Grammar* (London: Adam and Charles Black, 1906), 310–11. Abbot names this phenomenon the "they" non-pronominal. In one of several examples, he cites John 15:6, "'they' gather [severed] branches and cast them into the fire." As Abbott sees it, the common understanding of Jewish tradition would likely identify the "they" as "the powers of heaven," or "the angels." In other words, the context (historical or literary) may provide a fabric of understanding sufficient to allow a writer to introduce an unspecified "they" into a passage, that is a "they" with no exactly identifiable grammatical antecedent.

intending to highlight merely the intelligence or social standing of Nicodemus. A teacher of Israel would be thoroughly versed not only with the books of Moses in particular, but with the Scripture as a whole.[42] Somehow his mastery of Israel's scriptures should have readied him for Jesus' heavenly teaching on the New Birth. The irony at work in this dialogue, as generally agreed, is that Nicodemus is struggling to embrace matters he should already have known from the very Scriptures that supposedly were his field of expertise.[43]

These contextual clues present Nicodemus as one fully versed in the message of God's prophets to Israel over the centuries. Put another way, the context *does* make available to us, even if somewhat opaquely, meaningful speakers who have already spoken what Nicodemus has already declined to believe. A reasonable sense for "they" as the subject of εἶπον in 3:12 is discernable from the preceding context, and is seconded by the Fourth Gospel's assessment of Jewish unbelief. We propose that the linkage between 3:10 and 3:12 is therefore more vital than usually recognized: "You are the teacher of Israel [and fully familiar with the Scripture]? . . . If [the prophets of Israel] told you earthly things . . ."

## 2) The 'missing' emphatic ἐγώ

Godet's second objection sounds entirely reasonable, that Johannine style would almost certainly require an emphatic ἐγώ underscoring the particular contrast being urged: "If [earlier prophets] told you earthly things and you do not believe, how will you believe if *I* (ἐγώ) tell you heavenly things?"

If we wished, we could respond with a simple *tour de force*. Every stylistic pattern, we could say, has its exceptions. While acknowledging the great abundance of emphatic pronouns used throughout the Fourth Gospel, we could judge 3:12 simply to be an aberration from that norm, accepting this unlikelihood as the cost of advancing our interpretation of 3:12 (judging it a lesser cost than charged by the difficulties involved in the other interpretations). But more careful attention to the dynamics of the contrast at work in 3:12 will lead us more naturally (though not so obviously) to the conclusion that an emphatic ἐγώ should actually *not* be expected in this circumstance.

---

42. Schnackenburg, *Gospel according to St. John*, 375.

43. One can find additional support for the presence of OT scripture and its prophets/writers witing the fabric of the larger context by noting the post-ceding reference to Moses lifting up the serpent in the wilderness (see 3:14–15, drawing upon Num 21:4–9).

But first we begin by recalling 3:12 as traditionally translated with italic font highlighting the point of contrast between the two halves of the verse:

> If I told you *earthly* things and you do not believe,
> how will you believe if I tell you *heavenly* things?

With only one point of variation between these halves, our minds naturally select the point of difference, intuitively reading the verse (aloud) with vocal emphasis at that very point to bring the contrast into sharp focus.

Our translational proposal for 3:12 essentially adds a *second* point of difference between the two halves of the verse (both pairs indicated with italic font):

> If *they* told you *earthly* things and you do not believe,
>
> how will you believe if *I* tell you *heavenly* things?

Godet's intuition told him that such an additional point of difference should be emphatic (simply because it is a point of difference?), and that it should therefore have been marked (*a la* Johannine style) with an emphatic ἐγώ if this double difference (earthly things vs. heavenly things *and* they vs. I) were intended by the writer:

> If *they* told you *earthly* things and you did not believe,
> how will you believe if *I* (ἐγώ) tell you *heavenly* things?

Without an (emphatic) ἐγώ in the second half of the verse, reasoned Godet, no difference was intended between the one(s) who spoke earthly things, and the one(s) who spoke heavenly things. And since the parsing of the second verb of saying (εἴπω "if I tell you heavenly things") is unambiguously 1st singular, we should conclude that the first verb of saying (εἶπον) must also be read as a 1st singular ("if I told you heavenly things"). According to such reasoning our proposal for 3:12 appears less viable.

But another line of analysis leads in the opposite direction, perhaps even confirming our approach to 3:12. We begin by noting that an emphasis often (though not necessarily) implies a contrast.[44] When we hear an emphatic element in a sentence, our minds typically suspect that a (contrastive) substitute will be implied, if not actually supplied, in a balancing expression. In the following pairs of sentences consider how the listener is set up to expect corrective information at the initial point of emphasis:

> No, Jim didn't *sell* me a pearl necklace.

---

44. While emphasis and contrast often work together, they remain distinct and should be treated separately. Wallace, *Greek Grammar Beyond the Basics*, 321–23.

Jim *gave* me a pearl necklace.

As intuition teaches us, the emphatic word is likely the point at which an underlying contrast is at work (here, sell vs. buy). Emphasis often implies contrast, and such contrasts are typically marked with emphasis (whether spoken or written).

We can modify this example of single-point contrast to create one with multiple contrasts:

> No, Jim didn't *sell* me a *pearl* necklace.
> He *gave* me a *diamond* necklace.

The emphasis laid upon each word in the first sentence is designed to alert us to an element that will be changed in the second. In fact, every change showing up in the second sentence should already have been marked with emphasis in the first sentence. In such a scenario, change *requires* emphatic expression, if communication is to be clear.

To this point we have only explained the logic underlying Godet's critique of our proposal. If in 3:12 the Evangelist (in the words of Jesus) has crafted mirrored clauses that differ from each other in two features, should not both elements undergoing change bear marks of emphasis ("If *they* told you *earthly* things . . . If *I* (ἐγώ) tell you *heavenly* things . . ."). Should we not expect to find at least an emphatic ἐγώ in the second conditional clause?

But consider this complex contrast:

> If a brain surgeon repaired your aneurism just in the nick of time,
> and you never said thanks,
> why should I expect you to say thanks
> if a waitress refills your Diet Coke?

Here we have created a two-fold difference: *brain surgeon* vs. *waitress*, and *repairing an aneurism* vs. *refilling a drink*. Perhaps we should adopt the rule we generated from the earlier example, and recommend that both sets of differences be emphasized when writing or speaking these lines. But under closer scrutiny a crucial distinction emerges between the two examples, a difference regarding "entailment."[45] In the first example we can easily imagine that Jim could *either* have sold *or* given a necklace, and that the necklace could have been crafted *either* of diamonds *or* pearls. Each pair of variables appears to function independently of the other pair, allowing us just as easily to imagine that Jim could have *sold* a *diamond* necklace.

---

45. We are using the term "entailment" only as we describe it here, not as a technical term from any given system of linguistic analysis.

But the second example is different, since the repair of an aneurism presumes the agency of a surgeon, and the refilling of a drink (easily) presumes the setting of a restaurant and its staff. In other words, brain surgery *entails* a brain surgeon, and table service *entails* a waitress, making a cross-matching among these agents not easily envisioned.[46]

Another clue to the peculiar nature of our second example is that, unlike the first, mention of the agents *may be omitted* without damage to the basic idea in view. We shift to the passive voice to allow such omission:

> If *your aneurism was repaired* just in the nick of time,
> and you never said thanks,
> why should I expect you to say thanks
> if your Diet Coke *is refilled*?

This shows that some activities are so well understood to involve certain agents, that the outcome alone may be expressed, given its power to suggest to our minds the agents appropriate to each activity.

We conclude that when such entailment operates between elements within a clause, the power of entailment may permit only the actions (or the outcomes of actions) to be expressed for the concept to be complete, *even if the agents entailed by these actions differ from one clause to the next* (surgeon, waitress). Though surgeons and waitresses are absolutely necessary agents for these outcomes to take place, they need not be expressed, and therefore should be considered grammatically and stylistically *unemphatic*.[47]

This directly informs our response to Godet's concerns about our reading of 3:12. In alignment with our theological analysis of 3:31 above, it is our contention that an *entailment* is operating between elements within the two conditional clauses of 3:12. According to our assessment of the theological vision of the Fourth Gospel, *earthly* things are taught only by *earthlings*, and *heavenly* things are taught only by the one from above. If this claim of entailment is valid, then the dynamics we discovered in our second example are operative here in 3:12 as well. The elements of the second contrast ("they" vs. "I") need not even be expressed, or (if expressed) need not be expressed

---

46. That is, we would be puzzled by reference to a surgeon refilling our Coke, or to a waitress repairing an aneurism.

47. In fact, if entailment is at work, confusion could easily result if emphasis were added to both elements (agent and activity). If we were to say, "If a *surgeon* repairs your *aneurism*," I might inadvertently be leading the listener down a false trail, as if suggesting that I am entertaining the possibility of someone other than a surgeon performing the surgery. My point does not focus on who performed the surgery (as opposed to some other person), but upon one's response to that surgery (which would obviously have been performed by a surgeon).

emphatically. A radical paraphrase allows our whole claim to be viewed in one pass:

> If you were told *earthly* things
>   [which, of course, were taught by earthlings (God's prophets)],
>     (an optionally expressed and unemphatic entailment)
> and do not believe,
> how will you believe
> if you are told *heavenly* things?
>   [which, of course, are taught by me, the one from heaven]
>     (an optionally expressed and unemphatic entailment)

In short, we believe we have supplied strong responses to Godet's concerns about both a "missing subject" and a "missing emphatic ἐγώ," and have significantly enhanced the viability interpreting of 3:12 as we propose.

## NEW POSSIBILITIES FOR 3:11

In the limited space remaining, we should give some attention to how our reading of 3:12 might speak to the thought flow from 3:10 to 3:12. Within this sequence of verses stands 3:11, famous for its own interpretive challenge of identifying the "we/our":

> Truly, Truly I say to you, we speak of what we know,
> and bear witness to what we have seen;
> but you do not receive our testimony. 3:11

To this point in the story Nicodemus and Jesus have been referenced by singular pronouns, whether in their direct comments to each other or through the narrator's voice. But immediately after the solemn introductory formula of 3:11 ("Truly, truly I say to you" [singular]), all pronouns are plural ("we, our"; "you" [plural]). Most interpreters readily envision the "you" [plural] as a device for addressing the larger Jewish community through Nicodemus. But who joins Jesus in seeing, knowing, speaking and testifying?

Several options make good sense, and have been argued credibly by numbers of interpreters. Perhaps by the "we" Jesus means no one other than himself, "sardonically aping" the way Nicodemus began the whole conversation ("We know that you are a teacher from God. . . ." 3:2).[48] Perhaps Jesus has his own disciples in view, whether because they are right there with him in the room,[49] or because they will, in time, accompany him throughout his

---

48. Carson, *Gospel according to John*, 198–99.
49. Morris considers this view (attributed to Westcott) and does not dismiss it

earthly ministry.[50] Perhaps Jesus is speaking prolepticly of the whole Johannine community, who will, after the resurrection and in continuity with the original apostles, bear witness to the gospel throughout the world.[51]

But 3:12 is linked (in ways have already suggested) with 3:10, forming a bracket around 3:11 and raising the possibility that the flow between them is smoother than usually imagined. In Jesus' reference to Nicodemus as Teacher of Israel (3:10) we discerned the presence of the Law and Prophets in the logic of this rebuke. Then in 3:12 we discerned the presence of the Law and Prophets again, now entailed (according to the larger theology of the Fourth Gospel) in the revelation of earthly things. We now surmise that the "we" of 3:11 quite naturally represents Jesus in solidarity with the lineage of OT prophets (including John the Baptist), all of whom see, hear, speak and bear witness in God's behalf. Such solidarity connects nicely with the Fourth Gospel's claim that Jesus and the prophets must either be believed together, or disbelieved together.[52] Such solidarity also explains Jesus' presumption that a (genuine) belief in the message of the prophets should manifest itself (now on the part of Nicodemus, the teacher of Israel) by a full reception of Jesus' teaching on the New Birth.

If we are right in seeing the "we" of 3:11 as referring to Jesus in solidarity with the Israel's prophetic heritage, then 3:12 can be read as referencing a distinction within that solidarity. In 3:11 Jesus joins himself to the company of prophets as sharing in the unity of their acceptance or rejection by Israel, while in 3:12 Jesus distinguishes himself from these same seers by virtue of his heavenly origin and teaching. And yet the underlying unity between Jesus and Israel's prophets remains in place, that rejection of earlier earthly witnesses entails the rejection of Jesus' heavenly person and proclamation. Accordingly, 3:10–12 can now be read as a meaningful series of claims within the flow of a conversation, claims that comport well with the theological vision of the Fourth Gospel. An expansive paraphrase might read as follows:

> You are Israel's teacher, fully schooled in the Law and Prophets, and you do not know these things? (10)
> Truly I say to you, Nicodemus, God's prophets and I speak what we know,

---

outright, allowing a circle of association around Jesus that might have made the conversation with Nicodemus something other than strictly a one-on-one affair. Leon Morris, *The Gospel according to John: The English Text with Introduction, Exposition and Notes* (Grand Rapids: Eerdmans, 1971), 221–22.

50. Herman N. Ridderbos, *The Gospel according to John: A Theological Commentary*, translated by John Vriend (Grand Rapids: Eerdmans, 1997), 133–34.

51. Witherington, *John's Wisdom*, 98; Beasley-Murray, *John*, 49.

52. See again 5:46–47.

and bear witness to what we have seen,
but you and others do not accept the testimony that the prophets and I supply. (11)
But if the prophets spoke to you and others from their earthly perspective
and you and others do not believe,
how will you and others believe
when I speak from my heavenly perspective? (12)

## SUMMARY

We have argued that the parsing ambiguity of εἶπον in John 3:12 opens the door to consider the viability of reading that verb as a 3rd plural (as opposed to the 1st singular), resulting in the following translation:

> If they told you earthly things, and you do not believe,
> how will you believe if I tell you heavenly things?

We have on two bases urged that "they" are to be understood as Israel's prophets. First, since the Fourth Gospel explains Jewish unbelief in Jesus as flowing from prior unbelief in Israel's prophets (e.g. 5:46–7), we are invited to read 3:12 as likewise naming unbelief in the message of earlier prophets as the cause for unbelief in Jesus' teaching here. Second, we judge that the high Christology of the Fourth Gospel not only insists on the heavenly origin of Jesus as the "one coming from above," but implies that his teaching is delivered consistently and exclusively from that same perspective, and is therefore to be judged as thoroughly heavenly in character (3:31). Such an evaluation of Jesus' teaching should encourage us to identify the earthly things of 3:12 with prior divine revelation delivered through Gods' earthly (human) prophets, not through Jesus. We have also offered grammatical and stylistic defenses of our translation that account not only for the appearance of the (grammatically) unanticipated "they" opening our translation of 3:12, but also for the lack of an emphatic ἐγώ that many readers might expect to find in 3:12b. A possible benefit of our proposal is the ease with which 3:10, 11 and 12 may now be seen to be flowing together.

Our treatment of 3:12 relieves us of the task of identifying both earthly and heavenly elements within the teaching of Jesus, and renders unnecessary appeals to its putative Gnostic origin or to its status as a cliché of the day. Its focus upon the question of belief, not knowledge, inclines it in a specifically moral/religious direction, and its participation in the Fourth Gospel's analysis of unbelief bends its vertical orientation (of earthly and heavenly) to include a horizontal (salvation-historical) dimension (of prior revelation through the prophets and present revelation through Jesus). The message of 3:12 is not the pragmatic advice that simple things must be mastered before the difficult, but a dominical warning that rejecting God's first words delivered through the prophets will lead to rejecting God's fullest Word present in Jesus.

# 6

# With God on Our Side

*The Rhetoric of Economics in Revelation*

JASON A. MYERS

IT IS QUITE THE privilege to contribute this essay in honor of my *Doktorvater*, Ben Witherington III. I first became aware of the work of Dr. Witherington in my undergraduate coursework where I perused his commentaries for various assignments. In coming to Asbury, Ben has been not only a great mentor, but also a friend who has shown equal concern for the well-being of my wife and I.

Outside of biblical studies, one of Ben's main loves is music. It is not unusual for Ben to start off his classes with one of his favorite songs or a song that sets the theme for the class. One could also mention the infamous story of how Ben missed going to Woodstock in the summer of 1969! This intertwining of music and biblical studies is one of the many ways Ben engages popular culture and the biblical world bringing the two into constant conversation. In honor of his excellent work on Revelation and rhetoric and his love of music, I offer this essay on the rhetoric of economics in Revelation with a little help from Bob Dylan to set the tone.

In his 1964 song, *With God On Our Side*, Bob Dylan walks his listeners though a series of historical events in chronological order that ends with the eponymous line of the title. While points are raised along the way about these events, it is the penultimate verse that stands out for several reasons. For one, Dylan throws off the chronological constraints of the first six incidents by recalling the betrayal of Jesus by Judas. Second, unlike the other eponymous lines which were cast as objective statements, "with God on our side," Dylan now changes the nature of the statement in this last event by asking his listeners to decide *if* God was on Judas' side, his question of course begging a negative answer from his audience. This subtle rhetorical shift from an objective to inquisitive statement throws the entire song into a different relief. The listeners are now juxtaposed with the negative character of Judas and thus caused to question their own actions.

In this penultimate verse, the author has now played his hand, revealing that not only in this last incident, but every incident before that evoked the phrase "with God on our Side" is now thrown into question. In Dylan's invocation for the audience to wonder about how Judas thought about his betrayal, he has called into question the general notion that God invariably sides with one's own views and opposes those with whom the audience disagrees and thus never question the morality of their own actions. It is in the entirety of the song that the rhetorical punch comes into full picture and thus reveals that the innate and unquestioned assumptions of the previous verses.

Shifting analogies rather abruptly, Revelation is engaged in its own rhetorical tour-de-force whereby the first three chapters are written to the seven cities of Asia minor and the author engages them in a series of critical self-reflections calling into question various aspects of their communal lives. While Rev 1–3 is not subtle in its critique of some churches, here I want to argue that Revelation has saved one of its critiques for last and this critique, like Dylan's of his audience, casts the identity and life of one community into an entirely different relief. Through a series of rhetorical moves, the Laodicean church is caused to question the morality of their own actions, specifically their economic ties to the soon-to-be fallen Roman empire.

The thesis of this study is that the self-sufficiency of Laodicea as expressed in economic terms is characterized in Revelation as capitulating to the economic practices of the Roman empire that are also under judgment. It will be argued that both textual references within Revelation and intertextual references from the Hebrew prophets combine to offer a prophetic critique of Laodicea in Rev 3:14–22. Within the book, the economic critique of Rome in Rev 18 functions as a future point of warning for the church at Laodicea.[1] However, intertextually this critique is not the apocalypticist's

---

1. L. Hartman, "Form and Message. A Preliminary Discussion of <<Partial Texts>> in Rev 1–3 and 22,6ff," in *L'apocalypse Johannique Et L'apocalyptique Dans Le Nouveau Testament*, ed. Jan Lambrecht (Leuven: University Press, 1980), 129–49. "Rev 2–3

alone, rather the author draws upon the prophetic critiques of the Hebrew prophets (such as such as Jer 5:27; Hos 12:8; and Zech 11:5) to provide a negative evaluation of Laodicea's current position. Furthermore, the contrast with the other churches addressed in the first three chapters identifies economic affluence as a sign of consorting with the empire and thus standing under the coming judgment.

## LAODICEA: A QUICK GLIMPSE

Scholarly attention typically focuses on the lukewarm water (3:15–16) or the eye salve (3:18) in light of the local conditions present at Laodicea.[2] However, few have looked at Laodicea from within the socio-economic framework provided and indebted to the Roman Empire.[3] Scholars have primarily concentrated on Laodicea as its own wealth-producing city and neglected the possibilities made possible by the Roman Empire.[4] As such, the critique of Laodicea is usually seen as self-sufficiency rather than Roman-sufficiency. It will be argued that although self-sufficiency is a possible problem in Laodicea, the exact nature of the problem is not that the Laodiceans rely on themselves too much. Rather, the Laodiceans are too

---

should be regarded as prophetic messages that point to the real situation of the addressees, on which, from ch. 4 and on they will have further light shed on them from a higher divine perspective" (144). A similar point has been made by others regarding the connection between the letters and the rest of the Apocalypse.

2. For introductory issues to Revelation which cannot be discussed here, such as the issue of the letters to the body of the document, the nature of apocalyptic vs prophecy and issues of authorship see Richard Bauckham, *The Theology of the Book of Revelation* (New York: Cambridge University Press, 1993); Raymond E. Brown, *An Introduction to the NT* (New York: Doubleday, 1997), 773–813; Paul J. Achtemeier, Joel B. Green, and Marianne Meye Thompson, *Introducing the NT: Its Literature and Theology* (Grand Rapids: Eerdmans, 2001), 555–88; Frank J. Matera, *NT Theology: Exploring Diversity and Unity* (Louisville: Westminster John Knox, 2007), 400–22.

3. This is surprising as Revelation offers one of the most strident attacks on the economy of the Roman empire, an economy which is well documented. Everett Ferguson, *Backgrounds of Early Christianity: Third Edition* (Grand Rapids: Eerdmans, 2003), 82–96; David Mattingly, "The Imperial Economy," in *A Companion to the Roman Empire*, ed. David S. Potter (Malden: Blackwell Publishing, 2006), 283–97; Walter Scheidel, "Economy and Quality of Life," in *The Oxford Handbook of Roman Studies*, ed. Alessandro Barchiesi and Walter Scheidel (New York: Oxford University Press, 2010), 283–297; Scheidel, "Economy and Quality of Life," 593–609.

4. "The task of supplying the Roman empire's urban population involved both the state and private producers in a complex network of exchange." See Dennis P. Kehoe, "The Early Roman Empire: Production," in *The Cambridge Economic History of the Greco-Roman World*, ed. Walter Scheidel, Ian Morris, and Richard Saller (New York: Cambridge University Press, 2007), 543.

reliant upon the Roman Empire for their security rather than Christ and this has come at the cost of their witness.

Cities play an important role in Revelation. The importance of the "city" has been noted by Eva Maria Räpple who has noted an often-missed role that the city plays in Revelation.[5] She argues that the world depicted by John's apocalypse is intended to compel a new understanding of the world not only through critical evaluation as in the case of the seven churches and Rome, but also through the hopeful and the imaginative possibilities as seen in the example of the New Jerusalem. Much of her study builds on the philosophical role the city played in antiquity that allows her to compare and contrast the Apocalypticist's view of the "ideal city" with that of Plato and Aristotle.[6] She concludes in her study that the city in Revelation plays an evocative role that encourages the reader to think anew of the role of the ideal city amidst the pretenders that currently exist. Several parts of her thesis are important for our study of Laodicea and Rome.

One important aspect that Räpple raises is the connection between city and identity. The Apocalypse views cities as domains for human beings in community. The Apocalypse, "places the focus on the identity of a community as a community in relation with the beast . . . or God and the Lamb" that is, "the inhabitants . . . are freely choosing alliance with the beast or the conjugal bond with the Lamb."[7] She further notes that the choosing of this relationship will later on result in their weeping over the destruction of Babylon or by making them citizens of the New Jerusalem.[8] Her insights are quite helpful in negotiating the role of Laodicea and the words of Jesus. As will be shown below, the relationship between Jesus and the church is in disarray. Jesus encourages them to buy gold from him (3:18), which indicates that the current economic economic relationship is not with him. Jesus also stands outside the church, indicating a breach of relationship, whereby he is asking to fellowship with them again (3:20). Currently at stake is the identity of the Laodicean church and its relationship to Babylon-Rome and the New Jerusalem.

Another critical issue Räpple rightly notes is that the issue of the ideal community or city was a prominent topic in the Greco-Roman world. In

---

5. Eva Maria Räpple, *The Metaphor of the City in the Apocalypse of John* (New York: Peter Land, 2004). See also Peter Oaks, "Contours of the Urban Environment," in *After the First Urban Christians: The Social-Scientific Study of Pauline Christianity Twenty-Five Years Later*, ed. Todd D. Still and David G. Horrell (New York: T&T Clark, 2009), 21–35.

6. Räpple, *Metaphor*, 139–78.

7. Ibid., 127–8.

8. Ibid.

both the Apocalypse and other contemporary works, the well being of humanity is tightly linked to the *polis*. She rightly identifies that one of the primary concerns of the city imagery is the connection between "right identity, which finds its expression in right conduct, best suited for the city/community."[9] Suffice it to say, the Apocalypse is acutely aware of the triad of identity/ethics/community. As will be shown, Rome partakes in the exploitation of humanity to serve its own ends strikingly portrayed in the trading of human lives (18:13). Laodicea will be one of the primary targets of Rev 18:4 and the call to "come out of her my people." Laodicea has found itself intertwined with the economic practices of Rome and it must untangle and separate itself to restore fellowship with the Slain Lamb.[10]

Of keen interest for Rev 3:14–22 and 18 is the verbal and / or topical phenomena that create comparisons between the two cities. The verbal link is established by repeated formulaic phrases.[11] The verb πλουτέω only occurs in Revelation in 3:17–18 and 18 (3x).[12] The congregation of the verbal idea of "becoming rich" combined with socio-economic terms such as "to buy," and "gold," occur in both Rev 3:14–22 and 18 and thus provide a glimpse into the overall socio-economic discourse throughout the book and thus in 3:14–22 begin to form a "wealth motif."[13]

## Revelation 3:17–18

Wealth plays an essential role in the letter to Laodicea (Rev 3:14–22). This primary role will be examined through two textual features: 1) the phrase "I am rich, I have become rich and I need nothing"; and 2) the verb "to buy." In 3:17 it is reported that the Laodiceans say, "I am rich, I have become rich, and I need nothing" (πλούσιός εἰμι καὶ πεπλούτηκα καὶ οὐδὲν χρείαν ἔχω). This phrase is essentially repeated three times for rhetorical effect and

9. Räpple, *Metaphor*, 145. Cf. Aeschines, "It remains for you, fellow citizens, in view both of what has been spoken and what is left unsaid, yourselves to give the verdict that is just and for the city's good" (*Ctes.*, 260).

10. Räpple has an excellent section on wealth and luxury, as well as the condemnation of luxury in the Apocalypse (145–7).

11. Aune, *Intertextual Reading of the Apocalypse*, 123ff.

12. Although see the multiple ways the verb can be used in the OT and the Pseudepigrapha see Gen 30:43; Exod 30:15; Jdt 15:6; Ps 48:17; Prov 28:22; 31:28; Eccl 5:11; Sir 11:18; Hos 12:9; Zech 11:5; Jer 5:27; Dan 11:2; 2 *En.* 97:8; *Sib. Or.* 2:56, 109; 3:41, 241; 8:35; *T. Jud.* 21:6; *T. Gad* 7:4, 6; *T. Jos.* 12:2; *T. Benj.* 4:4; *L.A.E.* 24:3; Ps.-Phoc. 1:5, 109; *Odes Sol.* 1:9.

13. I am borrowing this term from the dissertation of Robert M. Royalty, *The Streets of Heaven: The Ideology of Wealth in the Apocalypse of John* (Macon: Mercer University Press, 1998).

is further emphasized through the threefold repetition of the first person pronoun.[14] This self-reported identification serves as part of the condemnation of Jesus towards the church, for in fact they are really poor (πτωχὸς), wretched, pitiable, blind, and naked.[15] The rhetorical effect from the first half of the verse carries into the second, as the five predicate nominative adjectives linked with *kai* rhetorically highlight the precarious position of the church.[16] Clearly the Laodiceans "think" that they are rich as indicated by the present active indicative (λέγεις) in 3:17. However, the criticism of Jesus towards the church raises the precise question of, "who is truly rich?"[17] There is already an implicit warning here as the only other occurrences of these ideas together are negative (Rev 18:3ff).

The phrase "I am rich" (πλούσιός εἰμι) is not entirely common in Graeco-Roman literature.[18] One of the often-noted parallels is found in Epictetus. In his recorded lectures, an exchange is given between Epictetus and another Roman where in the midst of Epictetus' diatribe on submitting pleasure to duty, the Roman responds, "But I am rich and need nothing" (ἐγὼ πλούσιός εἰμι καὶ οὐδενός χρεία).[19] The similarity with the words of the Laodicean church is apparent. The response of the Roman official highlights the value of wealth as one of the highest accolades and indeed self-sufficiency.

---

14. David Aune, *Revelation*, 3 vols. (Dallas: Word Books, 1997), 1:263. Also noted by Stephen S. Smalley, *The Revelation to John: A Commentary on the Greek Text of the Apocalypse* (Downers Grove: Intervarsity, 2005), 99; Joseph L. Trafton, *Reading Revelation: A Literary and Theological Commentary*, Revised ed. (Macon: Smyth & Helwys, 2005), 52.

15. Also Jürgen Roloff, *Revelation: A Continental Commentary*, trans. John E. Alsup and James S. Currie (Minneapolis: Fortress, 1993), 65; Robert H. Mounce, *The Book of Revelation*, Revised ed. (Grand Rapids: Eerdmans, 1997), 111; Witherington, *Revelation*, 108. For a discussion of the terms used to describe the Laodicean church see Grant R. Osborn, *Revelation* (Grand Rapids: Baker Academic, 2002), 208. Cf. Plutarch, *Demetr.*, 32.5—33.4.

16. Beasley-Murray, *Revelation*, 106; Aune, *Revelation*, 1:259; Smalley, *Revelation*, 99.

17. Royalty, *Streets of Heaven*, 69. More comparison between Smyrna and Laodicea will be considered later in the paper.

18. Demosthenes, *Eub.*, 52; Plutarch, *Cat. Maj.*, 18.5.5; Epictetus, *Diatr.*, 2.24.24; 3.7.29.1; Plautus, *Capt.*, 300–338. Contra Prigent who tends to see gnostic tendencies and finds parallels in the Gospel of Thomas 28 (*Apocalypse*, 216). The Jewish apocalyptic work of Enoch gives a similar warning, "Woe to you, you who gain gold and silver not by way of righteousness; and you will say, "We have grown rich with riches and we own and we have acquired belongings (*1 En* 97:8).

19. This is also noted by Aune, *Revelation*, 1:263; Keener, *Revelation*, 111. A full discussion of the text is provided by Royalty, *Streets of Heaven*, 207–209.

The notion of "needing nothing" is also key within Plato, Aristotle, and Plutarch to name but a few examples.[20] Within their discussions, the idea of "needing nothing" is in relationship to God and God's self-sufficiency. Aristotle remarks, in a discussion of friendship that God is not in need of having a friend.[21] Although this in the context of friendship it is still pertinent to the discussion for where Aristotle takes the conversation. In contrast to Laodicea that only looks in upon itself, Aristotle derives the opposite conclusion. Aristotle link's the self-sufficiency of God and needing few friends as a paradigm for human existence and society.

> For when we are not in need of something, then we all seek people to share our enjoyments, and beneficiaries rather than benefactors; and we can judge them better when we are self-sufficing than when in need, and we most need friends who are worthy of our society.[22]

For Aristotle self-sufficiency leads to the amelioration of the community. In light of Aristotle, we find both a comparison and contrast with Jesus' words to the church. The Laodicean church is critiqued from the viewpoint that their self-sufficiency and economic prosperity has separated them from the true source of wealth in God. The parallel can be drawn further; the Laodiceans have not used their self-sufficiency for the betterment of the Christian communities in Asia Minor, as in the case of Smyrna. In contrast to Aristotle, the words to Laodicea are not concerned with the church's relationship to their city, but with their relationship to the other churches. The censure of Jesus towards the church not only challenges their self-sufficiency but also the source of that self-sufficiency. The words of Jesus to the churches (Rev 2–3) further complicate the current reality of Laodicea by noting that Laodicea has enriched itself while at the same time the other churches are in need.

In Rev 3:18, the economic features continue as Jesus counsels the church to "to buy gold" from him. The verb, "to buy" (ἀγοράζω) occurs six times in Revelation (Rev 3:18; 5:9; 13:17; 14:3–4; 18:11) and comes from the

---

20. Plato, *Resp.*, 507d. Although compare with Plutarch, *Sept. sap. conv.* 12, 16, "The one way of avoidance and of keeping oneself pure, from the point of view of righteousness, is to become sufficient unto oneself and to need nothing from any other source. But in the case of man or beast for whom God has made his own secure existence impossible without his doing injury to another, it may be said that in the nature which God has inflicted upon him lies the source of wrong (16).

21. Aristotle, *Eth. Eud.*, 1244a. 1–19.

22. Ibid., 1244b.1–19.

business arena and refers to economic transactions.²³ Other than 3:17, the verb primarily refers to the people whom God has purchased / redeemed for himself (Rev 5:9; 14:3-4). These are the peoples from every tribe, tongue, and nation of the earth that God bought through the blood of the Lamb. The other two occurrences are also important for understanding the nature of "buying" in Revelation. In 13:17, only those who have the mark or number of the beast are allowed to "buy," that is only those who have aligned with Rome are able to participate in this activity. The final occurrence appears in Rev 18:11 thus linking these two passages again.²⁴ In chapter 18 the merchants of the earth weep after the judgment has fallen as no one "buys their cargo anymore" (18:11). Thus it appears that the first appearance of ἀγοράζω in Rev 3:18 sets up the twin themes of two different economic enterprises that are seen in the rest of the book, that of the economy of God who buys people from every tribe, tongue, and nation, and that of the Roman economy, who also buys people (18:13) but will ultimately come to its demise.

## Revelation 18

After the description hailing the fallen Babylon, a voice from heaven commands God's people (ὁ λαός μου) to "come out" (ἐξέλθατε) of Babylon before destruction falls (18:4). The imperatival verb carries the force of the command and is linked by two purpose infinitive clauses in 18:4b-5. The first purpose is so that God's people do not participate in the sins of the city (μὴ συγκοινωνήσητε ταῖς ἁμαρτίαις αὐτῆς). The second purpose, related to the previous one by the linking of καὶ, is so they do not participate in the plagues (ἐκ τῶν πληγῶν αὐτῆς ἵνα μὴ λάβητε) that are about to fall upon the city.

Richard Bauckham has shown that Rev 18 is a "remarkable patchwork of skillful allusions to OT prophecies of the fall of Babylon and the fall of Tyre."²⁵ Here John stands within the long prophetic line of "oracles against

---

23. Roloff, *Revelation: A Continental Commentary*, 65; Fiorenza E. Schüssler, *The Book of Revelation: Justice and Judgment* (Minneapolis: Fortress, 1998), 74; Osborn, *Revelation*, 208. Although Rowland has pointed out a reference to Sir 51:25 is similar (*Revelation*, 587).

24. Schüssler, *The Book of Revelation: Justice and Judgment*, 74; Leonard L. Thompson, *Revelation* (Nashville: Abingdon, 1998), 85.

25. Bauckham, *Climax of Prophecy*, 345; Boring, *Revelation*, 185. Aune describes it as a "prophetic taunt song" (*Revelation*, 2:976). Likewise, Mangina calls it a "funeral dirge" (*Revelation*, 204). For the debate concerning whether Rev 18 is a taunt song or a dirge see Adela Yarbro Collins, "Revelation 18: Taunt-Song or Dirge?," in *L'apocalypse Johannique Et L'apocalyptique Dans Le Nouveau Testament*, ed. Jan Lambrecht (Leuven:

the nations."[26] John's scriptural reservoir contains two major prophetic oracles, that of Jer 50–51 against Babylon and Ezek 26–28 against Tyre. The point of comparison by Bauckham deserves full quotation:

> If Rome was the heir of Babylon in political and religious activity, she was also the heir of Tyre in economic activity. For Tyre was the greatest trading centre of the OT period, notable not, like Babylon, for her political empire, but for her economic empire. So it is to focus his indictment of Rome for her *economic* exploitation and his pronouncement of judgment on Rome for aspect of her evil, that John reapplies to Rome Ezekiel's oracle against Tyre.[27]

Thus, both Laodicea and Rome are offered criticisms from the Hebrew prophets regarding their economic practices. However, John takes this further, it is not just that Laodicea and Rome happen to share some of the same economic features. Rather, from John's point of view Laodicea has been unduly influenced by the economic practices of Rome and thus is in a precarious position.[28] Satake has noted similarly that, "Er ist ein Ergebnis ihrer Kompromisse mit der Umwelt . . . gleichzeitig veranlasst er sie, ihr Leben in Seblstzufriedenheit zu fürhen, was wiederum auch ihr Glaubensverhalten prägt."[29]

Bauckham rightly notes that the language of, "come out of her" in 18:4–5 is not geographical, but ethical.[30] None of the seven churches were identified as Rome and it can be safely assumed that none of them were currently present in Rome.[31] Thus, as Bauckham has noted, "The command is

---

University Press, 1980), 185–204. Collins regards it as a dirge as it involves only the speeches of the characters, kings, merchants, sea-farers, contain no condemnation of the city but reveal that the judgements are deserved. She also points out that the call for rejoicing in vs. 20 also indicates that the primary aspect is a dirge (203). I disagree with Collins and concur with Aune that it is a prophetic taunt song, mainly as it is used dialectically to engage the churches to remove themselves from the Roman system of exploitation.

26. See a similar critique of Rome along parallel lines in *Sib. Or.* 8.

27. Bauckham, *Climax of Prophecy*, 346.

28. Craig R. Koester, *Revelation and the End of All Things* (Grand Rapids: Eerdmans, 2001), 164.

29. "It is a result of their compromise with the environment, that it led them to lead their lives in self-satisfaction (Seblstzufriedenheit), which in turn also shapes their faith conduct." Akira Satake, *Die Offenbarung Des Johannes* (Göttingen: Vandenhoeck & Ruprecht, 2008), 188.

30. Similarly noted by Boring, *Revelation*, 189; Reddish, *Revelation*, 341.

31. A similar analogous aspect is found in the "merchants of the earth" who are described as "your [Babylon's] merchants. As Bauckham has noted, "This does not mean

for the readers to *dissociate* themselves from Rome's evil, lest they share her guilt and her judgment. It is a command not to be in the company of those who are then depicted mourning for Babylon."[32] However Bauckham fails to specifically link which cities among the seven churches could specifically fall into this predicament. Out of all the churches mentioned in Rev 2–3 which would most likely be in a position to mourn the fall of Rome? Smyrna has exited the system long ago as made apparent in 2:9. Rather, Laodicea is the primary example from the churches in the letters that could be depicted in the role of a mourner. They are the ones who stand to lose the most with the fall of Rome as they already stand in an economically advantageous position. Stated more directly, if the economic system of Rome collapses it is the church at Laodicea who is an economically advantageous position that will suffer loss more than any other church in Asia Minor. This statement is not intended to be a historical description, for certainly an economic collapse would affect all the churches both poor and rich. Rather, from a literary point of view, Laodicea is the only church among the seven that from John's point of view appears to be financially solvent.

The verb πλουτέω also links the two passages (Rev 3:17; 18:3, 15, 19). The first reference comes in 18:3 and explains the cause of Rome's judgment as the seduction of other nations and rulers. Revelation depicts both the nations (τὰ ἔθνη) and the kings (οἱ βασιλεῖς τῆς γῆς) as committing fornication with the empire.[33] The merchants (οἱ ἔμποροι τῆς γῆς) have "grown rich" (ἐπλούτησαν) from their association with Rome and her luxury.[34]

---

that they were Romans, but simply that they did business with the city of Rome...Thus citizens of the cities where John's readers lived, especially Ephesus, will be included" (*Climax of Prophecy*, 373). I would also add that Laodicea, rather than Ephesus, bears a closer resemblance in terms of business. So also, Dagoberto Ramiréz Fernandez, "The Judgment of God on the Multinationals: Revelation 18," in *Subversive Scriptures: Revolutionary Readings of the Christian Bible in Latin America*, ed. Leif E. Vaage (Valley Forge: Trinity International, 1997), 88–9.

32. Bauckham, *Climax of Prophecy*, 377.

33. The account and charges here are similar to Rev 17:2. Smalley rightly identifies it as the "unholy relationship" (*Revelation*, 444). An important text-critical issue is present in this verse regarding whether the text reads, "have drunk" or "have fallen." "Have drunk" has a little support (1006c 2329 itMSS syrh), but it does fit the context of "wine." However the original reading most likely was "have fallen" (א A C 1006ᵃ 2053c syrh), the change probably resulted from wanting to make the explicitly connection between wine and the subsequent actions. However, drank can be easily assumed from what follows. See Bruce M. Metzger, *A Textual Commentary on the Greek NT*, 2 ed. (Stuttgart: United Bible Societies, 2006), 683. Also offering a helpful summary is Louis A. Brighton, *Revelation* (Saint Louis: Concordia, 1999), 457–9.

34. There is a three-fold emphasis on luxury that is seen in 18:3, 7, 9 (Keener, *Revelation*, 424). See also Tacitus *Ann.* 3.52.1–54.5; Seneca *Ep.* 86.1–7; Pliny *Nat.* 9.58.117–18; 13.29.92; Petronius *Saty.* 31.3–34.4; Pliny *Ep.* 2.17.

Blount is right to point out that, "the angel is more vague about the city's role" in Rev 18."[35] The account in Rev 18 focuses on the role of Babylon and the nations, kings, and merchants are but secondary actors on the scene for Rome's judgment.[36] However, if one wanted a closer picture of the view from the city, one might look to 3:14–22 to see a city's acceptance and reliance upon the empire and its seductive solicitation of economic power.

The two other instances are found in 18:15, 19 and continues the reflection on the destruction of Rome from the viewpoint of the merchants and seafarers which were introduced in 18:3 and picked back up in 18:11, 17 respectively. The role of the merchants more closely resembles that of Laodicea than the seafarers and thus will be the focus of this section.[37] The lament of the merchants parallels that of the kings in vs. 10, both stand off in fear of her torment, but only the merchants weep and mourn.[38] In 18:11, the merchants lament the fall of Rome as there is no one to buy (ἀγοράζω) their cargo anymore as the economic system has collapsed. Rev 18:12–13 presents the list of the merchants' cargo and gold leads the list.[39] From Rev

---

35. Blount, *Revelation*, 326.

36. Thompson is right to point out that the three are interrelated causes for Rome's fall (*Revelation*, 167).

37. The lament of the seafarers is the shortest and in some ways is only distinct by its focus on the sea. Although only the sea-farers note that, "What city was like the great city?" thus setting up a nice foreshadowing of the New Jerusalem. The sea is mentioned prominently through Revelation (Rev 4:6; 5:13; 7:1–3; 8:8–9; 10:2, 5–6, 8; 12:12, 18–13:1; 14:7; 15:2; 16:3; 18:17, 19, 21; 20:8, 13; 21:1). Further, the notion of "one hour" is key to the entire lament (Rev 17:12; 18:10, 17, 19). For a further description of the seafarers see Harrington, *Revelation*, 181; Osborn, *Revelation*, 652; Blount, *Revelation*, 335. It has been noted that, "far more Mediterranean shipwrecks are datable to the period 200 BC—AD 200 than for any other period before the sixteenth century. See Neville Morley, "The Early Roman Empire: Distribution," in *The Cambridge Economic History of the Greco-Roman World*, ed. Walter Scheidel, Ian Morris, and Richard Saller (New York: Cambridge University Press, 2007), 572. Cf. Demosthenes., *C. Phorm.*, 1.

38. Compare with the weeping in 2 *Esdr* 5:6, 8, 11, 27–28; 6:25–26; 3 *Bar* 0:2–1:1; 1:3; 4:14; 13:1; 16:1; 4 *Bar* 2:5, 10; 3:3, 20; 4:6–7, 11; 6:3; 7:15, 22, 29–31, 36; 9:8, 10, 24. On the mourning of cities see Plutarch, *Fab.*, 18.1–5; *[Reg. imp. apophth.]* 35; *Pomp.* 51.2; Livy *Hist. Rom.*, 22.56.1–8, 23.25.1, 31.30.2.

39. It has been noted by many that this list is reminiscent of the list in Ezek 27, although this is not without problems. See Fiorenza, *Revelation*, 99; Beale, *Revelation*, 909–910, Blount, *Revelation*, 334. Keener provides a full summary of the list of cargo (*Revelation*, 426) and Osborn (*Revelation*, 648–650). Plutarch remarks briefly on the unethical practices of a merchant in *[Apoph. lac.]*, 2.69. Likewise, Xenophon makes a brief remark that merchants sold children (*Ages.*, 1.20). On the importance of gold see Pliny, *Nat.*, 33.14–19; Seutonius, *Aug.*, 73; Plutarch, *Pyrrh.*, 20. Cf. The account of wealth by Petronius who also lists gold as one of the motivating factors for Roman imperialism, "if there were. . . any land that promised a yield of yellow gold, that place was Rome's enemy, fate stood ready for the sorrows of war, and the quest for wealth

18:11, 13 we see both the notions of buying and gold that further link 3:14–22 with Rev 18.[40] Rev 18:15 explicitly states that the merchants have "gained wealth" (πλουτέω) from her, indicating that the source of their wealth had come from Rome and is now laid waste (18:17).[41] Thus Laodicea is again reminded that the source of wealth is under impending judgment and will soon be laid waste, if they do not want to end up "weeping and mourning" as the merchants, the source of their wealth needs radical reorientation. The sweeping judgment is that if Rome's time is "over" then the time of everyone who is connected with Rome, be that the merchants or Laodicea, is also over.[42]

Bauckham has cogently argued that the attention directed to these two groups is to *accentuate the link between those who mourn and the seven churches, mainly those who are economically compromised.*[43] Ironically, Bauckham does not draw the connection with Laodicea, but with Smyrna. This is understandable in the sense that the economic criticism of Rome could serve as a comfort to those in Smyrna facing economic persecution. However, what Bauckham misses is that Laodicea is the only church called out for economic compromise. Thus the economic critique provides an eerie parallel for the church in Laodicea as they stand much closer to the role of the land and sea merchants than Smyrna. The analogy works on a much better level between Laodicea and Rome than Rome and Smyrna.[44]

---

wanton" (*Sat.* 119). Noted by Bauckham, *Climax*, 352.

40. Garments in Rev 3:4–5, 18; 4:4; 16:15; 19:13, 16. To Clothe appears in Rev 3:5, 18; 4:4; 7:9, 13; 10:1; 11:3; 12:1; 17:4; 18:16; 19:8, 13. The mention of clothing in vs. 18:16 also parallels the challenge in 3:18 for the Laodiceans to be clothed as well. The ethical implications of the clothing language in relation to the churches has been noted by Stephen Pattemore, *The People of God in the Apocalypse: Discourse, Structure, and Exegesis* (New York: Cambridge University Press, 2004), 82–7; Räpple, *Metaphor*, 93–94. Contra Peterson who argues that "Es handelt sich hier nicht so sehr um das moralische Problem einer falschen Anhänglichkeit an Gold oder Kleider, sondern um ein ontologisches Existentialproblem" [It is not so much to the moral problem of a false attachment to gold or clothes, but an ontological existential problem] (*Offenbarung des Johannes*, 57). Similar references are found in *Odes Sol.* 11:7; *Pr Levi* 1.

41. Caird notes two important features of this section: (1) the description of the city in vs. 14 is almost the exact description of the whore in 17:4 and (2) that the entire chapter shifts back and forth between John speaking of a woman and the city (*Revelation*, 226–227). So also Aune, *Revelation*, 3:1004. Keener notes the irony of their lament, as it was Rome itself who had set up the current economic system where no one could buy or sell without their "mark!" (*Revelation*, 426).

42. Fiorenza, *Revelation*, 99–100; Fee, *Revelation*, 252.

43. Bauckham, *Climax of Prophecy*, 377.

44. Entirely missing the point is G. W. Buchanan. "There is nothing in the chapter to direct the reader to Asia Minor." (*The Book of Revelation: Its Introduction and Prophecy* [Lewiston: Mellon, 1993], 489).

Another often missed aspect of most studies on wealth and economy in Revelation is the "tale of two cities" motif.[45] Other than the seven churches, the only two cities listed in Revelation are Babylon and the New Jerusalem. The juxtaposition of these two inversely proportionate cities with the seven congregations provides an important point of comparison for the churches in Asia Minor.[46] The rhetorical effect is akin to asking, "What city will you be like?" Will you follow the harlot city of Rome and head towards its destruction? Or will you offer honor and praise to the slain lamb and thus reflect the New Jerusalem? In the case of Laodicea, they seem to be headed towards destruction and the verbal and thematic parallels between the two sections raise the theological tension within the letter. It is clear which type of language is used to describe the church in Laodicea as Jesus seems to offer a lament over the city. The church at Laodicea seems to reflect a more economic theology of Rome than of New Jerusalem.

## AN ANCIENT CRITIQUE FROM THE HEBREW PROPHETS

The phrase, "I am rich" containing the verb πλουτέω in Rev 3:17–18 contains an allusion to several passages in the Hebrew Scriptures.[47] The verb appears in Hos 12:8 (9), Zech 11:5, and Jer 5:27 (LXX). We turn briefly took look at these allusions.

### Hos 12:8

Hosea records the judgment of YHWH on Ephraim in Hos 12:2, where YHWH condemns Ephraim for making an "illegal covenant" with Assyria without the permission of YHWH. In Hos 12:7, YHWH calls the Ephraimites, a Canaanite. Those in Ephraim would not have understood the term positively. The term is not a reference to the people or the nation. Rather the term Canaanite refers to the "trading, mercantile culture of Canaan," that is, "namely a merchant or trader." Thus as Macintosh has pointed out,

---

45. The "tale of two cities" language is adapted from the excellent work by Edith M. Humphrey, "A Tale of Two Cities and (at Least) Three Women: Transformation, Continuity, and Contrast in the Apocalypse," in *Reading the Book of Revelation: A Resource for Students*, ed. David L. Barr (Atlanta: SBL, 2003), 81–96.

46. It might also be noted that the only cities that receive a total negative evaluation are Laodicea and Rome. Also mentioned by Luke Timothy Johnson, *The Writings of the NT: An Interpretation Revised Edition* (Minneapolis: Fortress, 1999), 587.

47. Aune, *Revelation*, 1:258; Thompson, *Revelation*, 85; Lupieri, *Apocalypse*, 129.

"Ephraim, then, is indicted for having appropriated the values and mores of Canaan."[48] The practices of God's people are more similar to the pagan nation than to the call of God to "observe goodness and justice" (Hos 12:7).

Regarding Revelation, if the context of the Hosea allusion is brought forward, the connections between Ephraim and Rome are clear. Each group is involved in the socio-economic enterprise and each are identified as "traders" or "merchants" and are judged as having corrupt practices that involve the furthering of injustice and oppression. However, the allusion to Hosea in Rev 3:17, draws a connection between all three participants. Laodicea, in the role of historic Ephraim, is now paralleled with Rome in John's apocalypse. If John's use of the Hosea allusion is to indicate that Laodicea is a merchant then the Ladocians are a merchant like Rome. It is Laodicea who has made assumed the values and mores of Rome by making an "illegal covenant" and now they are part of impending judgment about to fall on Rome in Rev 18. John has thus drawn a direct line between Laodicea and Rome.

The actual allusion in Rev 3:17 recalls the similar verbal phrase in Hosea 12:8. Similar to Laodicea, Ephraim is described in first person speech. The self-representation is also similar in that Ephraim claims "I have become rich" (πεπλούτηκα). The boast here is especially dubious as it reveals that, "Ephraim rejoices in his wealth, with confidence that it was worth the oppression of others, the immorality, the religious infidelity, and with confidence also that it made him a secure nation."[49]

Ephraim is further characterized by a double wordplay, not only have they become rich they have also found wealth! The self-description of the Laodicean church also has a similar double wordplay, "I am rich and have become rich" (ὅτι πλεούσιός εἰμι καὶ πεπλούτηκα). The economic prosperity of both cities had been misinterpreted as a sign of God's blessing when in actuality it was the very reason why judgment was coming.

The Ephraim-Laodicea allusion provides the author with a pertinent ancient critique. Laodicea is not unique in their troubles. Rather, they like Ephraim of old have capitulated to the current empire in exchange for socio-economic prosperity. Laodicea like Ephraim has misidentified their wealth as a blessing from God. As Ephraim was brought under the chastisement of a prophet of God so will the Laodicean church. Both groups are warned that discipline waits if they do not repent. However, like Ephraim, both are reaffirmed that it is God's hope that they will "overcome."[50]

---

48. A. Macintosh, *Hosea* (Edinburgh: T & T Clark, 2000), 496.
49. Douglas Stuart, *Hosea-Jonah* (Nashville: Thomas Nelson, 1987), 193.
50. See similar point made by Ehud Ben Zvi, *Hosea*, The Forms of the OT Literature

## Zech 11:5

Zech 11:5 also contains a reference to "becoming rich" and has been noted by scholars to be a possible allusion in Rev 3:17.[51] In Zech 11, the prophet is charged by the Lord to be a shepherd to the "doomed flock" (Zech 11:4). Here the leaders of the people are referred to as shepherds who buy and sell the people (Zech 11:5). Zech 11:4-6 is a critique of the current leaders of the nation as they have sought their own benefit (both economically and politically) at the expense of the people. The critique of the prophet is that the current leaders look out for their own economic interests which is juxtaposed with the fact that they have no "pity" for the people under their care except to "become rich" off of them (11:5).[52]

Mitigating against such an allusion is the fact attested to by Lupeiri that, "both Zechariah and the Apocalypse contain threats against unworthy leaders."[53] However the charges in Rev 3:14-22 are not against the leaders per se, but the church at large. Unlike Zechariah, in Revelation there is no direct critique of the religious leadership at Laodicea. This is not to say that the book of Zechariah does not have a function within Revelation. As Marko Juahiainen has noted in his important study of Zechariah in Revelation, John uses Zechariah in important ways.[54] However, here in Rev 3:17, Juahiainen notes that, "It is difficult to identify any one text as the marked text of Rev 3:17, but the lack of evidence to the contrary suggests that Zech 11:5 is certainly not the first choice."[55] Although the same verbal phrase occurs in both Zechariah and Revelation, beyond that there is no direct parallel between the two. However, one further possible allusion may repay better results.

---

(Grand Rapids: Eerdmans, 2005), 243.

51. Aune, *Revelation*, 1:258; Thompson, *Revelation*, 85; Lupieri, *Revelation*, 129.

52. On Zechariah the prophet and his book see Brevard S. Childs, *Introduction to the OT as Scripture* (Philadelphia: Fortress, 1979), 472-87; Ralph P. Smith, *Micah-Malachi* (Dallas: Thomas Nelson, 1984), 369-70; Walter Brueggemann, *An Introduction to the OT: The Canon and Christian Imagination* (Louisville: Westminster John Knox, 2003), 254; Marvin A. Sweeney, *The Prophetic Literature* (Nashville: Abingdon, 2005), 202-7; Paul L. Reditt, "Introduction to the Prophets," Grand Rapids: Eerdmans, 2008), 321-44.

53. Lupieri, *Apocalypse*, 129.

54. Marko Jauhianen, *The Use of Zechariah in Revelation*, Wunt, vol. 199 (Tübingen: Mohr Siebeck, 2005). See his chart on the parallels between the two (130).

55. Ibid., 108.

### Jer 5:27

The prophet Jeremiah was in a similar socio-theological context as John the Seer. Both were commissioned to foretell an impending judgment through an oracle of YHWH. Jer 5:20–31 is structured as three poems on the unified theme of "people." Craigie has argued that the poems are the elaborations on the failure of the people and the coming judgment.[56] Jeremiah's word to those in Jerusalem begins with a call to "hear" which is similar to the way that each of the seven letters of Revelation end with a call "to hear" (Rev 3:22).

In 5:20–25 the focus was the failure of Israel to see YHWH as the provider of rain and thus socio-economic prosperity rather than the foreign deity Baal. The immediate context of Jer 5:27 is a shift in viewpoint. In 5:26–29 the focus shifts to the arena of socio-economic justice. Similar to Revelation, the words are spoken by God, addressed to the prophet, but directed at the people. Both John and Jeremiah function as mediators of the divine message to their audience.

Jer 5:27 indicates the manner by which Israel has "become rich" (ἐπλούτησαν). As indicated in the LXX through the use of the adverb of purpose (οὕτως) Israel has become rich by filling their houses with "treachery" (δόλος). The word denotes things gained by fraud or obtaining things through trickery.[57] The fraudulent activity is the means by which the rich have acquired their wealth and they have done so at the expense of the orphan and the needy (5:28). As Leslie Allen has noted, "The sins were ones of judicial omission as well as of economic commission."[58] The neglect of the poor and the needy at the expense of gaining wealth reveals that Israel has broken their covenant with YHWH. Brueggeman has pointed out that, "The outcome of Israel's infidelity is a society of rapacious exploitation."[59]

If this allusion is behind Rev 3:17 then the point of contact is not necessarily that the situation at Laodicea is the same, that, "rapacious exploitation" is taking place, as that does not fall under the purview of the proclamation in 3:14–22. No neglect of the needy or the poor is mentioned.

---

56. Peter C. Craigie, Page H. Kelley, and Joel F. Drinkard, *Jeremiah 1–25* (Waco: Word, 1991), 95.

57. *HALOT*, 2:636. See also J. A. Thompson, *The Book of Jeremiah* (Grand Rapids: Eerdmans, 1980), 250. William L. Holladay, *Jeremiah 1: A Commentary on the Book of the Prophet Jeremiah Chapters 1–25*, Hermeneia: A Critical and Historical Commentary on the Bible (Minneapolis: Fortress Press, 1986), 198.

58. Leslie C. Allen, *Jeremiah: A Commentary* (Louisville: Westminster John Knox, 2008), 81.

59. Walter Brueggemann, *A Commentary on Jeremiah: Exile and Homecoming* (Grand Rapids: Eerdmans, 1998), 68.

Rather the intersection of Jeremiah's words towards Israel and John's to Laodicea is to propose the question "how have you become rich?"

At the onset of the proclamation in 3:14–22 the allusion may be being used to raise suspicion of how the Laodiceans have gotten themselves into such a socio-economic condition. This is further supported by the previous referenced context of the other seven churches, mainly Smyrna. If economic poverty is the experience of the church at Smyrna as a result of their witness then what should be inferred by the economic prosperity experienced by the Laodiceans? The letter itself gives a further clue in the description of Jesus as the "faithful and true witness" (3:14). The use of an allusion to Jeremiah signifies that the opulent position of the Laodicean church reveals that they have gotten there by ill-gotten means, whether these are through improper financial transactions is not clear. However, what is clear is that their failure to be a faithful witness has been both economically and socially advantageous.[60]

The verbal allusions to these passages in the LXX thus serve as an ancient critique of self-sufficiency on the part of God's people. Each of the allusions come from a Hebrew prophet pronouncing a judgment on the people of God for their self-sufficiency and specifically that their wealth is through ill-gotten means.[61] It is not entirely clear which prophecy John is alluding to, although Hosea seems to fit the purpose better. Both Hosea and Jeremiah speak a word of condemnation to the people of God for their unholy economic practices and also issue a call to repentance on behalf of the people. It is not surprising then that John would turn to these texts(s) to call the people of God at Laodicea back to their covenant relationship with him.

## CONCLUSION

A socio-rhetorical reading of Rev 3:14–22 has shown that numerous parallels exist between this passage and Rev 18 and that when read together bring added clarity to the proclamation to the Laodicean church. Prophetic

---

60. Jack R. Lundbom, *Jeremiah 1–20* (New York: Doubleday, 199), 408. Lundbom has argued that on the basis of Jer 5:7; Deut 32:15; and Hos 13:6 that these, "indicators of prosperity can be and here are concomitants of arrogance" (408). This highlights another connection with the church at Laodicea, which was also marked by arrogance.

61. The possibility for ill gotten means is also noted in the Testament of Judah, "For just like on the sea the just and unjust are tossed about, some being taken into captivity, while some are made rich, so every race of humanity will also be in you: some will be impoverished, being taken captive, and others grow rich by plundering the possessions of others (Judah 21:6). A similar point is made in Ps.-Phoc. 5 "Do not become rich unjustly, but from holy means live."

criticisms along with several verbal, thematic, and conceptual parallels dominate both sections. John has structured his discourse to raise the Laodicean's awareness of their economic capitulation to the Roman Empire. John not only sees this as a perennial problem, through his use of Hosea and Jeremiah, but also as a future dilemma for the church of Laodicea whereas the nation they are indebted to is under judgment from God and about to fall. Therefore, John issues a penchant warning to the church at Laodicea. Both past and future witnesses demand their repentance in order to overcome and find their place with the slain lamb. John's warning thus affects a call for repentance on behalf of the people for their current social and economic practices that have left them in an economically advantageous position but at the cost of their witness to the slain and risen lamb. John calls for the Laodiceans to transfer their allegiance from Old Rome to New Jerusalem, from the evil empire to the glorious kingdom or else face the demise and the removal of their place among the people of God.

# PAULINE EPISTLES

# 7

# Paul's Prophesying Isa 28:11 in Context

*The Signs of Unbelievers and Believers in 1 Cor 14*

FREDRICK J. LONG

Ben Witherington III has explored ancient rhetoric and social-cultural backgrounds and interprets NT texts in this light. His commentaries and other writings—too many to cite here—are well-known. His first books appeared in 1984, *Women in the Ministry of Jesus* (his revised dissertation), and in 1988, *Women in the Earliest Churches*—both in the prestigious Society for NT Studies Monograph Series.[1] Inspired by the topic of women in ministry and interacting with Ben's work, I presented a paper in 2005 entitled, "Christ's Gifted Bride: Gendered Members in Ministry in Acts and Paul in the Greco-Roman Milieu," in which I argue, *"the NT gift lists in context are completely gender neutral. . . . nowhere in these texts is there the suggestion that these gifts have a restricted distribution or role according to*

---

1. Ben Witherington III, *Women in the Ministry of Jesus: A Study of Jesus' Attitudes to Women and Their Roles as Reflected in His Earthly Life*, SNTSMS 51 (Cambridge: Cambridge University Press, 1984) and *Women in the Earliest Churches*, SNTSMS 59 (Cambridge ; New York: Cambridge University Press, 1988).

*gender*."[2] Moreover, I maintain that the ancient audiences of Paul would not have understood any restrictions, since contemporaneous religious voluntary associations increasingly enjoyed women membership, with examples of women even holding the highest positions.[3] For example, at the turn of the first century, the names of two women are found even among the traditionally male-exclusive "dancing cowherds of Pergamum," who would recite prayers, sing hymns, and dance in reenactments of the foundation story of Dionysius, in which the god inspired his maenads to rip apart the herds as the herders watched stupefied.[4] Foundational to worship is "reenactment." Honor attended to persons of these associations to the extent that they enthusiastically patronized and celebrated in the worship. For the Corinthian Christians, what might have such a reenactment dynamic looked like?

In what follows, I offer a tribute to Ben in the form of an interpretation of a perennially difficult text in Paul: 1 Cor 14:22. So difficult is this verse that J. B. Phillips reversed the logic of the verse in his translation and added this note: "This is the sole instance of the translator's departing from the accepted [Greek] text. He felt bound to conclude from the sense of the next three verses [14:23–25], that we have here either a slip of the pen on the part

---

2. This paper was published in *Women, Ministry, and the Gospel*, ed. M. Husbands and T. Larsen (Downers Grove, Ill.: InterVarsity, 2007), 98–123, here quoting 99 and 101 (*italics* original).

3. In addition to Witherington's work, I interacted with Ramsay MacMullen, "Women in Public in the Roman Empire," *Historia* 29 (1980): 208–18, Bernadette J. Brooten, *Women Leaders in the Ancient Synagogue: Inscriptional Evidence and Background Issues*, BJS 36 (Chico, CA: Scholars Press, 1982), and James M. Arlandson, *Women, Class, and Society in Early Christianity: Models from Luke-Acts* (Peabody, Mass.: Hendrickson, 1997). For voluntary associations, see also the erudite collection of essays edited by John S. Kloppenborg and Stephen G. Wilson, eds., *Voluntary Associations in the Graeco-Roman World* (New York: Routledge, 1996), esp. Wayne O. McCready, "*EKKLĒSIA* and Voluntary Associations" (59–73), and the essay by B. Hudson McLean, "The Agrippinilla Inscription: Religious Associations and Early Church Formation," in *Origins and Method: Towards a New Understanding of Judaism and Christianity: Essays in Honour of John C. Hurd*, ed. B. H. McLean, JSNTSup 86,1 (Sheffield, Eng.: JSOT Press, 1993), 239–70. More recently, see Philip A. Harland, *Associations, Synagogues, and Congregations: Claiming a Place in Ancient Mediterranean Society* (Minneapolis: Fortress Press, 2003).

4. See Harland, *Associations*, 48. This sentence is from my essay.

of Paul, or, more probably, a copyist's error."[5] Gordon D. Fee, too, agrees that 14:22 contains "notorious difficulties."[6]

A large part of the difficulty lies in understanding the significance of Paul's quotation of Isa 28:11 in 1 Cor 14:21 within its immediate context.

> In the law it is written, "With **other** tongues and with the lips of **others** I will speak to this people; yet even so they will not listen to me," says the Lord.[7]

> ἐν τῷ νόμῳ γέγραπται ὅτι Ἐν ἑτερογλώσσοις καὶ ἐν χείλεσιν ἑτέρων λαλήσω τῷ λαῷ τούτῳ καὶ οὐδ' οὕτως εἰσακούσονταί μου, λέγει κύριος.

It is generally agreed that 14:20–25 is a section within which to read 14:21.[8] Specifically, 14:22 is normally taken as the logical conclusion for 14:21 (NRSV):

> Tongues, then, are a sign not for believers but for unbelievers, while prophecy is not for unbelievers but for believers.

---

5. J. B. Phillips, trans., *The NT in Modern English* (New York: Macmillan, 1958), 1 Cor 14:22–25. Phillips provides no discreet versification of 14:22–25, but this is his translation: "That means that tongues are a sign of God's power, *not* for those who are unbelievers, but to those who already believe. Preaching the word of God, on the other hand, is a sign of God's power to those who do *not* believe rather than to believers" (italics added). The italicized "not" indicates Phillips's complete reversal of Paul's logic.

6. Gordon D. Fee, *God's Empowering Presence: The Holy Spirit in the Letters of Paul* (Peabody, Mass.: Hendrickson, 1994), 236.

7. English translations are mine unless otherwise noted. Cf. the inaccuracies of the NRSV: "In the law it is written, 'By people of strange tongues and by the lips of foreigners I will speak to this people; yet even then they will not listen to me,' says the Lord." A better translation of 14:22a is "With *other* tongues and with the lips of *others* I will speak to this people. . . ." Paul has either altered the LXX or MT (presuming he had both in mind) or used a Greek translation that has strayed from the MT to emphasize "otherness" (ἑτερο-). It is unlikely that ἐν ἑτερογλώσσοις would particularly refer to "people" since the LXX (διὰ γλώσσης ἑτέρας) and MT texts do not refer to such. Furthermore, the preposition ἐν is not usually used for personal agency suggested by the "by" in the NRSV.

8. Identifying this as a unit does not get us very far unfortunately. Frank Thielman has recently stated that these verses are among the most difficult for interpreters ("The Coherence of Paul's View of the Law: The Evidence of First Corinthians," *NTS* 38 [1992]: 235–53 at 247). The view of Kenneth E. Bailey that 14:13–25 form a discrete unit has more in its favor, based upon his literary analysis based on recognition of parallelisms into cameos (*Paul Through Mediterranean Eyes: Cultural Studies in 1 Corinthians* [Downers Grove, Ill.: IVP Academic, 2011], 394–95).

ὥστε αἱ γλῶσσαι εἰς σημεῖόν εἰσιν οὐ τοῖς πιστεύουσιν ἀλλὰ τοῖς ἀπίστοις, ἡ δὲ προφητεία οὐ τοῖς ἀπίστοις ἀλλὰ τοῖς πιστεύουσιν.

Thus, Paul's quotation of Isaiah in 14:21 is understood to be intimately connected with 14:22, so that however one reads 14:22, so follows 14:21 and *vice versa*. Regardless of one's interpretation of 14:20-25, scholars agree that 14:22 is the key to understanding these verses.[9]

Apart from explaining the relationship of 14:22 to 14:21 and to 14:23-25, one particular difficulty is in the expression εἰς σημεῖον "for a sign" in 14:22. The use of the preposition εἰς is not the problem: it should be seen either as an equivalent to a predicate nominative or as having a slight telic force.[10] Critical is how σημεῖον "sign" would have been heard within the context of 1 Cor 12-14. Joop F. M. Smit has argued that σημεῖον should be understood against the rhetorical tradition as a technical term, here meaning "the distinctive sign of unbelievers/believers" instead of the commonly held interpretation "sign of God's judgment/favor for unbelievers/believers."[11]

---

9. Gerd Theissen states, "The crucial problem for interpreters is that the general conclusion (v. 22) does not correspond to the illustrating examples in vv. 23-25" (*Psychological Aspects of Pauline Theology*, trans. John P. Galvin [Philadelphia: Fortress, 1987], 75). The number of articles addressing ch.14 is voluminous. There are many that treat 14:22 more specifically, such as Joop F. M. Smit, "Tongues and Prophecy: Deciphering 1 Cor 14,22," *Biblica* 75 (1994): 175-90; David E. Lanier, "With Stammering Lips and Another Tongue: 1 Cor 14:20-22 and Isa 28:11-12," *Criswell Theological Review* 5 (1991): 259-85; B. C. Johanson, "Tongues, a Sign for Unbelievers?: A Structural and Exegetical Study of 1 Corinthians XIV.20-25," *NTS* 25 (1979): 180-203; Wayne Grudem, "1 Corinthians 14:20-25: Prophecy and Tongues as Signs of God's Attitude," *WTJ* 41 (1979): 381-96; P. Roberts, "A Sign—Christian or Pagan?" *ExpT* 90 (1979): 199-203; O. Palmer Robertson, "Tongues: Sign of Covenantal Curse and Blessing," *WTJ* 38 (1975): 43-53; and J. P. M. Sweet, "A Sign for Unbelievers: Paul's Attitude to Glossolalia," *NTS* 13 (1967): 240-57.

10. That the expression εἰς σημεῖον "for a sign" should be taken as a predicate nominative (tongues are a sign) is held by most. See Grudem for a discussion of this use of εἰς with εἰμί or γίνομαι ("Prophecy and Tongues, " 388 n 23). Fee leans away from this, though, since it would render the expression a Semitism. "More likely the preposition carries its more ordinary telic force (=tongues are meant as a sign). . . ." (*God's Empowering Presence*, 240 n.644). Fee is correct to loosen the expression from the Semitic background. The tendency among interpreters to import a Jewish religious background into 14:22, ignoring Paul's entire argument, misleads them.

11. "Tongues and Prophecy," 185. Theissen arrives at a similar meaning for the expression "sign enabling recognition"; but, this is with respect to whether someone is a believer or not. He argues as follows: the use of tongues cannot lead the ἰδιώτης to the desired "amen" (14:16-17); in fact, tongues does not allow for a proper appraisal of outsiders (whether they believe or not), only prophecy functions to mark off true believers (14:24-25). While one would have to agree with Theissen's broader argument that Paul offers prophecy as a functional substitute for tongues, one must also disagree with the

Certainly, a rhetorical context exists in 1 Corinthians.[12] However, Smit has not sufficiently treated two *even more relevant contexts* within which to interpret 1 Cor 12–14.

First, Smit has underestimated the religious context for the term σημεῖον within Paul's arguments. Indeed, 1 Cor 12–14 in particular (not to mention earlier portions of 1 Corinthians) contains highly technical religious terminology understood from ancient (pagan) philosophical and religious experiential descriptions.

| Hellenistic Religious-Philosophical Terminology of 1 Corinthians 12–14 |
|---|
| 1. "mute idols" (τὰ εἴδωλα τὰ ἄ φωνα): 12:2 (cf. "sound" [φωνή]: 14:7, 8, 10, 11). |
| 2. The divine enabling human gifts and operations (Spirit, Lord, God): 12:4–6 and *passim* |
| 3. "workings" (ἐνεργήματα) and "to work" (ἐνεργέω): 12:62, 10, 12 |
| 4. "healings" (ἰάματα): 12:9 |
| 5. "miraculous powers" (δυνάμεις): 12:10, 28, 29; cf. 14:10 |
| 6. "spirits" (πνεύματα):[A] 12:10; 14:12*, 32 |
| 7. "prophecy" (προφητεία): 12:10; 13:2, 8; 14:6, 22 |
| 8. "tongue" (γλῶσσα): 12:10, 28, 30; 13:1, 8; 14:2, 4–6, 9, 13, 14, 18, 19, 22, 23, 26, 27, 39e. |
| 9. "interpretation" (ἑρμηνεία): 12:10; 14:26 |
| 10. "prophet(s)" (προφῆται): 12:28, 29; 14:29, 322, 37 |
| 11. "I interpret" ([δι]ἑρμενεύω): 12:30; 14:5, 13, 27 |
| 12. "I prophesy" (προφητεύω): 13:9; 14:1, 3–5, 24, 31, 39 |
| 13. "ringing gong" (χαλκὸς ἠχῶν) or "clashing cymbal" (κύμβαλον ἀλαλάζον):[B] 13:1 |
| 14. burning one's body to demonstrate religious devotion or ecstasy:[C] 13:3 |
| 15. "mysteries" (μυστήρια): 13:2; 14:2 |
| 16. "perfection" (τὸ τέλειον): 13:10 and maturity (τέλειοι): 14:20 |

---

level of importance he places on the recognition of an outsider's status as either believer or unbeliever. Paul is more concerned that the "spiritual" Corinthians speak intelligibly.

12. There are several authors that are concerned with the rhetorical context of 1 Corinthians. For example, Margaret M. Mitchell, *Paul and the Rhetoric of Reconciliation* (Louisville: Westminster/John Knox, 1991) and Ben Witherington, *Conflict and Community in Corinth: A Socio-Rhetorical Commentary on 1 and 2 Corinthians* (Grand Rapids: Eerdmans, 1995). See also Smit, "Argument and Genre of 1 Cor 12–14," in *Rhetoric and the NT: Essays from the 1992 Heidelberg Conference*, ed. S. E. Porter and T. H. Olbricht, JSNTSS 90 (Sheffield, 1993), 211–30.

17. "vision" of God "face to face": 13:10
18. "through a mirror" (δι' ἔσοπτρον):[D] 13:10
19. "enigma" (αἴνιγμα):[E] 13:12
20. "mind" (νοῦς) and "spirit" (πνεῦμα) dichotomy: 14:13-17
21. "thinking" (φρήν): 14:20 (2x)
22. "sign" (σημεῖον): 14:22
23. "to be mad" (μαίνομαι—used for Bacchic and other religious mantic states):[F] 14:23
24. circle of evaluative prophets: 14:29-32
25. Also, it is possible that women speaking out disruptively in the service may fit here: 14:34-35

A. Witherington indicates, "Plutarch does speak of *pneumata* that affected the [Delphic] oracle (*Mor.* 402B; cf. 437c)" (*Conflict*, 278).

B. Copper was used in the making of cult images ("χαλκός," BDAG 1076.1-2). Clanging cymbals were regular features of "ritual observances" ("κύμβαλον," BDAG 575). See also Hans-Josef Klauck, *The Religious Context of Early Christianity: A Guide to Graeco-Roman Religions*, trans. B. McNeil (Minneapolis: Fortress, 2003), 114 and 124.

C. Keener believes the reference to casting oneself into fire "no doubt alludes instead to the standard Jewish tradition of martyrs, some of whom threw themselves into the fire to avoid being forcibly defiled" (Craig S. Keener, *The IVP Bible Background Commentary: NT* [Downers Grove, Ill: InterVarsity, 1993], s.v.). However, Iamblichus (*De Mysteriis*, III.4) describes how the newly converted Corinthians would have understood this in pagan context: "I want to make clear the characteristic signs of those who are truly possessed by the gods.... Here is the greatest evidence: for many, even when fire is applied to them, are not burned, since the fire does not touch them on account of their divine inspiration. And many who are burned do not react, because at this time they are not living the life of an animate being.... Their actions are in no way human, because what is inaccessible becomes accessible under divine possession: they cast themselves into fire and they walk through fire...." Translation and Greek text are from Emma C. Clarke et al. trans., *Iamblichus: De Mysteriis*, Society of Biblical Literature Writings from the Greco-Roman World 4 (Atlanta: Society of Biblical Literature, 2003), 128-31.

D. Such an artifact is in the Dionysian basket (Klauck, *Religious Context*, 113). Also, in the Isis cult parade at Cenchrea (very near Corinth) described in Apuleius (*Metamorph.* 11.9), processional devotees carried mirrors on their backs to reflect back the idol goddess which followed them: "Other women had reversed shining mirrors behind their backs to show respect to the goddess as she moved after them" (as quoted in Harold W. Attridge, "Making Scents of Paul: The Background and Sense of 2 Cor 2:14-17," in *Early Christianity and Classical Culture: Comparative Studies in Honor of Abraham J. Malherbe*, ed. J. T. Fitzgerald et al., NovTSup 110 [Leiden: Brill, 2003], 71-88 at 81).

E. See "αἴνιγμα," BDAG 27.2 for the Pythagorean philosophic use of such notions as described in Plutarch.

F. See Klauck, *Religious Context*, 107. Certainly there were other causes of madness for which μαίνομαι could be used, but this was a well-known one, and fits the entire religious-experiential context of 1 Cor 12-14.

Although particular words or phrases listed above enjoyed broader reference and use, taken as a whole, the impression is clear: Paul was writing to engage a world of religious experience and presented a fairly technical exposition of it pointedly from the perspective of God's revelation of Jesus the Messiah in the working of the Holy Spirit (12:3–6).

Indeed, we must observe that Paul has "framed" the entire section with 12:2: "You know that you were pagans to mute idols being led astray, however you were led astray" (Οἴδατε ὅτι ὅτε ἔθνη ἦτε πρὸς τὰ εἴδωλα τὰ ἄφωνα ὡς ἂν ἤγεσθε ἀπαγόμενοι). This verse, moreover, contains many types of "marked" constructions that bring prominence to critical notions.[13] First, Paul slows down the discourse using a "metacomment" construction, "You know that . . ." to highlight "the introduction of important propositions."[14] Second is the preposed notion of "pagan" (ἔθνη) before the verb.[15] Third, is the periphrastic participle construction (ἔθνη ἦτε . . . ἀπαγόμενοι) that ascribes emphatically the verbal attribute of "being led astray" to the subject "(you as) pagans."[16] Fourth, there is attributive emphasis on "mute" since it is in the 2nd attributive position, repeating the article.[17] Fifth is the adverbial clause of manner with the imperfect tense, which indicates both

---

13. I began to describe such features in "Emphasis and Prominence Markers in Greek: A Proposal and Case Study within 2 Corinthians" (presented at the Biblical Greek Language and Linguistics Session at the Annual Meeting of the Society of Biblical Literature, Chicago, November 19, 2012).

14. See ch. 5 of Steven E. Runge, *Discourse Grammar of the Greek NT: A Practical Introduction for Teaching and Exegesis* (Peabody, Mass.: Hendrickson, 2010), quoting here 124.

15. One way that sentence elements or constituents gain prominence is through relative placement within the sentence. Levinsohn maintains that Verb-Subject-Object is the unmarked or default Greek sentence order. Words, phrases, or clauses that are placed before the verb are called "preposed" and are in a marked position (*Discourse Features of NT Greek: A Coursebook on the Information Structure of NT Greek*, 2nd ed. [Dallas: Summer Institute of Linguistics, 2000], 17 and 37–40).

16. See Stanley E. Porter, *Idioms of the Greek NT* (Sheffield: JSOT, 1999), 46. Porter correctly concludes "grammarians who wish to stress that the periphrastic is more emphatic or significant, or that it draws attention to the participle and its modifiers, are probably correct." Also, see the discussion of Richard A. Young commenting on Gal 1:22 and the interpreters who acknowledge the emphasis denoted by the periphrastic participle there (*Intermediate NT Greek: A Linguistic and Exegetical Approach* [Nashville: Broadman & Holman, 1994], 152).

17. Wallace states that the *art-adj-noun* (first) attributive construction gives more emphasis to the adjective, while the *art-noun-art-adj* (second) attributive construction emphasizes both the substantive (noun) and the adjective, the adjective being somewhat climactic. In describing the difference between these two uses of the attributive, Wallace notes, "This difference in the placement of the adjective is not one of relation, but of position and emphasis" (*Greek Grammar*, 306). Also, F. E. Thompson says of *art-noun-art-adj* that it is "a specification by way of apposition" and suggests that one translate the phrase ὁ ἀνὴρ ὁ σοφός as "the man, that is, the wise man" with a sense of apposition (*A Syntax of Attic Greek* [London; New York: Longmans, Green, 1907], 47). Tim Christian, my research assistant, supplied these summaries.

"manner" and repeated action within a past time frame. Finally, Paul has poignantly repeated the verbal root ἀγαγ* "lead" and "lead astray" and in so doing explicitly evokes the Corinthians' not so distant pagan past. Thus, the Greek word order and special constructions of these verses are highly marked, emphasized, and prominent, thus supporting the critical role that 12:2 plays as a "frame" for what follows.

I am using "frame" here in a technical sense: "Framing has a selective function; it emphasizes certain aspects of reality and makes others less obvious. In this way, certain attributes are suggested to the audience."[18] In discourse analysis framing "can be thought of as a means of conceptualizing the way that background knowledge is used to make sense of and produce discourse."[19] The preponderance of contemporaneous religious language would have helped the original audiences navigate Paul's argument, to track it, and understand points of Paul's overstatement (14:5a), exasperation (14:18–19), disappointment (14:20), and focal generalization (14:22). We must ask, "Why would Paul thus frame his treatment of the Corinthians' misunderstanding about and misuse of spiritual gifts with a reference to their pagan past?" And, "what relationship exists between Paul's framing of his response and the problems with the Corinthian worship?"

Second, Smit sees the quotation of Isaiah as being (rather violently) extracted by Paul from its original context and supplied with a completely alien meaning in 1 Cor 14. Smit's treatment of Isa 28:11 in 1 Cor 14:21 is not untypical. He states, "In my opinion, the original context and meaning of this quotation are entirely irrelevant here. For Paul the text refers exclusively to the ecstatic speaking of his own day, occurring outside as well as inside the church-community. It still remains a difficult task to determine exactly which phenomena he has in mind."[20] Smit's last comment also reflects his casual treatment of the religious background behind tongues and "signs." However, the intertextual context of Isaiah has an instrumental bearing on the interpretation of 1 Cor 14:21–22 far beyond what is typically understood.[21]

---

18. Aurora Iorgoveanu and Nicoleta Corbu, "No Consensus on Framing? Towards an Integrative Approach to Define Frames Both as Text and Visuals," *Romanian Journal of Communication and Public Relations* 14, no. 3 (2012): 91–102 at 94.

19. Paul Baker and Sibonile Ellece, eds., *Key Terms in Discourse Analysis* (New York: Continuum, 2011), 48.

20. Smit, "Tongues and Prophecy," 186.

21. By "intertextual" I mean methodologically that which Richard Hays investigated over two decades ago in his *Echoes of Scripture in the Letters of Paul* (New Haven: Yale University Press, 1989). See the recent consolidation of intertextual study and methodology by G. K. Beale, *Handbook on the NT Use of the OT: Exegesis and Interpretation* (Grand Rapids: Baker Academic, 2012).

In this paper I am proposing that Smit's interpretation of σημεῖον in 14:22 to mean "the distinctive sign of unbelievers/believers" is correct but can be greatly improved upon when set within three critical interpretive contexts. First, when one recognizes the technical Hellenistic religious language of σημεῖον "sign" employed in 14:22 within the context of Paul's argument (1 Cor 12–14), we can better understand how Paul argued that unintelligible, enigmatic tongue speaking as the Corinthians were engaged in was a characteristic "sign" of and for unbelievers in pagan religious expression, since such unintelligible speech effectively marked off a person as possessed of a spirit. Second, 14:22 functions more broadly within the argumentative and discursive context of 1 Cor 14 as is suggested by the strategic use of the conjunction ὥστε there. Third, by recontextualizing Isa 28:11, Paul prophesied in an exemplary, contextual way for the Corinthians to recognize and understand. Paul's prophesying has several significant parallels with the situation and setting of 1 Cor 12–14.

This paper will proceed as follows. First, I will briefly summarize the Hellenistic technical discussion of inspired speech from Plato and Iamblichus showing that σημεῖον "sign" was a technical category by which to discuss divine possession. This background supports my interpretation of "sign" in 1 Cor 14:22 and thus my intertextual interpretation of Isa 28:11 in 1 Cor 14:21. Then, second, I will recapitulate the main lines of interpretation that have been offered with regard to "sign" in 14:20–25, concluding with a refinement of Smit's proposal. Third, I will argue that the ὥστε beginning 14:22 indicates that this verse concludes and summarizes Paul's argument in 14:1–21 and should therefore not be seen primarily with 14:21. Finally, I will explore the intertextual relationship of Isa 28:11 within 1 Cor 14, concluding that Paul's prophetic use of Isa 28:11 is his example of appropriate inspired speech as prophecy based upon the Word of God and surprisingly applied to the Corinthians themselves.

## THE HELLENISTIC PROPHETIC EXPERIENCE AND 1 COR 12–14

Jerome Murphy-O'Connor in *St. Paul's Corinth* quotes a description of the city from Cicero's *On the Republic* (2:7): "Maritime cities also suffer a certain corruption and denigration of morals; for they receive a mixture of strange languages and customs, and import foreign ways as well as foreign merchandise, so that none of their ancestral institutions can possibly remain unchanged."[22] While the severity of this last remark was polemically

22. *Saint Paul's Corinth: Texts and Archaeology*, Good News Studies 6 (Wilmington:

driven, Cicero's comments would certainly be true with respect to religious experiences. The Corinthian believers certainly had come from diverse backgrounds—and probably many of them had been involved in idol worship, as Paul reminded them (1 Cor 12:2). Although the Corinthians had embraced Paul's gospel message, they were being led to idolatry again in some form or another (8:1–6; 10:7, 14–22; cf. 2 Cor 6:14—7:1).

Many studies describe Hellenistic cult and prophetic experiences. Such settings extend beyond the Delphic Oracles.[23] There is no need to recite all the references here.[24] In what follows several excerpts from Hellenistic texts are given which, in my view, ultimately help reconstruct the cultural religious phenomenon of ecstatic tongues and prophecy in Corinth. From this one can better appreciate Paul's strategy in 1 Cor 12–14 in addressing the issues pertaining to "spiritual matters/people" (12:1). It is hoped that the specific line of argument offered above with regard to 14:20–25 will be enhanced once one recognizes this background.

The preponderance of religious terms in 1 Cor 12–14 indicates that Paul was combating what might be called "syncretizing influences."[25] Furthermore, it is no accident that Paul in 12:2, when recounting this past of some of the Corinthians, describes the worshiped idols as "mute" (τὰ εἴδωλα τὰ ἄφωνα). The fact is that humans, and particularly women, supplied the voice or tongue for the gods in the form of prophecies and ecstatic

---

Glazier, 1983).

23. Witherington's restriction of his excursus and his critique of scholarship to the Delphic Oracle severely limits the value of his remarks on 1 Cor 14 (*Conflict in Corinth*, 276–79).

24. See especially Engelson (*Glossolalia*, 1–23) and Arthur Adams Lovekin, *Glossolalia: A Critical Study of Alleged Origins, the NT and the Early Church* (Univ. of the South Masters Thesis; Ann Arbor: University Microfilms, 1962), 1–31.

25. It is remarkable the extent to which Paul appropriates this language in his attempts to dissuade the Corinthians not to engage in a Hellenistic style of prophecy. See Smit's construal of the antithetical parallelism between 14:27–28 and 29–31. He argues that this style of rhetoric emphasizes the dissimilarity of prophecy, as Paul understands it, and tongue speaking ("Tongues," 190, n.25). E. Earle Ellis argues for a Qumran background for the problems at Corinth with regard to the spirit and their seeking after spirits ("'Spiritual' Gifts in the Pauline Community" *NTS* 20 [1974]: 128–44). But, one may need to distinguish Paul's background at this point "from the Corinthians." Definitely the two worlds have clashed. Thus, Paul speaks of the head covering in ch. 11 for the sake of angels, which more than likely originates from Judaism, perhaps particularly from Qumran.

utterances.²⁶ These oracular expressions were not seen as separate experiences.²⁷ The fact that Paul needed to give "women/wives" special instruction for Christian worship (14:34–35) may reflect the special role and status that women could gain as recipients of divine inspiration.²⁸ Importantly, Paul valued women praying and prophesying (11:5, 13). It may be that Paul was providing in controlled prophesying a "functional substitute" for the enthusiasm that tongue speaking had gained.²⁹ Why? It may be that the Corinthians in their worship were encouraged to reenact the Pentecost event of Acts 2 with tongue speaking; such reenactment is standard in religious cult.

At this point we must acknowledge the excellent work of Thomas Gillespie, who rightly located the use of σημεῖον in 14:22 within Hellenistic religious culture.³⁰ When a person prophesied on behalf of a god, "signs" were sought after for authentication. Among the signs, tongues was highly respected: "unintelligible ecstatic utterance . . . was viewed as the *sine qua non* of the divine legitimization of the prophetic word."³¹ Speaking in unintelligible or enigmatic speech was the high point of prophetic expression and the spiritual legitimization in the Greco-Roman world. Tongues functioned to set apart a "truly" inspired person. Gillespie has argued that the form of prophecy in the Greco-Roman world contained three parts:

---

26. "From Greek writers and poets it is possible to obtain a fairly clear picture of the phenomenon of a god speaking through the mouth of ecstatic priestesses and mantics" (Engelson, *Glossolalia*, 7). Engelson cites an excerpt from Plutarch (*Pyt.Or.* 404E): ". . . the god of this place employs the prophetic priestess for men's ears just as the sun employs the moon for men's eyes. For he makes known and reveals his own thoughts, but he makes them known through the associated medium of a mortal body and soul that is unable to keep quiet, or as it yields itself to the One that moves it, to remain of itself unmoved and tranquil. . . ." One wonders whether this background lies behind Paul's admonition for women to be silent in 14:34–35, presumably during the interpretation phase of the service. That there was such a phase is suggested by Plato (see below).

27. For a discussion of this point see Terrance Callan, "Prophecy and Ecstasy in Greco-Roman Religion and in 1 Corinthians," *NovT* 27 (1985): 125–40.

28. For an (unsuccessful) attempt to reconstruct the exigency of 1 Corinthians around a problematic group of women prophets, see Antoinette Clark Wire, *The Corinthian Women Prophets: A Reconstruction Through Paul's Rhetoric* (Minneapolis: Fortress, 1990). However, Wire explores this possible background as Paul engages issues of gender and women prophets.

29. This notion is described in Charles H. Kraft and Marguerite G. Kraft, *Christianity In Culture: A Study In Dynamic Biblical Theologizing In Cross-cultural Perspective*, 25th Anniv. (Orbis Books, 2005).

30. "A Pattern of Prophetic Speech in First Corinthians" *JBL* 97 (1978): 74–95.

31. Gillespie, "Patter of Prophetic Speech," 82.

1. *The prophetic claim*, which employed the ἐγώ εἰμί formula and served to identify the divine subject who is the source of the prophet's inspiration.

2. *The prophetic message*, which conveys the redemptive word of revelation from the one for whom the prophet speaks.

3. *The prophetic confirmation*, which provides a "sign" through ecstasy that authenticates the prophecy as a whole.[32]

The prophetic confirmation is characterized by Celsus as follows: "incomprehensible, frenzied, and indistinct sounds, the meaning of which no intelligent person is able to discover; for they are without form or meaning, but to a fool or sorcerer they afford an opportunity to put upon the utterance any meaning he wishes."[33] The relevance for 1 Cor 14 is that Paul was desperately trying to separate prophecy from ecstatic tongue speaking, when the Corinthian's would have naturally held them together.[34] Interestingly, Paul's own demonstration of prophecy in 14:21 conforms more or less to Gillespie's form, excepting the final ecstatic expression.[35]

Plato was a very influential source in the ancient world for information on the nature of prophecy. In the *Timaeus* (72A–B) he discusses the gift of prophecy at some length:[36]

> And that God gave unto man's foolishness the gift of divination a sufficient token (ἱκάνον σημεῖον) is this: no man achieves true

---

32. Gillespie, "Pattern of Prophetic Speech," 82. He draws on Celsus's comments about the rather common, and from his view, vulgar prophecy that existed at his time (mid second century AD) arguing that Christians practiced the same kind.

33. The English translation is from H. Chadwick, *Origen: Contra Celsum* (London: Cambridge University, 1953) and is taken from Gillespie. The text is from Origen's *Contra Celsum* 7.9–23.

34. Antoinette Wire is right in noting that Paul is attempting "to dissociate prophecy from tongues" but fails to comprehend the negative effect of ecstatic utterance for the community and its distinct identity as the people of the one God, not gods (*Corinthian Women Prophets*, 140). Thus, for Wire to praise tongues as a prayer language is mistaken in the context from which the Corinthians operated. Uninterpreted tongues were a sign of superiority, but also of pagan religious ecstasy.

35. The prophetic claim is indicated not only by the introduction "in the Law it is written" but also in the change from "he [God] will speak" (LXX and MT) to "I will speak." The prophetic message is given (14:21, 23). Finally, the prophetic confirmation is provided in "says the Lord." Paul's prophetic model, of course, is Jewish. It is also interesting that in 1 Corinthians Paul appeals to the Spirit within him in 7:40 (cf. 2:4, 10–14).

36. Excerpted from Engelson, although the Greek supplied is only partially from him. The translation is from R. G. Bury (LCL; Cambridge: Harvard University Press, 1952).

and inspired divination when in his rational mind (ἔννους) but only when the power of his intelligence is fettered in sleep or when it is distraught by disease or by reason of some divine inspiration. But it belongs to a man when in his right mind (ἔμφρωνος) to recollect and ponder both the things spoken in dream or waking vision by the divining and inspired nature, and all the visionary forms that were seen, and by means of reasoning to discern about them all wherein they are significant (τι σημαίνει "it signifies something") and for whom they portend evil or good in the future, the past, or the present. But it is not the task of him who has been in a state of frenzy (τοῦ δὲ μανέντος), and still continues therein, to judge (κρίνειν) the apparitions and voices seen or uttered by himself; for it was well said of old that to do and to know one's own and oneself belongs only to him who is sound of mind (σώφρονι). Wherefore also it is customary to set the tribe of prophets (τὸ τῶν προφητῶν γένος) to pass judgment upon these inspired divinations; and they, indeed, themselves are named "diviners" by certain who are wholly ignorant of the truth that they are not diviners but interpreters (ὑποκριταί) of the mysterious voice and apparition, for whom the most fitting name would be "prophets (προφῆται) of things divined."

This passage could help explain several features in Paul's discourse on spiritual phenomena. First, the "sign" or "token" of Hellenistic prophetic activity is that the νοῦς or mind is not engaged. Paul must also admonish the Corinthians to engage their minds (νοῦς) along side their spirit (14:13–19). Second, prophecy must be discerned or judged. This is done by others who are in their right mind, not by the mantic (μανίς). These other persons are essentially interpreters or "prophets." This could explain Paul's constant juxtapositioning of tongues and translation/interpretation throughout (12:10, 30) and the need for the translation of tongues (14:27–28). Paul also instructs the prophecies to be judged (διακρίνω) by others (14:29), which would seem to be related to situation described by Plato above. One wonders whether Paul is here working within Plato's model or one like it.

Another instructive passage is found in Iamblichus' *On the Mysteries* (III, 4–5).[37] Although this document is dated ca. AD 300, it nonetheless has value in preserving information that is older.[38] In III.4 Iamblichus explained

---

37. Iamblichus lived c. AD 250–325 and was a neo-Platonist philosopher who studied under Porphyry at Rome or Sicily. He later founded his own philosophical school in Syria. "On the Mysteries" is specifically entitled "Reply of Abammon to Porphyry's *Letter to Anebo*" and is a defense of ritualistic magic (*OCD*, 538).

38. There was a trend in all of Greco-Roman thought in the second and third

that the most sure sign (τεκμήριον) of divine possession consisted in the ability not to experience pain by fire, daggers, etc.: "This proves that in their enthusiasm [i.e., their state of inspiration] they . . . live instead another and diviner kind [of life], which fills them and takes complete possession of them." This section is followed by III.5, a discussion of σημεῖα:[39]

> There are many different kinds (εἴδη) of divine possession, and there are different ways of awakening the divine spirit; consequently there are many different indications (τὰ πολλὰ σημεῖα) of this state. For one thing, there are different gods (οἱ θεοί) from whom we receive the spirit [i.e., are inspired= ἐπιπνεόμεθα], and this results in a variety of forms in which the inspiration manifest itself; further, the kinds of influence exerted are different, and so there are various ways in which the divine seizure takes place. For either the god takes possession of us, or else we are entirely absorbed in him, or else [thirdly] we co-operate with him (ἢ κοινὴν ποιούμεθα πρὸς αὐτὸν τὴν ἐνέργειαν). At times we partake of the lowest power of God, at others of the middle [power], at still others of the highest [i.e., first]. Sometimes it is a mere participation, again it is a communion [fellowship or sharing], or again it becomes a union of these [two] kinds. Now the soul enjoys complete separation; again it is still involved in the body, or [else] the whole nature is laid hold of [and controlled].
> 
> Hence the signs of possession (τὰ σημεῖα τῶν ἐπιπνεομένων) are manifold: either movement of the body and its parts, or complete relaxation; [either] singing choirs, round dances, and harmonious voices, or the opposite of these. [The] bodies have been seen to rise up, grow, or move freely in the air, and the opposite has also been observed. They have been heard to utter [different] voices of equal strength, or with great diversity and inequality, in tones that alternated with silence; and again in other cases harmonious crescendo or diminuendo of tone, and in still other cases other kinds of utterance.

First, this passage suggests the importance associated to a "sign" as an indication of inspiration. Second, this passage discusses a variety of expressions from a variety of gods. These expressions in which people

---

centuries to form authoritative "canons" on a variety of subjects. Dennis E. Groh cites authorities to this effect: "At exactly this point in time . . . the cumulative wisdom of Greek culture was brought together and systematized in handbooks and encyclopedias which were used throughout the middle ages" ("Hans von Campenhausen on Canon: Positions and Problems," *Int* 28 [1974]: 331–43 at 343).

39. This translation is from Fredrick C. Grant, *Hellenistic Religion: The Age of Syncretism*, The Library of Liberal Arts (Indianapolis: Bobbs-Merrill, 1953), 173–74.

"co-operated" with the divine are called ἐνέργειαι "manifestations." This section from Iamblichus shows a number of similarities with Paul's description of spiritual manifestation in 1 Cor 12. Of particular importance is the recognition that the Corinthian believers had once served gods among many diverse gods (12:2). Thus, it is no surprise that Paul's strategy was to prove that the one God lies behind the diverse manifestations and workings (ἐνεργήματα) in 12:4–6.[40] Paul carefully argues in such a way so as to subsume all activities of the Spirit not only to the body of Christ, but also to the purposeful unified activity of the one God (cf. 1 Cor 12:6, 28). But even the analogy of the functioning body of Christ is ultimately brought under God's direction (12:18, 24). Paul's argument eventually leads to ch.13—the critical excursus on love that must be the motivation for the use of spiritual gifts—and leads to ch.14 with its exposition on the notion of mutual edification in the public gathering.

## THE INTERPRETATION OF σημεῖον "SIGN" IN RHETORICAL AND RELIGIOUS SENSE

There have been many attempts to understand what exactly Paul means by εἰς σημεῖον "a sign" in 14:22, let alone Paul's argument in 14:20–25. The use of this word is rare in Paul, attested only seven times in the Pauline epistles.[41] As stated above, a majority of scholars hold "for a sign" in relation to tongues as a (prophetic) sign, either positively as reflecting God's presence[42] or negatively as a sign of judgment upon the unbelievers.[43] This

40. Smit makes this point well when explicating the rhetorical structure of ch.12 ("Argument and Genre," 218).

41. In Rom 4:11 Abraham is said to have received the sign of circumcision. In Rom 15:19 and 2 Cor 12:12 Paul speaks of his own signs which have been performed while doing his ministry. In 1 Cor 1:22 Paul portrays the Jews as demanding signs. These latter references are closest to what Paul intends in 1 Cor 14:22. Additionally, Paul refers to his signature at the end of 2 Thess 3:17 as a sign.

42. See, e.g., Robert H. Gundry, "'Ecstatic Utterance' (N.E.B.)?" *JTS* 17 (1966): 299–307 at 306.

43. As Witherington argues, "Here the word 'sign,' in view of the Isaiah quotation, surely means an 'ōt, a sign of judgment that they [the unbelievers (ἄπιστοι)] are out of touch with God. This is the effect of uninterpreted tongues on the nonbelievers in Corinth. They cannot respond positively but only say that tongues speakers are ecstatics" (*Conflict*, 285). See also, e.g., J. G. Davies, "Pentecost and Glossolalia," *JTS* 3 (1952): 228–31 at 230. That the sign of tongues here reflects negatively upon the Corinthians themselves and these unbelievers is often strongly implied, e.g., by A. C. Thiselton, "The 'Interpretation' of Tongues: A New Suggestion in the Light of Greek Usage in Philo and Josephus," *JTS* 30 (1979): 15–36 at 36 and especially by Fee who says, "'sign' in this sentence can function only in a negative way. That is, it is a 'sign' that functions to the

sign is directed for or against those persons mentioned in vv.23-25.[44] It is also generally recognized that Paul's argument in 14:20-25 is relatively complete. Gordon Fee has concisely summarized B. C. Johanson's rhetorical analysis of the passage:[45]

| 14:20 | Exhortation: Redirect your thinking (about the function of tongues) | | |
|---|---|---|---|
| 14:21 | OT text: Tongues do not lead people to obedience | | |
| 14:22 | Application: "So then..." | | |
| | Assertion 1: Tongues a sign | not for believers | A |
| | | but for unbelievers | B |
| | Assertion 2: Prophecy [a sign] | not for unbelievers | B |
| | | but for believers | A |
| 14:23 | Illustration 1: Effect of Tongues (1) | on unbelievers | (B) |
| 14:24-25 | Illustration 2: Effect of Prophecy (2) | on unbelievers | (A) |

Fee's interpretation of 14:22 is that the Corinthians' untranslated tongues are a sign of judgment upon unbelievers; it does not bring them to repentance (14:23). This is essentially, then, how Fee interprets Paul's use of Isaiah in 14:21, "Tongues do not lead sinners to obedience."[46]

But there is dissonance between 14:22 and the two assertions which follow, as Fee himself aptly admits: "one is led to expect something else from the two assertions...."[47] This difficulty in explaining the relationship be-

---

disadvantage of unbelievers.... Because tongues are unintelligible, unbelievers receive no revelation from God; they cannot thereby be brought to faith. Thus by regarding the work of the Spirit—tongues—as madness, they are destined for divine judgment—just as in the OT passage Paul has just quoted" (*God's Empowering Presence*, 239-41 at 241). According to Fee's understanding, it is hard to ignore that the situation reflects poorly on the Corinthians themselves. The view that a negative judgment attends to tongues speaking from their initiation in Acts 2 at Pentecost is argued by Blaine Charette, "'Tongues as of Fire': Judgment as a Function of Glossolalia in Luke's Thought," *Journal of Pentecostal Theology* 13 (2005): 173-86.

44. The reason why interpreters go this route is because of the use of σημεῖον in the LXX. But, there is no developed notion of "sign" that corresponds with how it functions in 1 Corinthians. For a discussion of σημεῖον in the LXX in relation to 1 Cor 14:20-25, see Wayne Grudem, *The Gift of Prophecy in 1 Corinthians* (Washington: University Press, 1982), 192-202.

45. This is taken exactly from Fee, *God's Empowering Presence*, 236.

46. Fee, *The First Epistle to the Corinthians*, NICNT (Grand Rapids: Eerdmans, 1987), 680.

47. Fee, *God's Empowering Presence*, 237 cf. 239. Fee's interpretation of the passage has several other problems that will be treated below. These include a failure to recognize how Paul uses ὥστε within the Corinthian correspondence, a failure to make

tween 14:21 and 14:22 and, consequently, 14:22 to the following assertions has been carefully analyzed by Johanson. He has argued persuasively that however one takes the sign—as a sign of judgment or as a positive sign—the logic of Paul's argument is very difficult to comprehend. Johanson helpfully diagrams both readings:[48]

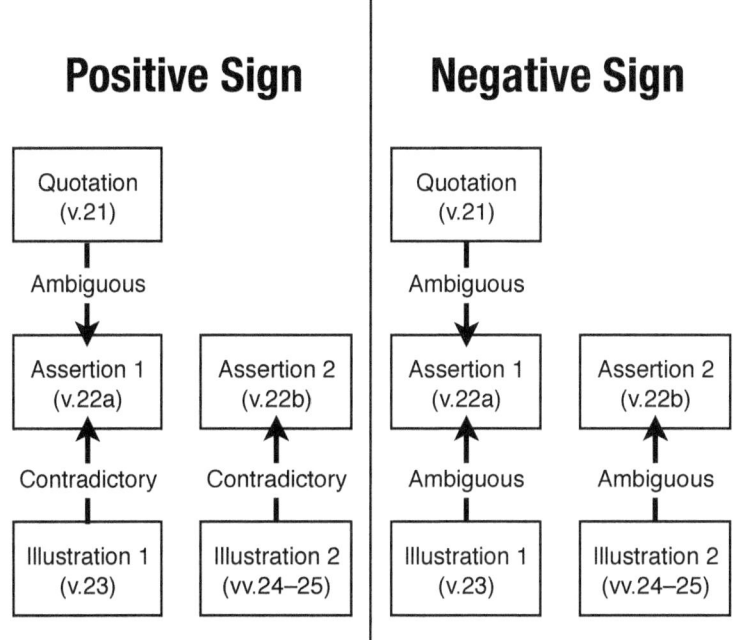

From this we visually see the problem: in either interpretation, it is highly problematic to take "sign" as either positive or negative. In actuality it would have to mean both—for tongues "sign" would be negative, but for prophecy "sign" would be positive. Thus, if one understands "sign" as referring to God's activity of "signing," the sense of 14:22 is very confusing since it must carry both a negative and positive meaning.

In view of this impasse Johanson offers a solution. He argues that 14:22 is a rhetorical question adapted to "the content of the glossolalists' childish thoughts." Thus, 14:22 would read as follows: "Are tongues, then, meant as a sign not for believers but for unbelievers, while prophecy is meant as a sign not for unbelievers but for believers?"[49] Such a use of ὥστε,

---

the most direct intertextual connection with the Isaiah passage (i.e., the disobedient people [Israel] = the Corinthian unintelligible speakers), and a failure to recognize the Hellenistic background to Paul's argument.

48. Johanson, "Tongues," 192.
49. Johanson, "Tongues," 193–94.

he argues, is found in Gal 4:16.[50] According to Johanson's reconstruction, the Corinthians considered corporate tongues to be a sign for the unbelievers benefit, since they were not effective for non-participating believers (ἰδιῶται; 14:16–17). Thus Paul uses Isa 28:11 as a "springboard" [Johanson's expression] for 14:22. And after redirecting the Corinthians' thinking by the use of a rhetorical question in 14:22, Paul continues his argument by showing that the Corinthians had it backwards: tongues are not for unbelievers (14:23), rather prophecy is (14:24–25).[51]

Although Johanson has provided a plausible reading which ameliorates some difficulties, it creates another. After analyzing the form of Paul's quotation in 14:21, he comments:

> If we are to hold that Paul has the OT context in mind when he quotes these verses, we must also hold that the precise wording of the quotation is not very important for him. This seems rather unlikely in the light of the fact that Paul seems to have either altered the text or chosen to quote from a version felicitous to his argument with deliberate intent. As a result, the possibility of the OT context being implied by the quotation looks somewhat dubious. That Paul uses scriptural quotations out of context is clear enough elsewhere.[52]

This conclusion respecting any intertextual meaning, not unlike Smit's, is very severe, and is not warranted as will be argued below. Furthermore, Johanson's analysis of the conjunctions ὥστε (14:22) and οὖν (14:23) is weak. As will be argued in detail below, the ὥστε in 14:22 is a concluding summarization of 14:1–21. Smit and others have also critiqued Johanson's position by pointing out that the οὖν in 14:23 expects 14:22 to be an assertion rather than a rebuttal in the form of a rhetorical question.[53] In the end,

---

50. Johanson, "Tongues," 193. Gal 4:16: ὥστε ἐχθρὸς ὑμῶν γέγονα ἀληθεύων ὑμῖν; "Have I now become your enemy by telling you the truth? (NRSV)" The problem with Johanson's interpretation is that he sees the ὥστε as somehow being instrumental to the form of the rhetorical question. I would argue that it is not. Instead, it functions to bring the discussion (14:12–16) to a summary and after that the argument advances along a somewhat different, although not dissimilar, line.

51. Johanson, "Tongues," 194. Johanson does take the sign positively when applied to prophecy. Accordingly the sign status for tongues would be positive in relation to believers. But, this is certainly not Paul's point since no one can understand what is being said (14:2, 6, 9, 11, 16–17).

52. Johanson, "Tongues," 182–83. For Johanson the form of the Isaiah passage is unimportant. But, this is precisely what should be carefully weighed and interpreted.

53. Smit, "Tongues," 177.

Johanson's interpretation is unconvincing, especially because it fails to take the Isaiah passage in 14:21 more seriously

Smit offers yet another reading of 1 Cor 14:22. He picks up Johanson's focus upon rhetoric as a means to solve the puzzling use of σημεῖον. Smit analyzes the argument of 14:20–25 as follows:

    14:20    Introduction

                *exhortatio* (14:20)

    14:21–25  Argumentation

                1. *iudicium* (14:21)

                ὥστε

                2. *propositio* (14:22)

                οὖν

                3. *exempla* (14:23–25)

The introduction is demarcated by the vocative "brothers" which suggests that Paul is moving to a new line of thought. A complete argument exists in 14:20–25 with logical connectors (ὥστε and οὖν).[54] The key verse, however, is 14:22, because it is sandwiched between 14:21 and 14:23–25. By working back from 14:23–25 Smit is able to achieve a very plausible reading of 14:22, namely, "tongues are a distinctive sign of unbelievers," i.e., "a sign of recognition."

Instrumental to Smit's interpretation are the classical rhetorical handbooks that discuss types of argumentative proofs, two of which are σημεῖον "sign" and ἔλεγχος "refutation." Significantly both types are often listed and treated together. Both word groups are found in 14:22–25: σημεῖον in 14:22 and ἐλέγχω ("I refute") in 14:25. In *Rhetorica ad Alexandrum* (14.1431b.2–4) the author explains the difference between the two:[55]

---

54. Smit observes, "We have already noticed that 1 Cor 14,20–25 form a coherent argumentation" ("Tongues," 186). See also Hanz Conzelmann, *A Commentary on the First Epistle to the Corinthians*, trans. J. W. Leitch (Philadelphia: Fortress, 1975), 241. But such a view is grossly overstated. Smit's statement that "vv.20–25 form a clearly defined part of a discussion" is more accurate, since these verses fall within Paul's larger argument ("Tongues," 178).

55. Text and translation are from Smit ("Tongues," 182), although I have altered "the judges" to "those judging." Smit cites other handbooks and authors, such as Cicero, as well.

> καί μὴν ἔλεγχος σημείου ταύτῃ διαφέρει, διότι τῶν μὲν σημείων ἔνια μόνον οἴεσθαι ποιεῖ τοὺς ἀκούοντος, ἔλεγχος δὲ πᾶς τὴν ἀλήθειαν διδάσκει τοὺς κρίνοντας.

> Moreover, a <u>refutation</u> differs from a <u>sign</u> because some <u>signs</u> only cause the hearers to think, whereas every <u>refutation</u> teaches those judging the truth.

The conclusion Smit draws is that Paul was using such a rhetorical distinction in his discussion of the spiritual phenomena under consideration in 1 Cor 12–14. When the unbelievers (ἄπιστοι) or outsiders (ἰδιῶται) enter into the congregation that is speaking in tongues they will pronounce "You are mad" (μαίνεσθε, 14:23). Thus, argues Paul, tongues are a sign of pagan religious mania. But when someone hears prophecy, he or she is refuted (ἐλέγχεται, 14:24). Such a person says, "God is truly among you" ("Οντως ὁ θεὸς ἐν ὑμῖν ἐστιν, 14:25).

Smit rightly argues, "[t]he choice of the verb μαίνομαι [in 14:23] is most significant. It evokes the entire range of religious, ecstatic phenomena, familiar to the Hellenistic world. In particular it conjures up the prophetic ecstasy of the Bacchantes."[56] Nils Ivar Johan Engelson has also studied μαίνομαι in reference to a religious ecstatic state.[57] From a Jewish perspective, too, this verb was applied to describe a setting aside of rational thought associated with pagan idolatry (Wis 14:27–28); the verb could also refer to a madness associated with false prophecy (Jer 36:26 [LXX]).[58] This negative association of μαίνομαι to religious experience supports Smit's reading of 14:22 that "tongues are not proper to the believers but to the unbelievers."[59]

Smit's interpretation of the rhetorical use of σημεῖον advances our understanding of Paul's puzzling statements. Moreover, Smit rightly acknowledges the religious context evoked by Paul's use of μαίνομαι. However, the interpretive gains of Smit's analysis come at the expense of appreciating how Paul utilized Isaiah in 14:21. Smit works his solution backwards from 14:22

---

56. Smit, "Tongues," 183; see n.17, which provides several ancient texts which use μαίνομαι in this way.

57. *Glossolalia and Other Forms of Inspired Speech According to 1 Corinthians 12–14*, Yale University diss. (Ann Arbor: University Micorfilms, 1971), 7–9.

58. In one other location, the madness results from God's judgment (Jer 32:16 [LXX]). The only other occurrences in the LXX are when Antiochus attempts to persuade the Jewish martyrs not to "be crazy" as the previous martyrs had been in refusing him (4 Macc 8:5; 10:13). Antiochus's appeal to this verb to describe Jewish faithful resistance (to the point of death through torture) indicates how desperate the appeal is, and draws upon the verb's negative connotations.

59. Smit, "Tongues," 185.

to 14:21. By assuming a tight logic between these verses, he concludes that Paul took Isa 28:11 completely out of its original context, as other interpreters have concluded.⁶⁰ But I question whether 14:22 must relate so directly to 14:21 so as to conclude that Paul disregarded the context of Isa 28:11. In fact, Paul's introduction of 14:22 with the conjunction ὥστε indicates that 14:22 concludes the entire argument in 14:1–21, and thus not singularly 14:21. Consequently, the use of Isa 28:11 in 14:21 must been seen within the larger context of 1 Cor 14 rather than be restricted logically to relate solely to 14:22.

## THE USE OF ὥστε IN 1–2 CORINTHIANS

The use of ὥστε by Paul, especially in 1 and 2 Corinthians, has been unappreciated among interpreters.⁶¹ In BDAG among the meanings of ὥστε are two basic categories: to introduce independent clauses or dependent clauses. The meaning given for the independent constructions is simply "for this reason, therefore, so."⁶² This is the most frequent use in 1 Corinthians. However, this understanding in and of itself is inadequate from a discursive perspective. As many have noted, we are in need of updated grammars and lexicons.⁶³ Recent developments in text-linguistic theory should play a significant role in the development of such tools.⁶⁴ One premise of discourse criticism is that meaning beyond the sentence level can be conveyed in language. Stephen Levinsohn recently has studied logical connectors used in the NT and has concluded that ὥστε marks "conclusion": "When *hoste* introduces an independent clause or sentence, it constrains it to be interpreted as the conclusion of a section or sub-section (+Conclusion)."⁶⁵

---

60. Smit argues, "For Paul the quotation [Isa 28:11] speaks about the pagan, Hellenistic environment, which is alienated from God. Ecstatic speakers form a characteristic feature of this world. They belong to the religious life of the unbelievers" ("Tongues," 187). In other words, for Smit the original context of the Isaiah passage had no bearing for Paul's use of it in 14:21.

61. E.g., Fee simply calls this particle a "strong inferential conjunction" and gives the references in 1 Corinthians (*God's Empowering Presence*, 239, cf. n.640). Cf. Grudem who assumes that 14:22 is the interpretation of 14:21 (*The Gift of Prophecy*, 192).

62. s.v. BDAG 1107.1.

63. E.g., this was called for by Micheal W. Palmer, *Levels of Constituent Structure in NT Greek*, Studies in Biblical Greek 4 (New York: P. Lang, 1994).

64. Recently there is the *Lexham Discourse Greek NT* (LDGNT) based upon the discourse grammar of Runge, *Discourse Grammar*. Although Runge advances the field, there are still many areas for improvement and LDGNT contains too many errors (I reviewed his work and LDGNT at the 2012 SBL Annual Meeting).

65. Stephen H. Levinsohn "'Therefore' or 'Wherefore': What's the Difference?"

Thus, from a discourse perspective, ὥστε concludes a larger argument. In my survey below, I will show that an independent ὥστε does not function to connect one sentence to the next inferentially, rather it focalizes by way of generalizing or summarizing the preceding argument as a conclusion. Just how far backwards the conclusion reaches must be determined in context.

In 1 Corinthians, when ὥστε is used with an independent clause, it has the discourse function of generalizing Paul's main concerns in the foregoing argument, whether this argument spans a couple verses or many verses. Occasionally, this is in the form of a summary.[66] It should be added that ὥστε represents Paul's formulation of ideas into memorable statements rather than indicates the slogans of others.[67] In the discussion below, I will evaluate and summarize the use of ὥστε in 1 and 2 Corinthians. I conclude that 1 Cor 14:22 does not relate primarily with 14:21 but rather focalizes Paul's argument in 14:1–21 in preparation for his subsequent argumentation.

The conjunction ὥστε is used twenty-one times in the Corinthian Correspondence. Of these occurrences, only six times does it function to introduce a dependent result clause (1 Cor 1:7; 13:2; 2 Cor 1:8; 2:7; 3:7; 7:7). In one other place at 5:1, ὥστε functions basically like a noun clause to give the actual content of the kind of sexual immorality reported to Paul.[68] In the remainder of the cases with independent constructions, ὥστε is used within the discourse to bring into focus Paul's point in his argument. Sometimes this argument runs only one or two verses. Thus in 1 Cor 3:5–7 the ὥστε in 1 Cor 3:7 succinctly summarizes Paul's point using the exact language of the preceding verses.[69] Likewise, the ὥστε in 1 Cor 4:5 brings into clearer focus

---

(presented at the SBL Greek Language and Linguistics Section, San Francisco, Calif., 2011), as stated in the abstract. I do not have a copy of Levinsohn's paper nor did I attend that session. My description of ὥστε described below is over ten years old, and is confirmed by Levinsohn's analysis.

66. The difference is that a summary statement contains elements that are reflective of the entire argument (see 1 Cor 3:7). On the other hand, a general statement is one that brings Paul's concern (in the argument) into clear focus (without summarizing the entire argument).

67. See particularly 3:7, 21; 5:8; 7:38; 10:12; 14:39 as Paul's own slogans. The function of ὥστε argues against the use of a Corinthian slogan in 14:22, as suggested by Johanson ("Tongues") and Thomas Gillespie, "A Pattern of Prophetic Speech in First Corinthians" *JBL* 97 (1978): 74–95 at 81.

68. Here the meaning is essentially "namely..." or "to the effect that...." The NRSV renders it "for" which is a rather poor rendering: Ὅλως ἀκούεται ἐν ὑμῖν πορνεία, καὶ τοιαύτη πορνεία ἥτις οὐδὲ ἐν τοῖς ἔθνεσιν, ὥστε γυναῖκά τινα τοῦ πατρὸς ἔχειν. "It is actually reported that there is sexual immorality among you, and of a kind that is not found even among pagans; for a man is living with his father's wife." Even here the idea of result is not totally absent.

69. We must note the repeated language in 3:7 that refers back particularly to 3:6:

Paul's point in 4:1–4.[70] In 1 Cor 5:8 ὥστε introduces an exhortation which is the main thrust of Paul's argument in 5:1–7. After 5:8, Paul's argument immediately continues (5:9–13). In 2 Cor 4:12 the ὥστε functions to clarify Paul's point in his discussion (4:1–11) and even prepares for that which continues in 4:13—5:10.[71] The back-to-back use of ὥστε in 2 Cor 5:16 and 5:17 emphasizes the main thrust of Paul's argument to that point (5:11–15). After 5:17, Paul's argument continues in 5:16–19. Paul uses a ὥστε in 1 Cor 7:38 as a general statement to his argument in 7:28–38. Likewise in 11:33 the ὥστε functions to present Paul's concerns concisely in the form of a supposition with a command. The argument unit extends from 11:17 through 11:32. In 1 Cor 14:39 the ὥστε functions to generalize Paul's concerns by providing a final exhortation. This particular ὥστε functions either to distill the second major unit of ch.14, namely, 14:26–38, or alternatively to summarize Paul's entire argument in ch. 14, as Gordon Fee argues: Paul "brings the preceding argument to a conclusion by way of a three-part summation. It is signaled by the strong inferential conjunction 'so then,' common to this letter. . . ."[72] In 1 Cor 15:58 ὥστε functions to conclude the whole argument of ch.15, although Margaret Mitchell has argued that 15:58 summarizes the entire epistle to this point(!),[73] a view that supported by Kenneth Bailey's extensive study.[74]

Thus far this survey of ὥστε suggests that it functions markedly to articulate the point that Paul is making. In a sense it represents the "distillation" of his main concern. Thus, it is not surprising that ὥστε often introduces an exhortation. This exhortation adequately generalizes Paul's central concern(s) in the argument. It should also be noted that the lines of argument that ὥστε generalizes vary in length. Sometimes they are short and span only a few verses. At other times ὥστε introduces a general statement which governs long segments or perhaps an entire chapter. It is notable that ὥστε spans increasingly longer and longer sections in 1 Corinthians. Lastly,

---

φυτεύω, ποτίζω, αὐξάνω.

70. In 4:5 the entire verse should be seen as the general statement since the sentences which follow the initial clause with ὥστε build upon it. 4:5 not only relates to 4:4, but to 4:1–2 as well: Paul and others are steward slaves and are only judged by the Lord.

71. The second part of 4:12 ("life is at work in you") is difficult to understand unless it pertains to Paul's larger argument and concerns, which supports the generalizing function of ὥστε.

72. Fee, *First Epistle*, 712.

73. Mitchell, *Paul and the Rhetoric of Reconciliation*, 290. She describes the function of 15:58 in her rhetorical outline, "ἐπίλογος *(Conclusion/Summation) to the Argument in the body of the letter.*"

74. Bailey, *Paul through Mediterranean Eyes*, 475–76.

it should also be said that ὥστε can mark either the relative conclusion to Paul's argumentation or some intervening point in Paul's argument.

In 1 Corinthians three other instances of ὥστε occur that are very significant: 3:21, 10:12, and 11:27. These cases are most like 14:22 in that ὥστε immediately follows authoritative teaching material, whether OT Scripture or Jesus traditions. In each case, as we would expect, the ὥστε generalizes or recapitulates Paul's concerns as relates to his broader argument. But more than this, the ὥστε *does not particularly relate or pertain to the authoritative/ traditional material*. Thus, Paul used ὥστε in 3:21 to summarize his argument in 3:1-18 while essentially not referring to two Scripture references in 3:19-20 that nevertheless support his overall argument.[75] In other words, ὥστε does not specifically relate immediately or directly to the Scripture that Paul just quoted. In the next example, after Paul has been working with OT events in relation to the Corinthians in 10:1-11, he then in 10:12 uses ὥστε to state the thesis of his argument. However, as in 3:21, the ὥστε in 10:12 does not function specifically with the traditional material immediately preceding.[76] In the final example, the ὥστε in 11:27 follows Paul's discussion of Jesus' teaching on the last supper in 11:23-26, but pertains more thematically to the opening material of his argument in 11:17-22. In other words, the ὥστε in 11:27 does not draw a conclusion from the immediately preceding traditional material concerning Jesus, but rather from the whole section (11:17-26).

If this evaluation of ὥστε is correct, then interpreters have been misled to consider 14:22 as *particularly* or *solely* relating to 14:21. Paul's use of ὥστε in 1 and 2 Corinthians would indicate that the conjunction has a broader discursive function to signal conclusion rather than immediate causation (i.e. building immediately from the preceding verse). The conjunction functions to bring Paul's larger argument into clearer focus. Put another way, ὥστε represents a generalizing, sometimes even summarizing, statement of an argument unit. Additionally, when one considers how ὥστε functions

---

75. In 3:18 Paul exhorts the Corinthians in such a way that reminds one of 14:20. In both places, OT Scripture follows this exhortation. In 3:19, however, γάρ is present to suggest the Scripture references are used in support of Paul's exhortation. In 14:21 there is no conjunction present, but instead an authoritative statement. This would suggest that 14:21 is an example of a prophetic pronouncement.

76. This case is also analogous to ch. 14 in that Paul argues until his conclusion midway in 10:12-13 (as in 14:21) and then continues in 10:14—11:1 (as in 14:26-40). That 1 Cor 14:20-25 is the mid-point in Paul's argument in ch. 14 is confirmed by a discourse analysis of the chapter: these verses form a transition from a discussion of the nature and function of tongues and prophecy (14:1-19) to specific instructions for community worship in relation to tongues and prophecy (14:26-40).

after Scripture or Jesus traditions, ὥστε never summarizes or particularly relates to this material.

For the interpretation of 14:22, the implication is that ὥστε in 14:22 serves to generalize or summarize Paul's argument, and this argument extends back to at least to 14:1, and possibly even 13:1. The reason for this conclusion is that 14:22 juxtaposes tongues *and* prophecy, and Paul has deliberately juxtaposed the pair throughout 14:1–19. Chapter 14 begins with a very pointed alternation between prophesying and tongue speaking, which is primarily one of contrast.

| | | |
|---|---|---|
| 14:1a | Pursue love. | |
| 14:1b | Now [δέ] you are seeking spiritual things [πνευματικά], | |
| | Prophesying | Tongue speaking |
| 14:1c | but [δέ] *seek* more in order that [ἵνα] you prophesy. | |
| 14:2 | | For [γάρ] the one speaking in a tongue does not speak to people but to/for a god/God. For no one comprehends/listens, but [δέ] with a spirit/the Spirit he speaks mysteries. |
| 14:3 | Alternatively [δέ] the one prophesying speaks to people for edification and encouragement and consolation | |
| 14:4a | | The one speaking with a tongue edifies himself. |
| 14:4b | Alternatively [δέ] the one prophesying edifies the church. | |
| 14:5a | | Now [δέ] I want you all to speak with tongues |
| 14:5b | but [δέ] *I want* more in order [ἵνα] that you prophesy. | |
| 14:5c | And [δέ] greater is the one prophesying | |
| 14:5d | | than the one speaking in tongues, unless [ἐκτὸς εἰ μή] he translates, in order that [ἵνα] the church receives edification. |

The juxtaposition and development of Paul's points are marked by seven instances of the conjunction δέ, which is difficult to translate consistently. Δέ marks a "new development" or next step in the argument; the semantics of contrast or comparison or something else must be determined by the context.[77] But Paul is clear in this regard because of the framing of 14:1–5 around purpose statements with ἵνα showing his preference for prophesying (14:1c, 5b) and that tongues speaking be translated (14:5d). Around this framing, Paul has then alternated between prophesying (14:1c, 3, 4b, 5b–c) and tongues speaking (14:2, 4a, 5a, 5d).

This alternation, however, is not for comparison, as if Paul presented both gifts equally or positively. To match Paul's explicit preference for prophesying are his unmistakably positive descriptions of prophesying. In 14:3 there is what I call "correlative emphasis" in the listing and specification of positive outcomes of prophesying using the repeated καί: prophesying leads to "edification *and* encouragement *and* consolation."[78] Then in 14:4b "the one prophesying edifies the church [ἐκκλησίαν οἰκοδομεῖ]." This view of mutual service and upbuilding is precisely what Paul had earlier established after affirming individual giftedness (12:7–11): "the body is not one member, but many" (12:14; cf. 12:12). In other words, in 12:25 Paul affirmed that God has so structured the body of Christ so that there be no schism (σχίσμα), but that its gifted "members should care for one another the same" (τὸ αὐτὸ ὑπὲρ ἀλλήλων μεριμνῶσιν τὰ μέλη). Conversely, tongue speaking is presented in ambiguous if not even in negative terms. This ambiguity is reflected in my translation of 14:2 precisely regarding 1) the source of the tongue speaking, 2) who receives/hears it, and 3) who benefits by it. The reason is that in 14:2 both "G/god" (θεῷ) and "S/spirit" (πνεύματι) lack an article and are unqualified. This is in marked contrast to Paul's previous unambiguous use of these terms to clearly refer to the Spirit and to the (one) God. For example, in chapter 12 Paul has consistently used the article to modify "Spirit" when referring to "the Spirit" (12:4, 7, 82, 92, 11) or has used other qualifiers like "of God" (12:3a), "holy" (12:3b), or "one" (12:132).

---

77. Runge, *Discourse Grammar*, 28–36. Particularly helpful is Runge's working with the example of 1 Cor 12:4–6 illustrating that δέ may need to be translated as "now" or "but" depending on the constraint of the context.

78. Correlative emphasis describes the marked set of two or more clauses, phrases, or words beyond the singular occurrence of a conjunction like καί and δέ. Correlative emphasis occurs through formal correlation using adverb-conjunction-particle combinations: εἴτε . . . εἴτε (*whether . . . or whether*); ἤ . . . ἤ (*either . . . or*); καί . . . καί (*both . . . and*); μέν . . . δέ (*on the one hand . . . on the other hand*); μήτε . . . μήτε (*neither . . . nor*); οὐ . . . ποτέ (*not . . . ever*); οὐκ . . . ἀλλά or δέ (*not . . . but*); οὔτε . . . οὔτε (*neither . . . nor*); ποτέ . . . νῦν (*once . . . now*); τε . . . καί (this and . . .); τε . . . τε (*as . . . so*) or (*not only . . . but also*).

Furthermore, we cannot assume that the Greek words for "spirit" and "god" are automatically in reference to the Holy Spirit and the one God, because in the immediate context of 1 Cor 12-14, let alone the broader book context, Paul has alerted the Corinthians to the existence of other or multiple "spirits" and "gods."[79] Within the context of 1 Cor 12-14, one can identify six ways in which Paul signals and acknowledges religious background in which religious phenomenon and influences (like spirits) impinged upon the Corinthians' understanding of God's working among them.

First, Paul has bracketed the whole discussion around "spiritual things/persons" and "ignorance" (12:1): "Now concerning spiritual things/persons, brothers, I don't want you to be ignorant" (Περὶ δὲ τῶν πνευματικῶν, ἀδελφοί, οὐ θέλω ὑμᾶς ἀγνοεῖν). Moreover, Paul returns to these terms ἀγνοέω ("to be ignorant" or "to ignore") and πνευματικός ("spiritual") at the close of the discourse signaled by 14:37. Since Paul used πνευματικός in 14:37 to refer to persons, it is likely that he had persons in view at 12:1, which should then be translated as "I do not want you to be ignorant about 'spiritual people.'" There is some ambiguity. An alternative translation would be "Now concerning spiritual things . . ." which would include both spiritual manifestations and persons.[80]

Second, Paul has framed the ensuing discussion by recalling the Corinthians' pagan past in 12:2, and how they were led astray "to the mute/voiceless idols" (πρὸς τὰ εἴδωλα τὰ ἄφωνα). That Paul drew attention to the "voicelessness" of the idols relates specifically to Paul's affirmation in 14:12 that the Corinthians are "zealous of spirits" (ζηλωταί ἐστε πνευμάτων) in types of inspired speech or tongues, because this was how the pagans heard from their mute idols, i.e. through the inspiration of spiritual people speaking for the god/idol.

Third, Paul immediately affirmed the "sameness" of the Spirit, the Lord, and God. In 12:4-6 Paul used the personal pronoun αὐτός indicating "same": "4There are varieties of gifts, but the *same* Spirit 5 and varieties of services and the *same* Lord 6 and varieties of workings but the *same* God who works all in every way." Paul strategically provided a "theology of spiritual gifts/manifestations" in 1 Cor 12 around the Triune God. Why? In view of a spiritual world in which various spirits were believed to inspire

---

79. In relation to idols and gods, Paul has done so pointedly in 8:1-6, esp. v.6: "there are those called gods whether in heaven or upon earth, just as there are many gods and many lords" (εἰσὶν λεγόμενοι θεοὶ εἴτε ἐν οὐρανῷ εἴτε ἐπὶ γῆς, ὥσπερ εἰσὶν θεοὶ πολλοὶ καὶ κύριοι πολλοί).

80. Paul used πνευματικός at 14:1 in reference to "spiritual *things/realities*" (cf. 2:13; 9:11; 10:3, 4). However, Paul has also used the term to refer to "spiritual people" (2:15; 3:1; cf. 15:44, 46).

certain phenomenon, Paul affirmed at the start God's unity in terms of "sameness"—in other words, there are not multiple competing or confusing spirits behind Christian giftedness/services/workings, but rather the singular (Triune) God.

Fourth, in addition to affirming the "sameness" of the Triune God, Paul emphasized the "oneness" of the Spirit at the start of his exposition: 12:9, 11, 13 (2x). In fact, in 12:11 Paul affirmed clearly that the origins of the various manifestations is "the one and the same Spirit." The cumulative effect is to clarify for the Corinthians that, even though they are "zealous of spiritual things" (ζηλοῦτε δὲ τὰ πνευματικά, 14:1) and "zealous of spirits" (ζηλωταί ... πνευμάτων, 14:10), there is but one holy fount from which the one body of the Church ought to drink: the Holy Spirit.

Fifth, in 12:10 Paul described a gift called "discernment of spirits" (διακρίσεις πνευμάτων) that Paul strategically placed after the gift of "prophecy" (προφητεία) and before "kinds of tongues" (γένη γλωσσῶν) and "translation of tongues" (ἑρμηνεία γλωσσῶν). Paul was acutely aware of other "spirits" that would influence spiritual utterances, and the need for the community's discernment. So, his strategic placement amidst prophecy and tongue speaking underscores Paul's message for the Corinthians.

Sixth, in the developing argument of chapters 12–14, Paul has framed chapter 14 with a command to "pursue love" (14:1a) and also acknowledged that the Corinthians are "seeking spiritual things/phenomena" (ζηλοῦ τε δὲ τὰ πνευματικά, 14:1b). Paul wanted the Corinthians to understand how to discern such things in the face of their being "zealous of spirits" (14:12a), a descriptive state of the Corinthians that is strategically followed with another repeated purpose statement "in order to that you edify the church" (14:12b). As Paul's argument continues, he will immediately repeat his plea that the Corinthians pray to translate tongues (14:13, 27–28; cf. 14:5d); he will argue that mind and spirit need to be held together when speaking in tongues (14:14–19); he will restrict tongues speaking to at most three (14:27); and finally he will call the Corinthians to control themselves: "the spirits of the prophets are subject to the prophets" (14:32). But amidst this call for translation and edification, Paul's tone changes to frustration at 14:20 due to the immaturity of the Corinthians: "Brothers [ἀδελφοί], stop being infantile in your thinking; but in regards to evil be infants, but in your minds be mature." The use of the vocative ἀδελφοί in 14:20 marks this change; however, as 14:6 and 14:26 indicate, the use of ἀδελφοί does not mark a completely new topic departure.[81] In 14:21, Paul strategically used Isa 28:11 to advance his argument; but how exactly?

---

81. The diatribal question at 14:26 (Τί οὖν ἐστιν, ἀδελφοί;) suggests a direct link

# ISAIAH 28:11 AS PAUL'S PROPHESYING IN CONTEXT

Paul quotes and interprets Isa 28:11–12 reordering it, changing words, and framing it as "prophecy." Because of this it is no wonder that interpreters have struggled to identify the text-type of Paul's quotation of Isa 28:11. In his careful study, C. D. Stanley has stated, "Determining the precise relationship between the wording of 1 Cor 14:21 and the text of the LXX is one of the greatest challenges in the entire corpus of Pauline citations."[82] Paul departs from the LXX and is much closer to the Masoretic text.[83] Some have argued that the apostle deliberately used Isa 28 because of its history as anti-Jewish *testimonia*,[84] although he adapted it here for his purposes.[85] Regardless of this possible background, E. Earle Ellis' view is sound: The passage is representative of a *pesher* method of interpretation, the goal of which is the application of Hebrew Scripture to the present community.[86] Anthony Thiselton agrees: "we argue that Paul combines exegesis and application" and "*Paul is simultaneously quoting and applying the passage*" (emphasis original).[87]

---

with 14:20–25. In both a corporate setting is described. In 14:6 the νῦν δέ likewise suggests Paul in 14:6–12 is building upon his discussion in 14:1–5. In both sections "edification" is Paul's concern.

82. Christopher D. Stanley, *Paul and the Language of Scripture: Citation Technique in the Pauline Epistles and Contemporary Literature*, SNTSMS 69 (Cambridge; New York: Cambridge University Press, 1992), 198. This quotation is found in Anthony C. Thiselton, *The First Epistle to the Corinthians: A Commentary on the Greek Text*, NIGTC (Grand Rapids: Eerdmans, 2000), 1120.

83. Fee surmises, "Paul follows neither the LXX nor the MT, although he is closer to the latter. Since there are some correspondences between this citation and the later (ca. 100 years) translation of Aquila (in the combined form ἑτερόγλωσσος, and in the inversion of 'tongues' and 'lips,' including the form ἐν χείλεσιν ἑτέρων), it is possible that Paul and he were both dependent on an earlier form of Greek text no longer available" (*First Epistle*, 679 n.20).

84. For a brief discussion see E. Earle Ellis, *Paul's Use of the OT* (Edinburgh: Oliver and Boyd, 1957), 108–13 and *Prophecy and Hermeneutics in Early Christianity*, WUNT 18 (Tübingen: Mohr, 1978), 182–87.

85. This is important since a *pesher* of Isa 28:11 is found at Qumran and has similarities to Paul's use of it here. Lanier is wrong to suggest that 14:22 is a midrash of 14:21. This erroneously leads him to treat 14:21 and 14:22 together in isolation. He argues that these verses speak of the Old Covenant where law is central, but still prophecy is superior to tongues; then, with 14:23 (οὖν) a new situation under grace exists in which again prophecy is better than tongues ("With Stammering Lips," 281). The problem is that the Law/Grace dichotomy is otherwise foreign to Paul's argument here.

86. Ellis, *Prophecy*, 179–81.

87. Thiselton, *First Epistle*, 1120 and 1122, respectively. Thiselton only

Many scholars have summarized in detail the differences between Paul, the MT, and the LXX.[88] In the charts below, I have displayed the texts involved to show where Paul has added using **bold**, what he has altered using underline, and leaving brackets [ . . . ] indicating material he has left out of his quotation:

| 1 Corinthians 14:21 | |
|---|---|
| NA27 | My translation |
| ἐν τῷ νόμῳ γέγραπται ὅτι | **In the law it is written**, |
| Ἐν ἑτερογλώσσοις καὶ ἐν χείλεσιν ἑτέρων λαλήσω τῷ λαῷ τούτῳ [ . . . ] | "With other tongues and with the lips of others I will speak to this people; [ . . . ] |
| καὶ οὐδ' οὕτως εἰσακούσονταί μου, λέγει κύριος. | yet **even so** they will not listen **to me**," says the Lord. |

| Isaiah 28:11–12 | | |
|---|---|---|
| NASB95 (based on MT) | LXX | LXX Translation |
| Indeed, He will speak to this people Through stammering lips and a foreign tongue, | διὰ φαυλισμὸν χειλέων διὰ γλώσσης ἑτέρας ὅτι λαλήσουσιν τῷ λαῷ τούτῳ | because of the contemptuousness of the lips, by means of another language: for they shall speak to this people, |
| [12 He who said to them, "Here is rest, give rest to the weary," And, "Here is repose,"] | [12 λέγοντες αὐτῷ τοῦτο τὸ ἀνάπαυμα τῷ πεινῶντι καὶ τοῦτο τὸ σύντριμμα] | [saying to them, 12 This is the rest to him that is hungry, and this is the calamity:] |
| but they would not listen. | καὶ οὐκ ἠθέλησαν ἀκούειν | but they would not hear. |

qualifies this with the possibility that Paul might have been using as *Vorlage* a Greek translation close to Aquila's as Origen maintained (*Philocalia*, 9); but, given the elaborate and contextually appropriate tweaking that we see, I find this very unlikely. The possibility that Paul here records a form of Aquila's translation is not as convincing as Conzelmann (*Commentary*, 242, see esp. n. 17) or F. F. Bruce would suggest (*I & II Corinthians* [NCBC; Grand Rapids: Eerdmans, 1971], 132–33). The text from Aquila (as Origen remembers it) is slightly different than Paul's (ἑτέροις instead of ἑτέρων). See Lanier, "With Stammering Lips," 268, n.30. One gets the impression that Origen was defending Paul's adaptation of the text. In any case, we must account for Paul's choice to use an Aquila-like Greek translation—a choice was made which version to use and such was applied to the Corinthian situation and in support of his argumentation.

88. Lanier has the most complete analysis of the text types ("With Stammering Lips," 283–84).

Fee summarizes the differences concisely as they pertain to 1 Cor 14:21 while at the same time explaining his interpretation:[89]

> To underscore his concerns Paul adapts the Isaiah passage in four ways. (1) He inverts the order of "stammering lips" and "other tongues" to put his interest, "other tongues," in first position. (2) He changes "stammering lips" to "the lips of others"; the "others" now being the Corinthian believers, whose speaking in tongues would have a deleterious effect on unbelievers. (3) In keeping with the MT, but against the LXX, Paul alters "the Lord will speak" to "I will speak" and concludes with the formula, "says the Lord," probably to increase its impact on the Corinthians. (4) Most significantly, he skips a considerable section in the Isaiah passage, picking up at the end of v. 12, where he modifies "and they would not hear (ἀκούω)," referring to the intelligible words of the Lord, to "and even so [referring now to the 'other tongues'] they *will not obey* (εἰσακούω) me." In Paul's context this refers to the outsiders of v. 23, who on hearing the Corinthian's speaking in tongues would declare them mad. For Paul such a reaction by unbelievers would thus "fulfill" this "word of the Lord"; . . .

It is helpful to understand Fee's interpretation in relation to the four stated differences he has observed. In what follows, I hope to show that there is another way to account for these differences that better depicts Paul's overall argument as expressed in 14:22 (*contra* Fee).

The first step in identifying how Paul might have envisioned Isa 28 to have some relationship with 1 Cor 14 is to determine the identity of the persons involved, how they are characterized in each respective context, and to note other potentially relevant information. In Isa 28 the people involved are the prophet Isaiah, "this people," their leaders, and those responsible for speaking other tongues. Who is "this people"? They are certainly the people of Jerusalem who were being led astray by their leaders (28:14; cf. 9:14–16). These leaders are "Priests and Prophets"—the religious leaders of the people (28:7). Those speaking other tongues are invading Assyrians (cf. Isa 8:7).

Next, how is each group characterized or how do they function? The prophet Isaiah is speaking the Word of the Lord to the leaders of Israel (28:9–14). Regarding the religious leaders we learn various details: 1) they are drunken and staggering while performing their religious functions, i.e., seeing visions and rendering decisions (28:7); 2) they are offended at the infantile level of Isaiah's message and contrast themselves with newly weaned

---

89. *God's Empowering Presence*, 239. The quotation is cited exactly as Fee has it.

children by use of two rhetorical questions (28:9); and 3) they mock Isaiah and his perceived pettiness by babbling back at him (28:10).⁹⁰ F. Delitzsch suggests that "in the repetition of the short words we may hear the heavy babbling language of the drunken scoffers."⁹¹ Lastly, what is the function of the Assyrians? They serve a rhetorical function of announcing impending judgment. They speak a different language than what the leaders are used to hearing, but *a language that was certainly understood to them dialectically.*⁹² What is important here is that the "other language" spoken was intelligible. Thus, the religious leaders will receive their instruction from someone different from Isaiah in a different tongue than they were used to speaking, and this is a message of judgment.⁹³

When we turn to 1 Corinthians, there are four groups of persons: Paul, his "spiritual" readers, gifted leaders, and the ἰδιώτης ("outsider"14:16) referred to as the ἕτερος ("other person" 14:17) along with the ἄπιστοι ("unbelievers" 14:23-24).⁹⁴ Since Paul joins ἰδιῶται and ἄπιστοι in 14:23-24,

---

90. The "babble" of Isa 28:10, 13 is important here (*ṣaw lāsāw saw lāsāw qaw lāqāw qaw lāqāw*). For the options on how to interpret it for 1 Corinthians, see Lanier, "With Stammering Lips," 260-64 and Grudem, "Prophecy and Tongues," 382-86. In any case, it is difficult to determine how Paul would have understood these babblings; the various translations of the Hebrew even struggled how to render them.

91. *Isaiah*, 2 vols., Vol. VII of *Commentary of the OT in Ten Volumes* by C. F. Keil and F. Delitzsch (repr. Grand Rapids: Eerdmans, 1976), II.304. Grudem agrees that 28:10 is spoken by the scoffers ("Prophecy and Tongues," 385-86).

92. Delitzsch explains, "The Assyrian Semitic had the same sound in the ear of an Israelite, as Low Saxon (a provincial dialect) in the ear of an educated German" (*Isaiah*, II.305). The way in which the scenario is depicted by the writer of Isaiah is that of reciprocating judgment, i.e., the sin is met with an corresponding judgment. See, e.g., Isa 5:8-17.

93. A. van Selms argues that the babble can be worked back to a series of Assyrian commands such as would be directed towards slaves ("Isaiah 28:9-13: An Attempt to give a New Interpretation," *ZAW* 85 [1973]: 332-39).

94. The ἰδιώτης or outsider in 14:16 should be considered a believer who does not speak in tongues. I do not agree with Bruce who argues that the ἰδιῶται in 14:23 are non-Christians, although 14:16 refers to a Christian (*I & II Corinthians*, 133); F. W. Grosheide argues the two are different as well: in 14:16 it refers to one not having the gift of tongues and in 14:23 it refers to those who do not know what is going on (*The First Epistle to the Corinthians*, NICNT [Grand Rapids: Eerdmans, 1953] 332). But, this is splitting hairs. Since ἰδιώτης is such a unique word, R. G. Brachter argues it must have the same meaning throughout (*Translator's guide to Paul's First Letter to the Corinthians*, Helps for Translators [London/New York/Stuttgart: United Bible Society, 1982] 316). Theissen would agree: "the outsider is a participant in the liturgy" (*Psychological Aspects*, 76). Also the ἄπιστοι or unbelievers in 14:22-24 should not be characterized as dis-believers. As Fee says, "it can only refer to those outside the Christian faith," not implying a rejection of faith; *The First Epistle to the Corinthians*, NICNT (Grand Rapids: Eerdmans, 1987) 681, n. 33.

they should be grouped together. Thus, we have Paul, the Corinthians, the "spiritual" ones or leaders at Corinth, and the ἰδιῶται or ἄπιστοι. How are each described? Paul was instructing the Corinthians and chastising the spiritual ones (leaders) not to be children (14:20).[95] The spiritual people are speaking in tongues in a way that is confusing to outsiders (14:16–17, 23). The outsider cannot say "amen" in 14:17; moreover, the outsider/unbeliever in 14:23 identifies the tongue speaking Corinthians as in a pagan religious state ("You are in religious mania" μαίνεσθε).

In fact, a significant number of intertextual features connect the main human participants in the communicative context of Isaiah and 1 Corinthians:

| Isaiah 28 | 1 Corinthians 14 |
| --- | --- |
| 1) Isaiah<br><br>• prophet<br>• instructing them in such a way analogous to children (28:9b, 10,13)<br>• forecasting a scenario of what will be | 1) Paul<br><br>• a prophetic pronouncement using "says the Lord"<br>• dissuading Corinthians from childishness (13:11; 14:20), and having to give step-by-step instructions (14:26–33)<br>• forecasts two scenarios in 14:23–25 |
| 2) "this people" = God's people, Israel<br><br>• here led astray by Priests and Prophets (28:7, 14)<br>• drunk and staggering (28:7)<br>• not able to give judgment (28:7)<br>• unorderly (28:7–8) | 2) The Church, People of God<br><br>• religious "elite" or tongue speakers leading astray the congregation (14:37–38; cf. 3:1)<br>• perceived as in religious "madness" (14:23)<br>• problems judging prophecies (14:29)<br>• Paul commands them to be orderly (14:33, 40) |

---

95. Earlier Paul had chastised the Corinthians as still being like babes (1 Cor 3:1–3).

| | |
|---|---|
| 3) Speakers of another tongue (Assyrians)<br><br>• speak some unfavorable message (28:10, 13) | 3) "Others" = outsiders and unbelievers who speak another recognizable (intelligible) tongue<br><br>• speak a unfavorable message (14:23—"you are in religious madness") |

Paul and Isaiah were each prophesying and instructing religious leaders acting disorderly. Isaiah is perceived to instruct them as newly weaned babes; likewise Paul instructs the Corinthians not to be babes. Furthermore, in both settings "others" speak a message to the religious leaders in another tongue; in the case of Isaiah it is the Assyrians and in the case of 1 Corinthians it is outsiders or unbelievers.

Does Paul's adaptation of the Isaiah passage (as elucidated above by Fee) lend itself to such an intertextual reading? It would seem so. Importantly, the content of Paul's prophesying in 14:21 is framed by "other tongues" by being preposed in relation to the verb. If some Corinthians were speaking an unintelligible tongue (this was Paul's complaint in 14:6-19), then the "other tongues" in 14:21 would be *intelligible* tongues. In the context of Isaiah, the Assyrians spoke a different but intelligible tongue. Paul had just urged the spiritual Corinthians to pray for the ability to translate their tongues (14:13), to conjoin spirit and mind in prayer and thanksgiving (14:14-17), to speak intelligible words in the church to instruct others by following his own example (14:18-19), and to not be childish with their "minds" (φρέσες 14:20).[96]

Second, this reading is also supported by the fact that Paul uses "lips of others [ἑτέρων]." Paul has already explained who the others are; "the other"

---

96. The word φρήν here is a *hapax legomenon*. It is a Greek anthropological term denoting that capacity of a person lost when under the influence of passion, etc., in this case religious ecstasy. When a person enters into an ecstatic state his or her φρήν is rendered useless. Josephus combines the disobedience of the mind with being out of one's mind (παρακοπὴ φρενῶν καὶ μανία) due to passion for a women (J.W. I.506). See the extensive review of the term and its cognates in the Greek literature starting with Homer by Georg Bertram, "φρήν κτλ." *TDNT* IX.922-24. In the LXX the word occurs infrequently, but refers to deficient mental capacity due to naivety, idolatry, adultery, passion, or youthfulness (e.g. Prov 6:32; 7:7; 9:4; 11:12; 12:11; 18:2; 3 Macc 4:16; 5:47).

It is also noteworthy that παῖς is used in 14:20, since παίζω is used in 10:7 to describe the idolatrous revelry of Israel. In other words, what Paul was arguing is that the Corinthians' childish focus on glossolalia, which he clarifies is mainly recognized as a pagan practice (14:22), could lead them into idolatry, which Paul has framed this whole discussion of spiritual gifts (12:2).

(ὁ ἕτερος) is the outsider (14:16–17).[97] The use of the plural in 14:21 does not detract from this reading, but actually supports it since in 14:23 "outsiders" and "unbelievers" are used in the plural when pronouncing judgment, whereas in 14:24 they are in the singular when convicted and converted.[98]

Third, Paul supplies three statements of authority in 14:21 when quoting from Isaiah: "law," "it is written," and "says the Lord." The quotation is extremely authoritative. Furthermore Paul's addition of "says the Lord" clearly demarcates the speech act as a prophetic statement.[99] Thus, Paul in 14:21 has spoken as a prophet—a role he was more than willing to accept for himself (Gal 1:15–16; cf. Isa 49:1–6; Jer 1:5). But more than this, he has spoken prophetically against the Corinthians.[100] At the same time he has given them a model of what appropriate prophecy is: interpretation and directed application of Scripture to a given ecclesial situation. "Prophecy" is exactly what Paul has been urging for Corinthians to do all along (14:1c, 5b–c).[101]

---

97. Grosheide also recognizes the significance of the repeated "other" (ἕτερος) here (*Corinthians*, 330).

98. To my knowledge there is no other explanation for Paul to switch from plural (14:23) to singular (14:24).

99. This expression is found six hundred and nineteen times in the LXX, the majority of which are in the Prophets. It is found twelve times in the NT: Acts 7:49; 15:17; Rom 12:19; 14:11; 2 Cor 6:17–18; Heb 8:8–10; 10:16; Rev 1:8.

100. A similar polemical use of Isa 28:11 is found at Qumran. "With stammering tongue and uncircumcised lips" (adapted from Isa 28:11) was used to "brandmark foes (1QH 2.18–19) and lying prophets (1QH 4.16) who seduce people." Theissen suggests that the "foreign tongue" used by these enemies is Greek. In other words, "[t]hese passages are scarcely thinking about speaking in tongues" (*Psychological Aspects*, 74, n.32). Paul's use of the passage is different, both in the formal introduction of the material (although 1 QH is poetry) and in keeping with the context of Isaiah.

101. For a comprehensive treatment of the phenomenon of ancient prophecy, see the work by David E. Aune, *Prophecy in Early Christianity and the Ancient Mediterranean World* (Grand Rapids: Eerdmans, 1983). However, very little attention is given to 1 Cor 14:21–22 (202; 343, n.31; cf. 12–13), because 14:21 is not considered prophetic. David Hill's treatment is of ch.14 is more helpful: Paul is combating Hellenistic prophetic influences (*NT Prophecy* [Atlanta: Knox, 1979], 121–35, esp. 121). Aune is interested, though, in challenging Ellis by arguing that inspired exegesis was *not* performed by Christian prophets. I would maintain, however, that 1 Cor 14:21 represents a convergence of "Christian Prophecy and Charismatic Exegesis" (a topic which Aune treats in an appendix [339–46]). Whether this ultimately supports Ellis's thesis (*contra* Aune) cannot be settled here. The form that Paul's prophecy in 14:21 takes may be rhetorically conditioned by the need of the Corinthian community. They were lacking in moral conduct and discipline (chs.5–6). So, throughout 1 Corinthians Paul cites OT scripture (1:19, 31; 2:9; 3:19; 9:9; 10:7–11; 15:45, 54). Furthermore, Paul's position in the community was being questioned (chs.1–4; ch.9; 14: 36–37; cf. 15:8–11). Thus, in one prophetic announcement using Isa 28 Paul is able to draw attention to his authority and the written word's.

Fourth, the modification of the text of Isaiah by Paul is not an adjustment from the "Lord's intelligible speech" to unintelligible speech (as Fee suggests), but *rather to the intelligible speech of "others."* We must remember that the Assyrian language was intelligible to the Israelites/Hebrews. Furthermore, the change to first person singular (εἰσακούω) is critical, because it underscores Paul's voice for God in urging the Corinthians to obey him as the mouthpiece of God.[102]

How then does 14:20–25 function? Verse 20 marks Paul's exasperation with some of the Corinthians. Verse 20 is a special plea using a rhetorical *topos* that is seen earlier in the argument: child-adult or maturity language (13:8–12; CF. 3:1–3). This prompts Paul in 14:21 to speak prophetically to these Corinthian tongue enthusiasts adapting Isa 28:11. "This people" refers particularly to the spiritual enthusiasts who are given a chastising message in a tongue different (i.e., intelligible speech) from what they themselves disruptively employ. Such a message is that the Corinthians, if all were to speak in tongues, are seen as being in a pagan religious ecstasy or "mad" (14:23). Verse 22 is the general point that Paul has been making in 14:1–21: prophesy is a sign demarcating believers whereas unintelligible tongues are not a sign of believers, but of unbelievers. In 14:23 Paul illustrates his prophesying in 14:21: outsiders declare the Corinthians as religiously mad/ecstatic. To urge the Corinthians to a more appropriate expression—prophecy—Paul showed alternatively the converse situation in 14:24–25: if all prophesy, an outsider would be convicted and announce intelligibly, "Truly God is among you!" (ὄντως ὁ θεὸς ἐν ὑμῖν ἐστιν).[103]

---

102. Paul's authority in the community had been questioned (chs.1–4; ch.9; cf.15:8–11).

103. One other striking feature is that Paul has argued in 14:19 that he would rather instruct others (ἄλλους- to be distinguished from ἕτερος?) using "five intelligible words" than by using ten thousand words in a tongue. Is it a coincidence that Paul, via the outsider in 14:25, speaks so few words, perhaps even five, to the Corinthians, urging them to a better understanding of the use of their gifts? "God is truly among you" ("Οντως ὁ θεὸς ἐν ὑμῖν ἐστιν). What looks like six Greek words is arguably only five, since ἐν ὑμῖν could be considered a single unit. This is potentially correct because 1) post-positive conjunctions do not always divide a prepositional phrase, thus suggesting prepositional phrases are a cohesive speech unit, and 2) the only word which cannot be used independently among these is the preposition ἐν; to be used in a sentence ἐν must have an object, whereas the definite article can be used independently and a post-positive conjunction will separate it from its substantive.

## CONCLUSION

In 14:20–25 Paul generalizes his main concerns and makes a transition.[104] This unit serves to conclude Paul's main concerns in 14:1–19; it does so with a prophetic punch. It also prepares for Paul's admonitions about the Corinthian corporate worship experience in 14:26–38. In other words, in 14:20–25 the "indicative" and the "imperative" of Paul's argument meet. If this is correct, then it is not surprising that Paul has so carefully and rhetorically constructed his presentation in ways that many have noted. The confusion, however, has resulted from three difficulties: 1) not appreciating the pagan religious background of "signs" and "vocal utterances;" 2) not properly understanding the discourse function of independent ὥστε to conclude and generalize extensive argumentation; and 3) not fully understanding Paul's prophetic reconfiguration of Isa 28:11 to apply to the Corinthians' situation.

It would appear that at least some of the Corinthians were influenced religiously and socially by such religious practices in which they once participated, which is why Paul had framed the whole argument in their pagan past (12:2). As many interpreters would agree, leadership had become defined by "spiritual status" (12:1; 14:37) rather than by mutual service, love, and edification that can result with inspired intelligibility, clarity, and order in worship. These two concerns—unity in the one God and mutual edification through love—were foreign to religious settings outside of the Christian communities, excepting Judaism. One could imagine the various motivations that would accompany the diverse religious manifestations; not least of all, they would elicit prestige and increased social standing. That the Corinthians were also highly motivated to display these gifts is suggested by the use of the verb ζηλόω (12:31; 13:4; 14:1, 39) and the cognate noun ζηλωτής (14:12). What was needed was a "functional substitute," and Paul pushed strongly for prophesying. Thus, Paul attempts to redirect their zeal to prophesy in 14:39, although he does so only after having provided them with *his own appropriate demonstration of prophecy* from Isa 28:11.

---

104. Engelson agrees when he says of 14:20 "[t]he appeal concludes the arguments of the preceding sections (vss. 1–19), but introduces at the same time a new line of thought, but one related to the same theme" (*Glossolalia*, 162).

# 8

# "Do Not Be Conformed to This Age"

## Rom 12:1–2 in Light of Environmental Determinism[1]

### T. MICHAEL W. HALCOMB

IT WAS NEARLY A decade ago, during my undergradate studies, that I first encountered the name "Ben Witherington III." Unsurprisingly, that encounter occurred with one of Ben's books. A couple of years later, this time while doing graduate work, I had the opportunity to take an exchange course at Asbury Theological Seminary, and it was there that I first met Ben in person. Listening to him lecture was not only inspiring but edifying. Despite the fact that the course was structured as a summer intensive, I remember leaving each day intellectually energized and spiritually fed. That class, NT 621: Exegesis of Romans, was something of a defining moment in my life as a student of the Bible. In fact, as soon as I finished my MDiv, I applied to Asbury's graduate program and started working on another masters degree. I took as many classes with Ben as I could.

Once I finished at Asbury I took a year off and then began applying to PhD programs. I had several very nice offers from various institutions but

---

1. An earlier version of this paper titled "Which Pattern, Which World?: A Thought Experiement Concerning the Moral Climates in Paul's Letter to the Romans," was presented at the Stone-Campbell Journal Conference at Lincoln, Ill (Saturday, Apr., 14, 2012).

one of the biggest draws to return to the Wilmore (Ky) campus was to work with Ben. Looking back on my time as a PhD student, I am probably aware now more than I have ever been that—to borrow a phrase from Ben—"we all stand on the shoulders of those who have gone before us." Having studied with some of the greats, such as George Kennedy and C.K. Barrett among countless others, I consider it a wonderful privilege to stand in that line of tradition and have it passed on to me. I hope that as a scholar and churchman I can continue to uphold and pass on this legacy.

Ben, I'm thankful for the many inspiring—and challenging—experiences I've had with you at Asbury. It has also been a joy—athough at first it was a little intimidating—to have both you and Ann in Sunday school over the last year or so. I offer the following exploration in your honor, Ben, an essay on Romans, the epistle I first heard you lecture on. Much like Wesley's experience with Romans, hearing those lectures left my heart strangely warmed and help set me on a path that opened up a new world of possibilities for my life and ministry. Thank you.

One of the practical outworkings of the doctrine of eschatology is often summed up in the maxim "What you believe about the end determines how you live in the present."[2] While for those of faith there is certainly merit to placing stock in the promise of Christ's return, the push in Christianity for a beyond-robust, future-oriented theology, has had some devastating effects. One of these unfortunate outcomes has been blindness to Paul's theology of two competing present tense spiritual realms. Indeed, after reading Paul's epistle to the Romans with these factors in mind, it might even be said

---

2. Such views can be found in the works of Albert Schweitzer, Jürgen Moltmann and Wolfhart Pannenberg among others. Schweitzer's term "Practical Eschatology" captures the essence of this comment quite well. For an excellent treatment of this topic, see Ara P. Barasam, *Reverence for Life: Albert Schweitzer's Great Contribution to Ethical Thought* (New York: Oxford University Press, 2008), esp. 111–15. For an interesting critique of such robust eschatologies, see Bruce J. Malina, "Christ and Time: Swiss or Mediterranean?" in *CBQ* 51 (1989): 1–31. In this article, Malina questions whether or not ancient peasants, whose internal clocks were set to a "present" tense Mediterranean time, could have adopted the dense eschatologies that modern persons, who are obsessed with time, tend to project back on to them. Still, one should also see the widely heralded as "groundbreaking" work by Victor P. Furnish, *Theology and Ethics in Paul* (Nashville, TN: Abingdon, 1968). In this work, Furnish, though he locates Paul's ethics in theology, Christology and eschatology, contends that eschatology is the center of Pauline ethics. See also Henry M. Shires, *The Eschatology of Paul in the Light of Modern Scholarship* (Philadelphia, PA: Westminster Press, 1966) who says, ". . . we shall be concerned with how this [future] hope alters our present life in Paul's thinking. . . ." (103). Cf. Michael Gilbertson, *God and History in the Book of Revelation: NT Studies in Dialogueue with Pannenberg and Moltmann*, SNTSMS 124 (Cambridge: Cambridge University Press, 2003).

that Paul has a stout theology of the present that can be summed up in the maxim "What you believe about the present determines how you live in the present."

Before continuing, I should note that this essay is a "thought experiment."[3] within this thought experiment I am not rejecting wholesale the notion of eschatology in Paul's thought-world. Most certainly there are eschatological elements evident in Pauline theology. Instead, I am pushing back against such views just a bit, attempting to show that the apostle's present tense views of the relationship between theology and ethics are important.[4] A major goal of this essay is to explore the hypothesis that Paul's epistle to the Romans bears similarities to the concepts of climatic determinism and personal/social change that were so prevalent prior to, during, and after his lifetime in the ancient Greco-Roman world.

This experiment's point of departure is Rom 12:1–2. I will begin by reviewing key textual and exegetical facets of this pericope, particularly within the history of its interpretation. After this, I will attempt to locate and situate what I refer to as Paul's "Two Realms Theology" within its ancient cultural and literary contexts by garnering insights from ancient sources that speak to the topics of environmental determinism and change. Next, I will draw attention to the socio-rhetorical shape of these verses while also considering the context and occasion for Paul's epistle. Subsequently, I will attempt to connect the dots by synthesizing the aforementioned materials, which will lead directly into discussions concerning theology and ethics. Finally, a brief summary and concluding remarks will be offered.

---

3. "Thought Experiment" is a term coined first in Latin & German (*Gedankenexperiment*) and then morphed fully into German (Gedankenversuch; see also the synonym Versuch) before being translated into English. The thinker H. C. Örsted is believed to be the originator of this term. For more on this see J. Witt-Hansen, "H. C. Örsted, Immanuel Kant, and the Thought Experiment" in *Danish Yearbook of Philosophy* 13 (1976): 48–65.

4. Perhaps one of the best accounts given to-date regarding the relationship between the past, present and future of Paul's theology and ethics is given by Peter Oakes. See his *Reading Romans in Pompeii: Paul's Letter at Ground Level* (London: SPCK, 2009), esp. 166–71. Again, I am not rejecting the notion that Paul had no eschatology. Indeed, it seems clear that for Paul, the "age to come" that has broken into the present calls believers to live in a way that anticipates God's final reign in the future. The goal here is not to deny this fact. Instead, the aim is only to step back from that view for a brief moment to survey the landscape of Pauline theology and ethics, and to show that beyond the *parousia*, there are ways that individuals should live which are intrinsic to the worldly and spiritual realms in which they dwell and walk right now. As will be shown below, there are certain characteristics and mores embedded in each realm, which both find their origin and shape in the here-and-now.

## ROM 12:1–2 IN THE HISTORY OF INTERPRETATION

Any exegete of Rom 12:1–2 is bound to be aware of the linguistic idiosyncrasies embedded within these verses. Indeed, Paul's onslaught of unfamiliar words has proven to be a challenge for interpreters through the centuries. Additionally, there are historical, rhetorical and contextual facets within this handful of verses which merit the reader's attention. Here I shall interact with the works of other scholars on these matters and where necessary, offer critiques, affirmations, and/or new suggestions.[5]

At this point in his letter Paul utilizes the familiar request formula so prominent in ancient letters and paraenesis.[6] Interestingly, the particle

---

5. Against the view of Walter Schmithals who argues that Romans consists of two letters pieced together (parts A and B), where 12:1–2 is a portion of part B, I accept the unity of Romans as a whole. I discern no stitched-together epistle but rather as will be shown in the tables below, especially in terms of ethics, I find a great deal of continuity throughout the entire letter. For more on Schmithals's view, see his *Der Römerbief als historisches Problem*, SNT 9 (Gütersloh: Gerd Mohn, 1975). For a concise but forceful argument against Schmithals, see A. J. M. Wedderburn, *The Reasons for Romans* (London: T&T Clark, 1991), 25–29. See also, the work of Moo, *Epistle*, 5–9.

6. For an in-depth study of paraenesis in general but in relation to this pericope in particular, see C. J. Bjerkelund, *Parakalô: Form, Funktion, und Sinn der parakalo-Sätze in den Paulinischen Breifen* (Oslo: Universitetsforlaget, 1967). Bjerkelund finds in the Pauline paraenetic sections a formula that is structured as follows: 1) a παρακαλέω introduction; 2) a special construction of a singular verb, with a conjunction following οὖν or δέ and an object; and 3) The sentence often utilizes the vocative, is followed by a prepositional phrase and/or contains an infinitival or imperative clause preceded by ἵνα. These elements, of course, are noticeably at work in Rom 12:1–2. For more on paraenesis see Willi Marxsen, *Introduction to the NT*, trans. G. Buswell (Oxford: Basil Blackwell, 1968), esp. 95–104; T. Y. Mullins, "Petition as a Literary Form" in *NovT* 5 (1962): 46–54; G. Sigma, "Romans 12:1–2 and 15:30–32 the Occasion of the Letter to the Romans" in *CBQ* 53 (1991): 257–73 and Wedderburn, *Reasons*, esp. 70–86. Though I agree with Joseph A. Fitzmeyer, *Romans: A New Translation with Introduction and Commentary*, AB 33 (New York, NY: Doubleday, 1993), 637 that Rom 12:1–2 contains paraenetic material, I do not adopt his overall divisions of the text. For an interesting discussion on whether or not the terms "paraenetic" and "ethics" should be used at all, see Philip F. Esler, "Social Identity, the Virtues, and the Good Life: A New Approach to Romans 12:1–15:13" in *BTB* 33 (2003), 52–61. Esler's main complaint is that these terms have been so generalized that they have lost any sense of particularity. He appeals to the works of Martin Dibelius—the first to write on paraenesis in the field of NT studies and who follows closely the research of Rudolf Vetschera, *Zur Griecheschen Paränese* (Prague, Czech Republic: Rohlicek & Sievers, 1912)—contending that scholars who have used his terminology have veered from its original meanings. While this claim may be valid, Bjerkelund's work makes clear what paraenesis is and what it consists of. Certainly, it has to do with ethics/morals and is at work in Rom 12. For more on Dibelius, see his *James: A Commentary on the Epistle* (Philadelphia, PA: Fortress Press, 1976), 3 and *A Fresh Approach to the NT and Early Christian Literature* (London: Ivor

οὖν along with the initial verb παρακαλέω have sparked much controversy. Regarding the conjunction, debates focus on the distance to which it points backwards in the letter. Is this a remark referring to what was said at the end of chapter 11 or is it a totalizing statement that leads into a summary of chapters 1–11? To put it differently, is it rooted only in its immediate literary context or is it cumulative? Given that Paul in his other letters uses the phrase παρακαλέω οὖν ὑμᾶς in connection with his immediately preceding remarks (1 Cor 4:16; Eph 4:1), the broad review reading that some have espoused should be approached with caution.[7]

More evidence against placing too much back-looking weight on this pivotal particle can be found later in the sentence where Paul uses the term οἰκτιρμός, which is clearly linked back to the content of 11:30–32 and in particular the triple use of ἐλεέω.[8] Gaugler and Leenhardt have made a compelling case that despite the two different Greek terms, in Hebrew, these words share a common root in רחם.[9] Tied to this is the διά, which also points back to the contents of 11:30–32 and bears an instrumental force thus having the sense of "by means of God's compassion." In short, Paul is saying that the only reason he can make any type of appeal is because he himself has experienced the compassion of God (as he actually says in 12:3 and which acts as a reiteration of the point here).[10]

---

Nicholson and Watson, Inc., 1937), 217.

7. This is not at all to deny that themes present earlier in the letter are totally unconnected from this section of the work. In fact, as I will show, chapter 12 seems to be very much linked to chapters 1 and 8. However, acknowledging such connections does not merit placing so much stress on the οὖν of 12:1. Such links fail to provide the basis for a cumulative statement here. Indeed, the claim that Paul intended the division between chapters 11 and 12, despite the weight that most modern exegetes lay upon this division, seems to be lacking in evidence. For example, in the other two instances where Paul uses this phrase, they occur in the middle of letters (1 Cor 4:16; Eph 4:1). The case for a totalizing summary statement is more likely to be found at the end of an epistle rather than near the beginning or middle. Paul's phrase of choice for all-encompassing summaries seems not to be παρακαλέω οὖν ὑμᾶς but rather ὥστε followed by an admonition (1 Cor 15:58; Php 4:1; 1 Thess 4:18;). Again, the assertion that Paul reuses words from chapters 1–11 here as proof for such a view, seems rather weak. In fact, Paul uses words found earlier that are found after this section too (e.g. παρίστημι in 14:10 and 16:2). He also uses words here that are repeated later but which make no earlier appearance (e.g. παρακαλέω in 12:8, 15.30 and 16.17). Moreover, he uses words in previous sections that are not found here, some of which readers would expect to encounter if this is a major summarization of preceding materials (e.g. εὐαγγέλιον in 1:1, 9, 16; 2:16; 10:16; 11:28, etc.).

8. So James D. G. Dunn, *Romans 9–16*, WBC 38B (Dallas, TX: Word, 1998), 706–7 and Furnish, *Theology*, 102.

9. Ibid.

10. Kathy Ehrensperger, "Reading Romans 'in the Face of the Other'" in *Reading*

His appeal challenges the Romans to παραστῆσαι τὰ σώματα ὑμῶν (offer your bodies) as θυσίαν ζῶσαν (living sacrifices) that are holy and pleasing to God. This is not a matter to be taken lightly because such an act both defines and encompasses λογικὴν λατρείαν (spiritual worship).[11] It seems evident enough that παραστῆσαι has a cultic-sacrificial background to it. What makes this section confusing is that here in 12:1 Paul's use of σώματα seems to refer to the bodies of individuals while in 12:5 he appears to use it collectively. The question arises: How does individual sacrifice or abstinence of individual sacrifice affect the collective body?

One answer seems to be found be found in the oxymoronic phrase θυσίαν ζῶσαν (living sacrifice). By default a sacrifice assumes death. However, Paul says here that living sacrifices can be made. To unravel this perplexing statement he offers an extended analogy. The analogy suggests that just as persons have one body with many body parts there is also one body of faith with many limbs or body parts. When those body parts function according to the "grace given" to persons they are confessing "death" to their old selves, which is a testimony of and to the new "life" that the Spirit has initiated within them. Worship in and of the Spirit is what Paul deems λογικὴν λατρείαν (spiritual worship). Despite the debate over λογικός, it seems most appropriate to understand it in terms of functionality, which may have the connotation of "spiritual."[12]

---

*Romans with Contemporary Philosophers and Theologians*, ed. D. Odell-Scott, RTHCS (London: T&T Clark, 2007) is close to the mark when she says, "Thus, the sequence of Paul's argument in the transition from 11:36 to 12:1ff. is not coincidental but necessitated by the reference to the mercy of God which continues the theme of chapters 9–11, introduced in 9:15" (141).

11. Among exegetes λογικός has been widely debated. Basically there are two camps: 1) Those who understand this to mean "rational"; and 2) Those who take this to mean "spiritual." Of course, some have attempted to merge the two ideas. For a more detailed discussion of this, see Xavier P. B. Viagulamuthu, *Offering Our Bodies As A Living Sacrifice To God: A Study in Pauline Spirituality Based on Romans 12,1*, TGSS 7 (Roma: Pontificià Universita Gergoriana, 2002), 329–30.

12. Dunn, *Romans 9–16* has a great discussion of scholarly debate on this term. While many opt for readings such as "logical" or "reasonable" or "sensible act of worship," given the context and following the arguments of *BDAG* (598), *TDNT* (4:142–43), C. K. Barrett and Leon Morris, "spiritual" seems most accurate here. However, Douglas Moo's connection between the renewed "mind" and "logical" worship is worth acknowledging. See his, *The Epistle to the Romans*, NICNT (Grand Rapids, MI: 1996), 757. Still, as Barrett notes, "This is better described as 'spiritual worship' than 'rational,' for Paul is not thinking of what is meant in modern English by 'rational'" (213). Cf. 1 Pet 2:2, 5. See C. K. Barrett, *The Epistle to the Romans*, BNCT (Peabody, MA: Hendrickson Publishers, 1991), 213–14 and Leon Morris, *The Epistle to the Romans*, PNTC (Grand Rapids, MI: Eerdmans, 1988), 434. Other proponents of this view are Ernst Käsemann, *Commentary on Romans* (Grand Rapids, MI: 1980), 329; Otto Michel, *Der*

Another answer is found in comparing chapter 12 with chapters 1 and 8. Though I do not go as far as seeing the οὖν in 12:1 as a summary of all that has come before or as a transition point which moves from doctrine to praxis,[13] nevertheless, I do affirm connections with portions of the material that precede and follow it.[14] In fact, as Michael Thompson has shown, 12:1 actually "represents a reversal of the downward spiral depicted in Rom 1."[15]

---

*Brief an die Römer*, MeyerK 4 (Göttingen: Vandenhoeck & Ruprecht, 1978), 292; D. E. Hiebert, "Presentation and Transformation: An Exposition of Romans 12:1–2" in *Bsac* 151 (July-September, 1994): 317–18; F. J. Leenhardt, *L'Épître de saint Paul aux Romains* (CNTDS 6; Genève: Labor et Fides, 1995), 171; W. Sanday and A. C. Hedlam, *A Critical and Exegetical Commentary on the Epistle to the Romans*, ICC (Edinburgh: T&T Clark, 1962), 353; B. J. Malina and J. J. Pilch, *Social-Science Commentary on the Letters of Paul*, (Minneapolis, MN: Fortress Press, 2006), 276–77; V. P. Furnish, *Theology*, 103 and Michael J. Gorman, *Cruciformity: Paul's Narrative Spirituality of the Cross* (Grand Rapids, MI: Eerdmans, 2001), 247. One of the more detailed analyses of this term is found in Viagulamuthu, *Offering*, 329–362. Viagulamuthu, after surveying scores of ancient and contemporary literature concludes that textually and contextually, Paul's terminology of "spiritual worship" here is meant to have cultic ramifications.

13. Contra Morris, who says, "It is something of a pattern with Paul to begin a letter with a strong doctrinal section and follow this with an exhortation to live out the Christian faith. . . . But there can be no doubt that in these concluding chapters the way Christians live preoccupies the apostle to a far greater extent than in his earlier argument" (*Epistle*, 431). C. S. Dodd, *The Epistle of Paul to the Romans*, MNTC (London: Hodder & Stoughton, 1932), 188 and Matthew Black, *Romans*, NCB (London: Oliphants, 1973), 150 also make such arguments. This is even expressed in the early work Pseudo-Constantanius, *The Holy Letter of St. Paul to the Romans* [cited in G. L. Bray, *Romans*, ACCS NT VI (Downers Grove, IL: IVP, 2005), 296)]. Similar thoughts are found in the works of Ambrosiaster and Martin Luther. For more on Ambrosiaster's thoughts here, see Henricus I. Vogels, *Ambrosiastri Qui Dicitur Commentarius in Epistulas Paulinus: Pars Prima: In Epistulam ad Romanos*, CSEL 86 (Vienna, Austria: Hoelder-Pichler-Temsky, 1966), 293 and for more on Luther's comments, see Gilbert C. Meilaender, *The Theory and Practice of Virtue* (Notre Dame, IN: Notre Dame University Press, 1984), 107–08, 101–21.

14. Again, I accept Romans as a "whole" and therefore, see it as a unity. However, it appears that this unity is more fluid and/or dynamic than many suggest. For more on this, see footnote 5 above. Even Esler ("Social Identity"), who finds much fault with others who take this view, seems to up adopting it himself—albeit with some nuances. He writes, "Rather than positing some sharp distinction between 'theology' or 'doctrine' (in Romans 1–11) and 'ethics' or 'paraenesis' in Romans 12:1—15:13, we may treat Romans 1–11 as setting out Paul's view of the foundations, nature, and goals of the (re-categorized as Christ-believing) group of Judeans and non-Judeans in Rome he is addressing, while Romans 12:1—15:13 covers the norms necessary for the maintenance and enhancement of the identity of that group. Paul sets out his vision of reality-in relation to this particular group comprised of two sub-groups in Chapters 1–11 and then lays-out the norms which the members must accept and internalize for this vision to be realized" (55). It is still not clear to me that such a division is merited, however, Esler's view raises many good points.

15. Michael Thompson, *Clothed With Christ: The Example and Teaching of Jesus in*

While Thompson's findings are illuminating, he stops short of making the important connection regarding the two different realms being espoused in these sections, namely, the worldly and spiritual realms.

In fact, so strong is Paul's view of these opposing realms that he appears to be able to articulate a catalogue of ethical attributes or characteristics that are inherent to and ingrained in each of them. In other words, it appears that Paul believes that one's walk in the worldly realm presupposes certain types of ethical values, as does a one's walk in the spiritual realm. We shall look at this idea in greater depth below, along with a few connections of this pericope's link to chapter 8. For now, however, we need to consider the content of 12:2.

In the second verse of chapter 12, Paul begins with the negative command καὶ μὴ συσχηματίζεσθε τῷ αἰῶνι τούτῳ (And do not conform to this age . . .). While many translations take αἰών to mean "world," a rendering that on the surface would appear to bolster my overall argument, the word "age" is still probably a more accurate reading.[16] Thus, while αἰών is certainly not unrelated to κόσμος, it nuances such an idea by referring to this world's present state, which is characterized by ἀδόκιμον νοῦν (1:28). This suggestion is made even stronger by acknowledging Paul's use of the infinitive συσχηματίζεσθε, which is often used in ancient astronomical texts and has to do with seasons and natural phenomena. For example, Ptolemy, in his astronomical work *Tetrabiblos*, contends that all earthly ecosystems conform their habits and patterns to the movements of the sun and moon.[17] Using this same word and idea, Paul seems to have been arguing in a similar manner that humans conform their ways of thinking and living to the head of the realm in which they dwell (e.g. Self/Satan or the Holy Spirit).

---

*Romans 12.1—15.13*, JSNTSS 59 (England: Sheffield Academic Press, 1991), 82.

16. See Rom 1:24; 9:5 and 11:36.

17. Ptolemy, *Tetrabiblos* 1.24.4.6; 3.6.2.2, 13.9.5; 4.3.2.3, 3.4.3. This term also occurs in 1 Pet 1.14, where it has an ethical "two realms" sense to it. Those who are now believers, that is, persons walking in the Spirit Realm, should not do the things they did when they previously walked in the worldly realm. In Aristotle the term has to do with the conforming of definitions to their proper meanings in the process of argumentation. In other words, if one's opponent is misusing a word, it is the orator's job to demolish their use and definition of the word and to reconstruct it to make it conform to one's own meaning, which should inherently be clearer (*Topics* 151b8.). A similar meaning to this is found in Plutarch (2.83c). Ptolemy garnered much of his material from Hipparchus, who he called a "lover of truth." Hipparchus seems to have been a proponent of environmental determinism, which is discussed in more depth below. For more on Hipparchus and Ptolemy, see P. S. Laplace, *Exposition du système du monde* (Paris: Courcier, 1884), 413.

Paul further elucidates this point by using the term μεταμορφόομαι, which sets up a contrast.[18] This term is found in documents concerning nature and astronomy. This contrast is incredibly important as it points to Paul's view of two realms. One realm is conformed to this earthly age or realm and the other is conformed to the Spirit's realm. In the realm led by the Spirit, a new realm or realm of newness, there occurs a ἀνακαινώσις (renewing) of the mind, which is quite the opposite of the mind mentioned in 1:28. This renewal enables the believer to prove (δοκιμάζω) what God's good, pleasing and perfect will is.[19] Furthermore, this renewing of the "mind" seems to work in conjunction with offering one's "body" as a living sacrifice, which suggests conformity to the life of Christ.[20]

I want to suggest that at this point in the thought experiment we temporarily sideline the views of those who take Paul's language of "age" here—which is followed up by a contrast with the work of the Spirit—as drawing a distinction between the old "age of the Law" and the new "age of Christ." Instead, let us attempt to envision a setting where there is no pitting of ages based on ethnicity against one another in this section, especially where one is viewed as less because it is in the past and one is embraced because it is situated in the present.[21]

Alternatively, let us hypothesize that Paul is speaking of two present tense worldly and spiritual realms. Indeed, even in the preceding chapter Paul alludes to this when he says that God has imprisoned not just persons of a past or present age to disobedience, but *all* who are now living (11:32). By default, all share in the same present worldly fate whether Jew or Gentile. However, when persons allow themselves to be transformed by the Holy Spirit, which is proof that they are walking in and according to the ways of the spiritual realm, they will share not only a new life but also new ethics.

Having worked through some of the intricacies of Rom 12:1–2, more attention must now be given to Paul's "Two Realms" theory. In the following section we will review ancient ideals regarding environmental determinism

---

18. Against Karl Barth, *The Epistle to the Romans*, trans. E. C. Hoskyns (Oxford: Oxford University Pres, 1968), 424, who adopts the variant infinitival reading, I am going here with the imperatival reading, which is more strongly attested (P46, B, Alex., WH, etc.).

19. The appositional reading is accepted here.

20. Gorman, in his *Cruciformity*, touches the nerve of the matter when he says of Rom 12:1–2, "This is faith. Fundamental to this renewing of the mind—though Paul does not say it quite this way—is the adopting of the mind of Christ, a mind of cruciform love" (247).

21. Contra the proponents of "Two-Age Dualism" such Harry A. Hahne, *The Corruption and Redemption of Creation: Nature in Romans 8.19–22 and Jewish Apocalyptic Literature*, LNTS 336 (London, T&T Clark, 2006), 218.

and personal-social change. In turn, this will put us in a position to understand with more clarity Paul's "Two Realms" theory as espoused in Rom 12:1-2 in particular and the whole of Romans in general. To these matters we now turn our attention.

## ANCIENT VIEWS OF ENVIRONMENTAL DETERMINISM AND PERSONAL-SOCIAL CHANGE

In the early 19th and 20th centuries theorists tagged a name to a scientific phenomenon that had preceded them by thousands of years, a theory which they named Environmental Determinism.[22] This theory re-arose to fame with the publication of Ellen Churchill Semple's 1911 publication *Influences of Geographic Environment*.[23] In essence, Semple argued that because human beings are a "product of the earth's surface," they cannot correctly be studied apart from the grounds they till, they lands they travel or the seas that they tread upon.[24] Or as Allik & McRae have more recently stated the case, "From antiquity to the present day, people have assumed that personality traits are distributed geographically. Where one lives reveals what one is like. In part, these beliefs refer to stereotypes of national character and may reflect judgments about ethnicity or culture."[25]

As has already been noted, this theory contained roots that stretched back to antiquity. In fact, this idea's earliest attestation is found in Hippocrates' *Airs, Waters, Places*.[26] In chapter twelve of this work we find the

---

22. Known synonyms for this name are Climactic Determinism, Geographic Determinism or Environmental Conditioning. On this last term, which is nuanced quite a bit from author-to-author, see an interesting write-up by Daniel Hillel, *The Natural History of the Bible: An Environmental Exploration of the Hebrew Scriptures* (Columbia, SC: Columbia University Press, 2006), 23–24. See also Nancy Erhard, *Moral Habitat: Ethos and Agency for the Sake of the Earth*, SUNY (Albany, NY: State University of New York Press, 2007). Erhard shares a similar view saying, "I theorized that local topography and biota participate in (though they do not determine) many of the elements which are woven together in the construction of a set of cultural values and norms, its landscape of moral imagination" (94).

23. Ellen Churchill Semple, *Influences of Geographic Environment: On the Basis of Ratzel's System of Anthropo-Geography* (New York: Henry Hold and Company, 1911).

24. Ibid., 2.

25. Jüri Allik & Robert R. McRae, "Toward a Geography of Personality Traits: Patterns of Profiles Across 36 Cultures" in *JCCP* 35/1 (January, 2004): 13.

26. While this work is included in the Hippocratean Corpus, many have doubted that Hippocrates himself wrote it. For more on this debate, see Benjamin H. Isaac, *The Invention of Racism in Classical Antiquity* (Princeton, NJ: Princeton University Press,

following statement: "Now I intend to compare Asia and Europe and to show how they differ in every respect, and how the nations of the one differ entirely in physique from those of the other. It would take too long to describe them all, so I will set forth my views about the most important and the greatest differences."[27] Around this same time Herodotus was espousing similar views. In his *Histories*, he writes, "Apart from such precautions, they [the Egyptians] are, I believe, next to the Lybians, the healthiest people in the world—an effect of their climate, in my opinion, which has no sudden changes.[28] Herodotus is also responsible for the aphorism, "Soft land breeds soft men."[29] Columella is found to cite a different but similar apothegm from the "shrewd" and tough Carthaginians who said that "the farm should be weaker than the farmer" else "the land shall prove stronger and crush the master."[30]

Thales of Miletus shares similar thoughts saying, "I hold that Asia differs widely from Europe in the nature of all its inhabitants. . . . For everything in Asia grows to far greater beauty and size; the one region is less wild than the other, the character of the inhabitants is milder and more gentle. The cause of this is the temperate climate, because it lies towards the east midway between the risings of the sun, and father away than is Europe from the cold."[31] Aristotle commented that, "The nations inhabiting the cold places and those of Europe are full of spirit but somewhat deficient in intelligence and skill. . . . The peoples of Asia on the other hand are intelligent and skillful in temperament, but lack spirit, so that they are in continuous subjection and slavery. But the Greek race participates in both characters, just as it occupies the middle position geographically."[32]

---

2006), esp. 61n21. Near the end of writing this paper, I found the insightful work of Italian scholar Federico Borca. In his *Luoghi, Corpi, Costumi. Determinismo ambientale ed etnografia antica* (Roma: Edizioni di storia e letteratura, 2003), Borca engages several of the authors mentioned in this paper and wrestles with their views on environmental determinism in relation to ethnographic categorizing.

27. Hippocrates, *Airs, Waters, Places* 12.1–7. Translation taken from W. H. S. Jones, *Hippocrates: With an English Translation*, Vol. 1, LCL 147 (Cambridge: Harvard University Press, 1957), 104.

28. Herodotus, *Histories* Book II. Translation taken from G. Rawlinson, *Herodotus: The Histories* (Lawrence, KS: Digireads.com Publishing, 2009), 82.

29. *Histories* 9.22.

30. Columella, *On Agriculture* 1.9. Translation taken from H. B. Ash, *Columella: Extant Works: De Re Rustica, De Arboribus*, Vol. 1, LCL 361 (Cambridge: Harvard University Press, 1941), 49.

31. As cited in Hippocrates's, *Airs, Waters, Paces* 12.

32. Aristotle, Politics 7.1327b2. Translation borrowed from Hugh Rackham, *Aristotle*, Vol. 21, LCL 264 (Cambridge: Harvard University Press, 1944). A common theme

Plato echoes these sentiments when he gives advice on settling a territory. He says, "And that's another point about the choice of sites, Clinias and Megillus, that we mustn't forget. Some localities are more likely than others to produce comparatively good (or bad) characters, and we must take care to lay down laws that do not fly in the face of such influences. . . . The sensible legislator will ponder these influences as carefully as a man can. . . ."[33] In the Aristotelian text *Problems*, the entirety of chapter 14 is devoted to this matter. There we encounter the following:

> Why are those who live under conditions of excessive cold or heat brutish in character and aspect? Why are the Ethiopians and the Egyptians bandy-legged? Is it because the bodies of living creatures become distorted by heat, like logs of wood when they become dry? Why is it that in damp regions copulation is more likely to lead to the birth of female offspring? Why is it that those who live in airy regions grow old slowly, but those who inhabit hollow and marshy districts age quickly? Why are the inhabitants of warm regions cowardly, and those who dwell in cold districts courageous?[34]

Strabo also makes mention of such ideas. In his *Geography*, he says of the Gauls, "The whole race which is now called both 'Gallic' and 'Galatic' is war-mad, and both high-spirited and quick for battle, although otherwise simple and not ill-mannered. . . . Now although they are all fighters by nature, they are better as cavalry than as infantry; and the best cavalry-force

---

in Hellenistic works was the superiority of Greece and/or Rome over other lands and climates. One of Aristotle's students, Dicaearchus of Messana, once stated the matter poetically when he said, "If you've never seen Athens, your brain's a morass; If you've seen it an weren't entranced, you're an ass; If you've left without regrets your head's solid brass." Cited in Tony Perrottet, *Pagan Holiday: On the Trail of Ancient Roman Tourists* (New York, NY: Random House, 2003), 116.

33. Plato, *Laws* V.747d–e. Translation taken from Trevor J. Saunders, *Plato: The Complete Works*, ed. J. M. Cooper (Indianapolis, IN: Hackett Publishing Company, 1997), 1427.

34. Ps.-Aristotle, *Problems* 909a17—910b9. Taken from the work of C. A. Ruelle, H. Knoellinger & J. Klek, *Aristotelis Problemata physica*, trans. E. S. Forster (BiTeu; Leipzig; Teubner, 1922). A Chinese document dated to the second century BCE also advocates this idea. It says, "Now the water of [the state of] Qi is forceful, swift and twisting. Therefore its people are greedy, uncouth, and warlike. The water of Chu is gentle, yielding, and pure. Therefore its people are lighthearted, resolute, and sure of themselves." See Guanzi Zhong, *Guanzi: Political, Economic, and Philosophical Essays from Early China: A Study and Translation*, Vol. II, trans. A. Rickett (Princeton, NJ: Princeton University Press, 1998), 106.

the Romans have comes from these people. However, it is always those who live more to the north and along the ocean-coast that are the more warlike."[35]

Asclepiades of Bithynia, commenting on "the Brits" said that it was their "cold climate" that allowed them to "live one-hundred years."[36] Xenophon also spoke of climatic determinism. He once remarked, "Now the Chaldaeans carried each a wicker shield and two spears, and they were said to be the most warlike of the peoples in that region. They also serve for hire when anyone wants them, for they are fond of war and poor of purse; for their country is mountainous and only a small part of it is productive."[37] Pliny in his *Natural Histories* seconds such sentiments:

> ". . . Ethiopians by reason of the sun's vicinity, are scorched and tanned . . . in the frozen and icy regions the people have white skins and yellow hair long and growing downward and they are fierce and cruel by reason of the rigorous cold air. . . . But in the middle of the earth there is a wholesome mixture from both sides . . . manners of the people are civil and gentle . . . their wits pregnant and capable of all things within the compass of nature."[38]

Later, Tacitus would write, "When they are not entering on war, they spend much time in hunting, but more in idleness . . . by that curious incongruity of temperament which makes of the same men such lovers of laziness and such haters of quiet."[39] Polybius, in his *Histories*, speaks along the same lines when he says, "For we mortals have an irresistible tendency to yield to climactic influences: and to this cause, and no other, may be traced the great distinctions which prevail amongst us in character, physical formation, and complexion, as well as in most of our habits, varying with nationality or

---

35. Strabo, *Geography* 4.4.101–105. Translation taken from H. L. Jones, *The Geography of Strabo*, Vol. 2, LCL 50 (London: William Heinemann, 1923), 239.

36. Plutarch, *Epit.* 5.3. Taken from Hermann Diels, *Doxographi graeci: collegit recensuit prolegomenis indicibusque instruxit Hermannus Diels* (Berkeley, CA: University of California Press, 2008), 443–44. For more on this, see also the article by Elizabeth Rawson, "The Life and Death of Asclepiades of Bithynia" in *CQ* 32/2 (1982): 362n29.

37. Xenophon, *Cyropaedia* 3.2.7. Translation taken from Walter Miller, *Xenophon: Cyropaedia Books 1–4*, LCL 467 (London: William Heinemann, 1914), 187.

38. Pliny the Elder, *Natural Histories* 78. Translation is my own, which is a revised form of Philemon Holland's. See his work *Plinius Secundus: The Historie of the World*, Book II (London: Adam Islip, 1601).

39. Cornelius Tacitus, *Germania* 15. Translation taken from W. Peterson & M. Hutton, *Tacitus: Dialogueus, Agricola, Germania*, LCL 35 (London: William Heinemann, 1914), 284–85.

wide local separation."⁴⁰ The doctor Galen, using the theory of Posidonius, thinks along these same lines when he says:

> ". . . all broad-chested and warmer creatures and humans are more spirited by nature, the broad-hipped and colder, more cowardly. And environment contributes to considerable differences in human character with regard to cowardice, daring, love of pleasure or toil; the grounds for this are that the emotional movements of the soul follow always the physical state, which is altered in no small degree from the temperature in the environment."⁴¹

In a similar vein, Virtruvius, in his *On Architecture*, even argues that when constructing a building the climatic and geographical features of those who will use it must be taken into consideration. He notes, "Since then, it is climate which causes the variety in different countries, and the dispositions of the inhabitants, their stature and qualities are naturally dissimilar, there can be no doubt that the arrangement of buildings should be suitable to the qualities of the nations and people, as nature herself wisely and clearly indicates."⁴² Varro, in his treatise on agriculture and geography says, ". . . healthfulness, being a product of climate and soil, is not in our power but in that of nature, still it depends greatly on us, because we can, by care, lessen the evil effects."⁴³ Chrysippus is known for arguing this point too, upholding the view that environment shapes persons. He contended that the "delicate air in Athens rendered the Athenians clever" while in Thebes, where the air is "gross and heavy" the "Boeotians are proverbially sturdy and stupid."⁴⁴

Given the widespread view of environmental determinism in antiquity, many who felt trapped by their ecosystems attempted to break free

---

40. For more on Polybius and/or ancient views on climatic/environmental determinism, see Brian McGing, *Polybius' Histories*, OACL (Oxford: Oxford University Press, 2010) and Craige B. Champion, *Cultural Politics in Polybius's Histories* (Berkeley, CA: University of California Press, 2004).

41. Galen, *De Placitis Hippocratis et Platonis* F169f. Evidently, this view is supported too by Panaetius Fg 76. For more on this, see Frank W. Walbank, *Polybius, Rome and the Hellenistic World: Essays and Reflections* (Cambridge: Cambridge University Press, 2002), 197n27.

42. Vitruvius, *On Architecture* 6.1.12. For more on this, see the entire first section of Book VI. Translation taken from Joseph Gwilt, *The Architecture of Marcus Vitruvius Pollio* (London: Priestly & Weale, 1826).

43. Varro, *On Agriculture* 1.4.4. Translation taken from W. D. Hooper & H. B. Ash, *Cato and Varro*, LCL 284 (London: William Heinemann, 1934), 187.

44. As cited by Cicero, *On Fate* 4.1–8. Translation taken from H. G. Bonn, The Treatises of M. T. Cicero: *On the Nature of the Gods; On Divination; On Fate; On the Republic; On the Laws; and On Standing for the Consulship*, BCL (London: 1934), 267.

by traveling.⁴⁵ Despite his reticence toward persons who desired to wander the earth, even Cicero contended that changing climates could often be beneficial for health reasons.⁴⁶ Seneca shared a similar mindset believing that "[God] gave the winds to enable exploration of distant regions: for human beings would have been ignorant creatures, without much experience of the world, if they were confined by the boundaries of their native soil."⁴⁷ Celsus was quite adamant that one's change in climate could better their health. He argues repeatedly that physicians should, for part of their diagnoses and treatments, take into consideration the influence of good and bad climates.⁴⁸ Cicero contended that the overcoming of one's environment was most certainly possible and recognizable in the first place by one's diction.⁴⁹

These last several statements are particularly important as they accomplish two things for our purposes here: 1) They reiterate the fact that in antiquity one's environment presupposed certain character/ethical norms; and 2) Despite the fact that one's environment was so very influential, moving beyond the bounds of such an environment, especially in terms of ethics/morals, was not considered impossible. This second point is quite stunning

45. Nuancing this view, the geographer Eratosthenes (also known as Erathosthenes) seems to believe that while climate and geography do affect persons, it seems less appropriate to judge their complete character by these things and more suitable to judge them by their good and bad characteristics (F 155). Much of what we know about Eratosthenes is contained within the work of Strabo as citations. See Strabo's *Geography* [1.4.9].

46. Horace, *On Travel* 1.11. For more on this fascinating topic, see Rachel I. Skalitzky, "Horace On Travel (*Epist.* 1.11)" in *CJ* 68/4 (April-May, 1974): 316–321. Evidently, Robert D. Ward had not considered the concept of moving when he said, "Man's climatic environment affects him in many ways. . . . But he cannot change his climate" (735). See his article "Climate and Man" in *BAGS* 39/12 (1907).

47. Seneca, *Natural Questions* 5.14. Translation borrowed from Harry M. Hine, *Lucius Annaeus Seneca: Natural Questions* (Chicago: Chicago University Press, 2010), 86. The Egyptian writer Hecataeus argued that the land of the Hyperboreans was a type of climatic and geographic utopia, which contained the best soils and lacked sickness. See his *Egypt* and also the work of John Dillery, "Hecataeus of Abdera: Hyperboreans, Egypt and the 'Interpretatio Graeca'" in *Historia: Zeitschrift fur Alte Geschichte* 47/3 (1998), 255–75.

48. Celsus, *Medicine* 3.27.2. Translation taken from George F. Collier, *A Translation of the Eight Books of Aul. Corn. Celsus on Medicine* (London: Simpkin and Marshal, 1831), 120. See also pages 6, 13, 20, 28, 67, 79–80, 104, 114 and 159.

49. In *Brutus*, he says, "Cotta, who, by his broad pronunciation, threw off all resemblance of the elegant tone of the Greeks, and affected a harsh and rustic utterance, quite opposite to that of Catulus, acquired the same reputation of correctness by pursuing a wild and unfrequented path" (para. 258–59). Translation borrowed from Edward Jones, *Cicero's Brutus: Or History of Famous Orators* (Columbia, SC: Columbia University, 1776), 178. This is all the more interesting when set aside his discussions on fate and determinism. See his *On Fate*.

since, in antiquity, change was not only met with resistance on practically all fronts but was also met with great skepticism when it did take place.[50]

Plato's comment, which is characteristic of the ancient mindset says, "Change (μεταβολή), we shall find, except in something evil, is extremely dangerous. This is true of seasons and winds, the regimen of the body and the character of the soul—in short, of everything without exception (unless, as I said just now, the change affects something evil)."[51] Any sudden or dramatic change in a person's life would have demanded proof(s).[52] As I begin to construct the theory of Paul's "Two Realms" in Romans, the next best place to turn is to Paul's rhetoric and ethics in said epistle, for it is there that we find the apostle's moral distinctions between these opposing worlds being drawn.

## PAUL'S "TWO REALMS" THEORY: RETHINKING ROM 12:1–2

Since Hans D. Betz's monumental rhetorical commentary on Galatians, rhetorical studies in Pauline literature have abounded. In particular, Paul's epistle to the Romans has received very much attention. Without revisiting each and every view that has been espoused, it is enough here to state my position on this matter and to illustrate how such a view fits within the scope of this thought experiment. Once this has been accomplished, the topic of the apostle's ethics will surface.

We have already asserted above that Rom 12:1–2 is paraenetic in function. Abraham Malherbe has shown quite persuasively that paraenetic

---

50. I have done a considerable amount of research on "change" in the ancient world. For more on this topic, see T. Michael W. Halcomb, "The Role of Change in Galatians: Examining the Exordium," Annual Meeting of the Stone-Campbell Journal, Cincinnati, OH, March 2007; "Innovations & Galatians: A Comparative Case Study," Annual Meeting of the Stone-Campbell Journal, Cincinnati, OH, April 2008; "A *New* Reason For Jesus' Death: Reading Mark Socio-Culturally," The Midwest Region of the Society of Biblical Literature, Bourbonnais, IL, February 2009; "All Things to All People: Rethinking the Social Context of a Pauline Axiom," The Midwest Region of the Society of Biblical Literature, Valparaiso, IN, February 13, 2010 and "'Plotting To Kill Jesus': The Social Context Of Jesus' Death in Mark's Gospel," Annual Meeting of the Stone-Campbell Journal, Cincinnati, OH, April 2010.

51. Plato, *Laws* VII.797b–800a. Translation from Trevor J. Saunders, "Laws" in *Plato: Complete Works*, eds. J. M. Cooper and D. S. Hutchinson (Indianapolis, IN: Hackett Publishing, 1997), 1466. Dan 2:21 remarks that it is God who "changes time times and seasons."

52. For examples related directly to Paul's life, see my "The Role of Change" and "Innovations & Galatians."

material contains either traditional or familiar content, relies on examples of vice / virtue, and demonstrates a close relationship between the addresser and addressee(s).[53] This fits well within the overall rhetorical tenor of Romans, which is deliberative, meaning that its instrumental force lies in its ability to reinforce values and give advice or consent.[54] One aspect of such reinforcement comes in the way of moral/ethical principles.[55]

Clearly, there is conflict in Rome and as such the believers there fall under the umbrella of Paul's moral and theological directives. Yet, what was the problem and how might understanding it help elucidate the moral admonitions the apostle gives? This is precisely what Ben Witherington seems to be getting at when he contends, "when it comes to ethics, it matters who the audience is."[56] However, being more than two thousand years removed from Paul's epistle, we cannot know exactly the identities of Paul's recipients. The best we can hope for is reconstruction and regarding this topic, of the making of books there seems to be no end.[57]

One thing we can be confident of is that they are Christians (1:6-8, 13; 7:1, 4; 8:12, 29; 10:1; 11:25; 12:1; 15:14, 30; 16:17). However, exactly what and how much they do and/or do not know, especially as it relates to Paul's writing, we must simply plead ignorance to. Despite this, Robert Jewett's position that the addressees of Paul's letter met in a home seems quite plausible.[58] Recently, Peter Oakes has challenged exegetes to consider the notion

---

53. Abraham J. Malherbe, "Exhortation in First Thessalonians" in *NovT* 25 (1983): 238-56.

54. So Ben Witherington III and Darlene Hyatt, *Paul's Letter to the Romans: A Socio-Rhetorical Commentary* (Grand Rapids, MI: Eerdmans, 2004), 16 and Neil Elliot, *The Rhetoric of Romans: Argumentative Constraint and Strategy and Paul's Dialogueue with Judaism* (Minneapolis, MN: Fortress Press, 2007), 99.

55. I will use the terms ethic(s) and moral(s) synonymously throughout this paper.

56. Ben Witherington III, *The Indelible Image: The Theological and Ethical Thought World of the NT*, Vol. 2 (Downers Grove, IL: IVP, 2010), 603. Both Stephen C. Barton, "The Epistles and Christian Ethics" in *The Cambridge Companion to Christian Ethics*, ed. R. Gill (Cambridge: Cambridge University Press, 2001) and Wolfgang Schrage, *The Ethics of the NT*, trans. D. E. Green (Edinburgh: T&T Clark, 1988) both press this notion a little farther. Barton says, "The NT does not present abstract reflection of a philosophical kind on the nature and grounds of moral action. It is not a compendium of systematic reflection on the good. . . . It invites its readers to a new way of life under the one true God revealed in Jesus Christ" (63). Likewise, Schrage says, "Now the NT is certainly not a handbook or compendium of Christian ethics, with universal rules or detailed descriptions of conduct" (2).

57. For a brief review of discussions concerning Romans and audience see Moo, *Epistle*, 9-13.

58. Robert Jewett, *Romans: A Commentary*, Hermenia (Minneapolis, MN: Fortress Press, 2007), 64-65. Jewett's bibliographic material on this section is extensive and covers research conducted between 1939-1992 on the topic of house churches and

that the text may have been written for a quite diverse audience. If this is the case, as he notes, one "important analytical step is to consider how the text would sound to people from each part of the audience."[59] Marshaling data from architectural, social, economic and religious spheres, Oakes attempts to recreate the identities of four different ancient Pompeian persons in an effort to hear the epistle from each vantage point.

Oakes' research calls into question the validity of the prevailing concept among scholars to rebuild communities whose identities are depicted as homogenous.[60] Recognizing the diversity among earliest Christian communities puts us in a place where we can only attempt to tease out perceived similarities and differences.[61] Two of those likenesses have already been mentioned (i.e. they were Christians and they met in a home) and a third and fourth may be added here.

The third addition, following Oakes—whose data nuances the reconstructions of decades of scholarship on Romans—is that these were Gentiles with "no great interest in Judaism" and were probably "embarrassed by the fact that Christian life has a Jewish basis."[62] Fourthly, and in light of the previous point, I might add that the Gentile recipients may have started to draw

---

tenements. In Josephus's *Against Apion* 92.190–219, paraenetic materials are linked directly to the household order.

59. Oakes, *Reading Romans*, 127.

60. Oakes says, "It is therefore an important exegetical enterprise to ask how NT texts would have sounded to such people—as also to various other social types. Scholars cannot avoid this task simply on the grounds that the texts do not mention such people. An author's likely expectation that the text would be received by such people is part of the nature of the text in its context" (178).

61. Wedderburn contends that in Romans, Paul is "in fact" addressing "an audience that is divided" (140) and then goes on to base numerous suppositions about the audience on this model. It is not clear to me, however, that the division is as obvious as he assumes and that the major division in the house church(es) has to do with observance/non-observance of the Law (141).

62. Ibid. This seems to sit well with the theory offered by Witherington that Romans was written in the wake of a Jewish Christian expulsion from Rome, where these founders of the Roman church returned to find their congregation taken over by Gentile Christians. If this is the case, Romans appears to be a rhetoric-laden epistle aimed at teaching the Gentiles the riches of their Jewish heritage, which he thereby hopes will squash the reluctances of the Gentiles towards the returning Jewish Christians. See Witherington, *Romans*, 11–16. Several of Witherington's conversations partners should also be consulted on this matter, namely J. C. Walters, "Romans, Jews and Christians" in *Judaism and Christianity in First-Century Rome*, eds. K. P. Donfried and P. Richardson (Grand Rapids, MI: Eerdmans, 1998), 175–95; Hans D. Betz, "Christianity as Religion: Paul's Attempt at Definition in Romans" in *Paulinischen Studien* (Tübingen: Mohr Siebeck, 1994), 106–39 and Mark D. Nanos, *The Mystery of Romans* (Minneapolis, MN: Fortress Press, 1996).

thick lines of demarcation between themselves and their Jewish-Christian brothers and sisters. In sum, it seems likely to me that there may have been a certain amount of embarrassment on behalf of the Gentile believers receiving this letter, who did not want to base their faith in tenets carried over from Judaism. To prevent this from happening they began erecting barriers between themselves and the brand of (Christian) Judaism local to them.

If this was the case, it explains why Paul's letter was corrective in nature. The apostle may be suggesting to the Gentiles that they should not be separating themselves from the heritage or story of Israel but the "world" (i.e. the worldly realm) that has been corrupted by sin. To reiterate, Paul is telling them not to draw such a clear distinction between this young Christianity and certain aspects of Judaism but rather to draw a fine line between the worldly and spiritual realms. Judaism is not the threat; that fault belongs rather to the "world" and its evils! Now, this is not to say that Paul is advocating a Jewish gospel or even some form of escapism. Instead, it is to say that Paul's belief of "being in the world but not of it" is what is in view.

The apostle detects serious moral flaws in the Romans and he proceeds to link those directly to the created world. This may be why Paul stresses and re-stresses the concepts of a creation corrupted by the ongoing sinfulness of humans while at the same time constantly reiterating that dying and decaying within this cosmos is not the only option.[63] Through Christ's work new life in the spiritual realm is possible (6:4). This life is both characterized by a new mind (12:2) and characteristic of persons living in the new ways of the Spirit (7:6; 8:5).

For Paul, however, ways of living or ethical standards are different depending on which realm one is speaking of.[64] Both the worldly realm and the spiritual realm, which stand in contrast to one another, each have their own moral climate or environment. Much in the same way that ancient geographers spoke of climates and environments affecting human traits, personalities, and characteristics, Paul also suggests that the worldly and spiritual realms affect people. However, while Paul's thinking is quite congruent with this, the major difference has to do with the fact that he is speaking not of physical climate (e.g. heat, water, air, etc.) but rather moral climate. Just as climatic elements have features inherent to them that pre-

---

63. One might argue, however, that this need not be part of the audience's identity for Paul to mention it. This is certainly a legitimate point for Paul could have been pushing his own views on the letter recipients. However, given the prominence of the concept this seems less likely than the alternative suggested here.

64. For a nice overview of the discussion of Pauline over the last four decades, see Nijay K. Gupta, "The Theo-Logic of Paul's Ethics in Recent Research: Crosscurrents and Future Directions in Scholarship in the Last Forty Years" in *CBR* 7 (2009): 336–61.

suppose certain attributes and qualities (e.g. dark skin, curly hair, ignorance, broad-chests, tolerance for pain, proneness to war, etc.), the "two realms" also have a moral fiber embedded in them that play a role in determining how someone within those environments does ethics.

Generally speaking, ethics has to do with the meaning of moral teaching. More specifically, for our purposes here we are speaking of Pauline ethics in Romans, which has to do with the meaning of moral teaching in this letter.[65] The division of the two realms (worldly and spiritual) is perhaps seen nowhere better than between the ethical distinctions that Paul exegetes from each of them. I have worked through the entire epistle taking note of the moral principles and their end-results, both of which Paul believes are predetermined in each realm. I have compiled those findings in the following two tables:[66]

| Predetermined Ethics and Their Outcomes in the Worldly Realm in Romans[A] |
| --- |
| The wath of God, godlessness, wickedness, suppression of truth (1:18); failure to glorify God, failure to thank God, futile thinking, foolish/dark hearts (1:19); idolatry (1:23); sinful desires, sexual impurity, degrading of bodies (1:24); exchanging truth for lies (1:25); shameful lusts, unnatural sexual relations (1:26); shameful acts, due penalties received for shameful acts (1:27); depraved minds, doing what ought not be done (1:28); every kind of wickedness, evil, greed, depravity, envy, murder, strife, deceit, malice, gossips (1:29); slanderers, God-haters, insolence, arrogance, boasting, inventions of evil, disobedience to parents (1:30); no understanding, no fidelity, no love, no mercy (1:31); death, approval of doing things against God and his law (1:32); judgment, condemnation (2:1); |

---

65. This is essentially the simple definition espoused by Schubert M. Ogden in "Paul in Contemporary Theology and Ethics: Presuppositions of Critically Approaching Paul's Letters Today" in *Essays in Honor of Victor Paul Furnish: Theology & Ethics in Paul and His Interpreters*, eds. E. H. Lovering Jr. & J. L. Sumney (Nashville, TN: Abingdon, 1996), 296.

66. At the risk of blurring the lines too much between ethical and theological values, I have only listed the self-evident moral matters found in Romans. For example, I have ignored the concept of being called by God to be an apostle (1:1–2), which is inherent to the spiritual realm because, even though it may have ethical implications, it is not directly referring to a moral-ethical issue. Note that these two tables wholly challenge the notion that the first half (or chapters 1–11) of Romans is doctrine or theology while the second half (or chapters 12–16) is ethics! Indeed, Paul is concerned with practical ethical matters all through Romans, just as he is concerned with theology. This is against such views as Morris, as stated above in footnote #13.

contempt (2:4); stubbornness, unrepentant heart, storing up of God's wrath (2:5); self-seeking, reject truth, following evil, anger (2:8); trouble, distress (2:9); blindness, darkness (2:19); stealing (2:21); adultery, robbing temples (2:22); dishonor, breaking the law (2:23); blasphemy (2:24); outward circumcision (2:25); unfaithful (3:1); unrighteousness (3:4); falsehood (3:7); slander (3:8); under the power of sin (3:9); misunderstanding, no one seeking God (3:11); becoming worthless (3:12); throats are open graves, tongues practice deceit, poisonous words (3:13); mouths full of cursing and bitterness (3:14); bloodshed (3:15); ruin, misery (3:16); no peace (3:17); no fear of God (3:18); sin increases (5:20); ruled by sin (6:6); slaves to sin (6:20); shame (6:21); sinful nature, sinful passions (7:5); coveting (7:8); unspiritual (7:14); doing what is hated (7:15); war against the mind, prisoner to sin (7:23); mind set on what sinful nature desires (8:5); hostility toward God, rejection of God's law (8:7); misdeeds of the body (8:13); creation waits (8:19); creation subjected to frustration (8:20); creation in bondage and decay (8:21); creation groaning (8:22); hardship, persecution, famine, nakedness, danger, sword (8:35); not God's children (9:8); hardened heart (9:18); self-righteousness (10:3); rejection of the Good News (10:16); obstinate people (10:21); retribution (11:9); backs bent (11:10); spiritual stumbling and falling (11:11); rejected by God (11:15); sternness of God (11:22); cut off from God (11:22); bound to disobedience (11:32); rebellion against authorities, rebellion against God (13:2); punishment for wrongdoers (13:4); smooth talk, flattery (16:18).

A. Where traits or end-results are duplicated throughout Romans, I will not re-list them here or supply every verse number where they might show up. Instead, I have listed here only the first occurrences of where these items appear.

### Predetermined Ethics and Their Outcomes in the Spiritual Realm in Romans

Grace, faith, obedience (1:5); holiness (1:7); prayer (1:10); spiritual gifts (1:11); mutual encouragement (1:12); eagerness to preach the gospel (1:15); not being ashamed of the gospel, salvation, belief (1:16); righteousness (1:17); truth (2:2); kindness, forbearance, patience, repentance (2:4); persistence in doing good, honor, glory, everlasting life (2:7); peace (2:10); no favoritism (2:11); law written on hearts, consciences bear witness (2:15); boasting in God (2:17); knowing God's will, approving of what is superior (2:18); guidance, light (2:19); knowledge (2:20); inward circumcision, praise from God (2:29); no difference between Jew and Gentile (3:22); justified freely (3:24); transgressions forgiven, sins covered (4:7); justification (4:25); peace with God (5:1); access to God (5:2); perseverance (5:3); character, hope (5:4); no shame, God's love, gift of the Holy Spirit (5:5); reconciled to God (5:10); grace increases (5:20); new life (6:4); united with Christ (6:5); set free from sin (6:7); dead to sin (6:11); release from the law, service in the Spirit (7:6); spiritual (7:14); delight in God's law (7:22); deliverance, servant / slave to God's law (7:25); Spirit gives life (8:2); mind set on Spirit's desires (8:5); indwelling of the Spirit (8:9); led by the Spirit of God, become children of God (8:14); no fear, adoption by God (8:15); Spirit testifies with our spirit (8:16); heirs of God, co-heirs with Christ, share in Christ's sufferings, share in his glory (8:17); creation liberated (8:21); firstfruits of the Spirit, redemption of our bodies (8:23);

> Spirit helps us in our weakness, Spirit intercedes for us (8:26); God works for our good (8:28); predestined to be conformed to the image of God's son (8:29); we are glorified (8:30); God is for us (8:31); we are more than conquerors (8:37); inseparable form God (8:39); conscience related to Holy Spirit (9:1); God's mercy (9:16); richly blessed when calling on God (10:12); a remnant chosen by grace (11:5); kindness of God (11:22); irrevocable call and gifts (11:29); offering of body as sacrifice, pleasing God, true worship (12:1); nonconformity to the age, transformation, renewing of the mind, proving God's will (12:2); not thinking too highly of oneself, sober judgment (12:3); prophecy (12:6); teaching (12:7); encouragement, giving generously, leading diligently, showing mercy cheerfully (12:8); sincere love, hating evil, clinging to good (12:9); devotion (12:10); zeal, spiritual fervor (12:11); joy, patience, faithfulness (12:12); sharing, hospitality (12:13); blessing persecutors, no cursing (12:14); rejoicing, mourning with mourners (12:15); living in harmony, no pride, no class distinctions (12:16); no retribution, doing what is right (12:17); no revenge (12:19); overcoming evil with good (12:21); submission to governing authorities (13:1); paying taxes (13:6); paying debts, paying revenue, paying respect (13:7); no outstanding debts (13:8); loving neighbor as self (13:9); no harm to neighbor (13:10); putting aside deeds of darkness, putting on armor of light (13:12); behaving decently, no carousing, no drunkenness, no sexual immorality, no debauchery, no dissension, no jealousy (13:13); acceptance, no quarreling (14:1); no contempt (14:3); no plotting against others (14:13); no distressing others (14:15); bearing burdens of others, not pleasing oneself (15:1); unity (15:6); spiritual and material blessings (15:27); spiritual refreshing (15:32); absence of divisions (16:17); wisdom about good, innocent of evil (16:19).

These two tables show that for Paul ethics was important. They also reiterate the fact that for the apostle, each realm had a certain predetermined ethical environment that would shape the persons living in it. However, for the apostle, one was not confined to either of these realms forever. Instead, in the same way that Cicero, Seneca, and others contended that environments could be overcome and or left, Paul was of the mentality that persons could move from the realm of vice into the realm of virtue.[67] He himself believes that persons can "overcome evil with good" (12:12) and that freedom from the worldly realm, the domain of sin, is possible (6:7, 18, 20, 22; 8:2). Just as geographic bounds are traversable and escapable, the "worldly landscape" can also be left behind for the "spiritual" one.

Thus, whereas John Barton argues that "Paul is not telling his readers how to advance in the moral life, but describing the effects of conversion," I would contend that Paul is indeed telling his readers how to advance in the moral life and also laying before them the ethical effects and results of

---

67. We recall footnote #51 above, that, according to Plato, such a "change" was the only acceptable type of change.

choosing one moral climate over the other.[68] In fact, Rom 12:1-2 connects with Rom 1 and 8 by way of Paul's creation language and imagery. For the apostle, the created world has become subdued by sin (8:20-21) and groans for its release from captivity (8:22). As shown by the table above, it also stands poised against the spiritual world (1:18; 2:8; 7:23, etc.). The root of this problem, as articulated in Rom 1:18-32 and 8:19-22, is human immorality. As Harry Hahne notes, "the period during which creation is corrupted depends on the cause of the problem. . . . When the corruption is due to ongoing human sin, corruption is also a characteristic of this age."[69] It is obvious, then, as Hahne points out, that Rom 8:19-22 "focuses on corruption and futility as ongoing characteristics of creation."[70] It would seem then that this, in addition to the other data given above, suggests that the investigation into a "two realm" theory in Paul's letter to the Romans can be sustained in a number of ways and on a number of levels. Let us now briefly review our findings.

## SUMMARY AND CONCLUSIONS

In this experiment I have worked through some of the linguistic tangles of Rom 12:1-2 showing that while these two verses are not the hinge on which the epistle hangs, they do in fact contain themes that come prior to and after them. One of those themes is the contrast between the created world and the spirit world, a concept that I referred to as Paul's "Two Realms" theory. This is the premise that Paul had a present tense theology that posited the existence of these two competing realms, each of which contained major present tense ethical ramifications. In my hypothesizing, I attempted to show points of connection between this concept and ancient ideas concerning climatic or environmental determinism. Such theorizing helped us better understand the moral/ethical climates of each of these two spheres.

It was shown that in the same way that the ancient geographers believed environments to have predetermined characteristics that would shape people in specific ways, Paul believed that the present worldly and

---

68. John Barton, "Virtue in the Bible" in *SCE* 12 (1999), 15. Though used in reference to the narrative flow of Galatians, the statement by Ian W. Scott, *Paul's Way of Knowing: Story, Experience, and the Spirit* (Grand Rapids, MI: Baker, 2009) can be recontextualized to make our point here: ". . . this initial reconstrual of the world will simply heighten the cognitive tension for the outsider . . . paradigm shifts of this magnitude also involve a decision to leave one way of living and embrace a new one. . . ." (282, 285).

69. Hahne, *Corruption*, 213.

70. Ibid., 214. This is already detected early on in the work of John Chrysostom who said, "The form of this world is groveling and worthless. . . ." (*Homilies on Romans* 20).

spiritual realms contained ethical environments with predetermined mores. Depending on which landscape one found themselves in they would either be walking according to the ways of the Spirit of God or the ways of Satan or self. A complete list of each predetermined ethic in relation to its specific realm was given to further test this theory. It was also shown that the apostle had the mentality that persons were not forever confined to these locations but could leave or enter them at one's discretion.

This experiment also helped make sense of Paul's uses of deliberative rhetoric and paraenetic pleadings, along with one of his reasons for writing the epistle. In sum, a great deal of Paul's house church audience(s) consisted of Gentile believers who were embarrassed for having to root their faiths in Judaic tenets. With resistance, the Gentiles began drawing dividing lines between themselves and Christianity's Jewish roots. Paul's letter, which was corrective in nature, urged them to forego such thinking. Instead of perceiving Judaism as a threat, Paul insisted that they should instead understand the "world" and its evils as such. To combat such dangers the Gentile Christians should walk in and according to the spiritual realm thereby letting the Holy Spirit "renew" their minds.

As with most projects, this thought experiment has raised many questions and possibilities for further research. Diving even deeper into the concept of environmental determinism in antiquity might prove beneficial, especially in relation to Stoicism and Hellenistic Mystery Religions. For example, Troels Engberg-Pedersen has done some great work on Stoicism in relation to Rom 12, however, this concept has not been discussed.[71] Likewise, given the ancient view within that initiation into Hellenistic Mystery Religions could free persons from determinism, how might the work here affirm or challenge a connection of Romans to the Mystery Religions?[72]

---

71. See his *Paul and the Stoics* (Edinburgh: T&T Clark, 2000); "Paul, Virtues, and Vices" in *Paul in the Greco-Roman World: A Handbook*, ed. J. P. Sampley (Harrisburg, PA: Trinity Press International), 608–33; "The Relationship with Others: Similarities and Differences Between Paul and Stoicism" in *ZNW* 96 (2005): 35–60 and "Paul's Stoicizing Politics in Romans 12–13: The Role of 13.1–10 in the Argument" in *JSNT* 29/2 (2006): 163–72. See also Runar M. Thorsteinsson, "Paul and Roman Stoicism: Romans 12 and Contemporary Stoic Ethics" in *JNT* 29/2 (2006): 139–161 and Philip F. Esler, "Paul and Stoicism: Romans 12 as a Test Case" in *NTS* 50 (2002): 106–24.

72. See for example, Samuel Angus, *The Mystery Religions: A Study in the Religious Background of Early Christianity*, 2nd ed. (New York, NY: Courier Dover Publications, 1975). Angus says, "Astrology shackled the ancient world in determinism, from the burdens of which men sought escape in the Mysteries and in magic. In this way, the Mystery-Religions sought to provide a way of escape from the capricious acts of fortune, from the unbridled will of demons, and from the oppressive sense of fatalism concomitant with Astralism" (251). If this is correct, then explorations into Paul's view(s) of evangelism might be nuanced because in this schema, salvation and rescue take on

Robert Jewett, after all, when speaking of Rom 12:1-2, does contend that "The Pauline concept of transformation is oriented to this life rather than the next, and in contrast to the philosophers and mystery religions, it is corporate rather than individual."[73] On the surface at least, such a view would appear to mesh well with some of the suggestions made in this essay.

In light of the data this essay has offered, another interesting area of discussion might be the relationship of environmental determinism to predestination and freedom of choice. For example, reconsidering the notion that Paul had a "two realms" theory at work in which he understood each realm to have its own set of embedded or predetermined ethics and/or traits changes the theological discussion about predestination and predeterminism in quite a substantial way. Also, one wonders how the notion of Rom 7 being a pre-Christian diatribe might be further substantiated or challenged by this work? Certainly, more study on the matrices between theology and ethics, as well as the shape of the moral world(s) of the earliest Christians in light of climatic/environmental determinism deserves more attention.[74] Additionally, contributions from the field of physiognomy, especially in relation to Mediterranean antiquity, would prove helpful.[75] Of course, this essay has pushed back a bit against overpowering eschatologies and has attempted focus more on Paul's view of the "two realms" that exist in the present. Without a doubt, more studies on time in Romans, Paul's other works, and Greco-Roman antiquity in general would bear fruit in helping us understand the moral climates of Paul's congregations.

---

nuanced meanings.

73. Jewett, *Romans*, 733. Richard S. Ascough lists numerous scholars who have found links between the house churches or congregations in Paul's letters and Greco-Roman associations (*collegia*). See his 71–94. On this same topic, Alicia Batten has written a well-researched paper wherein she concludes that seeing correlations between the moral worlds of these associations and Paul's churches has the potential to offer many insights. See Ascough's, *What Are They Saying About the Formation of Pauline Churches* (Mahwah, NJ: Paulist, 1998) and Batten's, "The Moral World of Greco-Roman Associations" in *SR* 36 (2007): 135–51.

74. One work worth bringing more into this discussion is that of Wayne A. Meeks, *The Moral World of the First Christians*, LEC 6 (Philadelphia, PA: Westminster, 1986). The other texts in the LEC series would also prove to be good conversation partners.

75. In particular, engaging the work of social-science scholars such as Bruce J. Malina and Jerome H. Neyrey, *Portraits of Paul: An Archaeology of Ancient Personality* (Louisville, KY: WJK, 1996).

# GENERAL EPISTLES

# 9

# Centering the Decentered Self
*1 Peter and Identity in the 21st century*[1]

**RUTH ANNE REESE**

## INTRODUCTION

RECENTLY, WHILE VISITING LAGOS, Nigeria, I attended "God Bless Nigeria Church." The membership of this church is mostly made up of ex-cons, ex-prostitutes, ex-drug addicts, and others who come from difficult situations. After more than an hour of intense dancing and singing before the Lord, the pastor got up to preach. And the title of his sermon was, "Who Am I?" He began his sermon by asking the members of the congregation to think about the origins of their identities. He suggested a number of sources for one's identity. For example, is identity based on the work we do? Is identity based on the social networks we have? Do we believe the identity that we hear from others when they name us as people who are dirty or evil or deformed? Even more, do we get our identity from internal voices that

---

1. This paper is dedicated to my friend and colleague, Dr. Ben Witherington III, who has always been as concerned with application as much as with interpretation.

condemn us? These might be the voices that say that we are worthless, hopeless, and undeserving.

## IDENTITY IN THE 21ST CENTURY

These questions and concerns about identity are not unique to a particular church, whether in the United States, Nigeria, or elsewhere. Nor are these questions confined to the church. Nor are concerns about identity unique to a particular group, whether that is determined by social status, race, or other factors. The exact way in which these questions about identity are posed may differ across cultures and locations, but questions of human identity (for example: Who am I? How do I know who I am? Do I have a core identity? What do others say about me? Who am I like? Who am I different from? Where do I belong? etc.) cross cultural, social, and political boundaries.

Human identity comes from multiple sources. Some aspects of identity develop in the very genes that we are born with (for example, biological sex, eye color, hair color, and other aspects of genetic determination). The debate about the relationship between identity formation and its connection to nature or nurture has been long-standing and is on-going. Even a popular magazine like *Smithsonian* had a recent cover entitled "Born to be Bad? The New Science of Morality."[2] The article explored the question of whether or not moral choices are embedded in our genes rather than a matter solely of upbringing. While some aspects of identity are biological, others are environmental and social. Identity is formed by family, by experiences, by choices that are made, by the impact of individuals on one another, by words spoken, by actions done or received, by geography, and by communities, to name several sources. As such, identity is a complex area of exploration and research. This complexity has only been expanded by the introduction of the web, social networking, computerized machines (e.g., robots, Siri), and the always on, always connected, 24/7 world we live in. There is always someone somewhere with whom we can connect and who will, whether consciously or unconsciously, engage in the ongoing process of shaping human identity. In addition, even if, by chance, we arise at a time when all our networks are asleep, we often find advertisements and other items that are striving to mark our identities. Take, as one example, a recent advertisement for the Droid phone on the Verizon cellular network. After showing a man fusing with a phone, the commercial ends with the

---

2. Abagail Tucker, "Are Babies Born Good?" *Smithsonian*, January 2013, (http://www.smithsonianmag.com/science-nature/Are-Babies-Born-Good-183837741.html).

tagline, "It's not an upgrade to your phone, it's an upgrade to yourself."[3] The advertiser seeks to sell a product by indicating that the product will make the one who buys it a stronger, better person. This tagline is itself part of another identity formation device—storytelling. One of the ways that humans produce a coherent understanding of their identity is by weaving the disparate parts of their lives into a unified narrative that enables them to account for the many different factors connected to identity. In addition, storytelling allows humans to connect their past identity with their present identity. Such stories usually include transition points, turning points, and other elements that show both similarity and difference between previous and current understandings of the self.

On an individual level, some people struggle to put together a coherent identity. Sometimes the pieces of a life become so fragmented that it seems impossible to put together all the different pieces. Identity, as stated above, is a complex reality. Questions of identity are influenced by biological factors, contextual factors, and by the synthesizing work done by individuals within their own cultural narratives and contexts (whether modern or postmodern, Western or majority world, etc.). Most of these cultural contexts are changing at a rapid pace. More and more people across the globe have access to the always on, always connected digital world. One of the fascinating aspects of the digital world is the ability to remake one's identity in a virtual world or worlds. There is no requirement that the persona or personas (it is easy to have multiple identities, user names, and habits in the online world) that are "inhabited" on the web are the same as the identity inhabited in everyday offline lives. Many people "try out" new identities on the web. In Sherry Turkle's work on the digital world and identity she writes:

> The Internet has become a significant social laboratory for experimenting with the constructions and reconstructions of self that characterize postmodern life. In its virtual reality, we self-fashion and self-create. What kinds of personae do we make? What relation do these have to what we have traditionally thought of as the 'whole' person? Are they experienced as an expanded self or as separate from the self? Do our real-life selves learn lessons from our virtual personae? Are these virtual personae fragments of a coherent real-life personality?[4]

---

3. *Verizon Commercial—Droid DNA "Hyper Intelligence,"* 2012, n.p. [cited 7 January 2013]. Online: http://www.youtube.com/watch?v=IYIAaBOb5B0&feature=youtube_gdata_player. Accessed: 2013-01-07.

4. Sherry Turkle, *Life on the Screen: Identity in the Age of the Internet* (New York: Simon & Schuster, 1995), 180.

The internet has created a whole new arena in which millions of people are exploring, consciously or unconsciously, issues of identity. Because identity is no longer tied to the face-to-face or even voice-to-voice engagement of previous times, identity is no longer dependent upon presence. It is this disconnection from physical presence that presents the very opportunity for exploration of multiple aspects of identity (whether that is seen as multiple pieces of the same self or as multiple selves). One place to see this being worked out is in the role playing games that abound on the internet. "Traditional ideas about identity have been tied to a notion of authenticity that such virtual experiences actively subvert. When each player [of online games] can create many characters and participate in many games, the self is not only decentered but multiplied without limit."[5] A college student can "play" a soldier or a violent drunk or a geek or all of these characters at once. Some may see these characters as aspects of themselves (whether those are acted out in offline life or not), others as things that they "try on" for a period of time, and still others as completely disconnected from their offline self. The digital age provides (is the impetus for?) the perfect setting for the aspect of postmodern narrative that tells a story of displacement, of an unsettled feeling, a loss of solid foundation, and in this context questions of identity continue to have a significant place.

At first glance identity may have seemed like a simple issue, but our brief discussion shows that it is complex and dependent upon a variety of factors. In addition, the means available for working out questions of identity have changed significantly in the last 30 years as the internet has become a significant part of the lives of billions of people. In the complex context that we inhabit, can Scripture speak meaningfully about identity? And can its message help us in an age where more and more people are experiencing a decentered sense of identity?

## INTRODUCTION TO IDENTITY IN 1 PETER

Here, I turn to 1 Peter because the opening portion of the epistle (1:1—2:10) is specifically addressed to issues of identity. First Peter is an epistle most likely written to a church that consisted mostly of Gentiles.[6] The letter was

---

5. Turkle, *Life on the Screen*, 185.

6. Although some commentators argue for a Jewish audience (e.g., John Calvin, *Commentaries on the Catholic Epistles* (Grand Rapids: Eerdmans, 1948), 25), especially because of the references to exile and dispersion as well as the prevalence of OT metaphors and quotations, the majority of commentators (e.g., J. Michaels Ramsey, *1 Peter*, Word Biblical Commentary (Waco: Word Books, 1988), xlvi) argue for a Gentile audience. Many of these point to the phrase "futile ways of your ancestors" in 1 Pet 1:18 and

sent to communities of believers living in Asia Minor (present day Turkey), an area that had been heavily colonized during the reign of the Emperor Claudius (AD 41–54).[7] These communities faced a number of challenges related to identity. First, they were living in exile, which we will discuss further below. As such, they were intimately aware of alienation. In the context of exile, 1 Peter speaks about a new familial identity. These are the two identity markers to which we will give attention in the remainder of this essay.

## EXILE

1 Peter uses a variety of words connected with the experience of exile. In the opening sentence, the audience is identified as παρεπιδήμοις ("strangers," "sojourners," or "resident aliens"). They live in the Diaspora—a word intimately connected with the OT backdrop for exile. In the OT the southern tribes were removed from Jerusalem and deported to Babylon. This deportation forms the context of the Jewish Diaspora. For although some returned to Jerusalem some 70 years later, many did not return. The Jews were now a scattered people many of whom did not live in their homeland. The language of 1 Peter points to an audience who cannot rely on their citizenship as a means of security within their cultural location. Their status as "strangers" is reinforced by the use of παροικία, which refers to "being in a strange locality without citizenship."[8] This identity as aliens, strangers, or exiles is highlighted at the beginning of the next section. There 1 Peter uses πάροικος ("alien") and παρεπίδημος ("sojourner, exile") to call the audience to a life of good conduct among the nations (2:12). This conduct is to serve as a means of identification. Those around them may want to name them as "wrongdoers," as people who are not living in accordance with the expectations and laws of their society, but their good actions are a way of lessening that accusation. Although, unbelievers who experience those good actions may not fully understand them until the end of time when their eyes are opened by God's visitation. 1 Peter's audience is addressed in terms that set them on the margin. They are not citizens at the center of society but rather

---

to 1 Pet 4:3–4 and its identification of the audience as those who may have formerly participated in such things as "licentiousness, passions, drunkenness, revels, carousing, and lawless idolatry" as evidence that this is not a Jewish audience. In contrast, Karen Jobes argues that both Jews and Gentiles are addressed by book and reliance on any tradition, whether Jewish or not, over against reliance on God is seen as futile by Peter (*1 Peter*, Baker Exegetical Commentary on the NT [Grand Rapids: Baker Academic, 2005], 24).

7. Karen H. Jobes, *1 Peter*, 29–33.
8. BDAG.

people with a tenuous status who exist within contexts where they cannot sit easily within the seat of power.[9] One of the realities of this group is that they are marked as "strangers." They are people who in some way "do not belong" to the culture in which they reside. Although they are present, they are not at home. Where does the person on the edges find their identity? What helps them survive in a world that overlooks and devalues them? How are these exiles—these strangers, these people on the margins—to live and act in the place where they find themselves? These are important questions in the 21st century as well. While 1 Peter's readers experienced "strangeness" because of their faith, many in this century and in the culture of the developing world also understand themselves as alienated from the world around them. They may experience estrangement from family, disconnection from friends, or being out of step at work. How might 1 Peter speak in this new "exile"?

## FAMILY

To the imagery of exile and strangeness, 1 Peter adds the motif of family. Family is an important marker of identity. When we get to know another person we often learn about their relationships with parents whether this includes a traditional mom and dad, a single-parent family, stepparents, a grandparent or grandparents raising a child, a homosexual couple, or other variations of "family." Often, we also learn about siblings (or the lack of them) and about the tragedies, challenges, or triumphs of growing up and living in a particular family. For many in the West "family" has come to be understood flexibly to mean something along the lines of "the people that you grew up with." And an invitation to "tell me about your family" may extend beyond the people with whom one grew up to also include a larger circle of family—aunts, uncles, stepparents, grandparents, and "adopted" family. In this discussion of family, no matter how independent any one individual appears to be, there is always a story of dependence. Even those who are disconnected, estranged, or marginalized have some originating connection to family. Children are not created out of nothing but rather from a joining together. Even for those children who come into existence by way of a donor, there is a creation story—a story of how the child came to be. And in this way there is always a pre-story. There is always a story that begins before the existence of that particular individual. The individual may

---

9. For the purposes of this essay it is not crucial to resolve the debate over whether the people addressed are physically exiles or whether they have become like exiles or strangers by joining the way of Christ.

not even know all the twists and turns that bring him or her to that place at that moment, but the story is still there, and it points to the dependent nature of existence. Existence is never self-determined. Rather it is marked by forces prior to birth and by continuation after death.

Just as family is an important identity marker in our own cultural context, family was also an important identity marker in the Greco-Roman world in which 1 Peter was written. In the first century context, the identity of one's father was one of the most significant identity markers. The status of children was often determined by the identity of the child's father. Birth from noble ancestors was a cause for elevated status, and both biblical books (e.g., Matthew) and Greco-Roman occasions of honor often began with a recounting of the ancestry of the main person.[10] To put it simply, the identity of one's family was an important key to one's own identity. The importance of "family" as a marker of identity extended beyond the very real bonds created by birth, adoption, and marriage to the larger societal sphere. Within the context of the larger Greco-Roman culture the concept of "family" was tied to the Roman Emperor, who was viewed as the "father of the country." Thus, Rome and her empire could be viewed as a vast household under the emperor's leadership and control. Using the metaphor of kinship in this way creates a "fictive kinship" among people who do not share family ties based on biology or marriage.[11] So, it is not surprising that 1 Peter, written in this context, also points the book's audience to an identity that is marked by fictive familial kinship language.

1 Peter 1:1—2:10 has a lot to say about familial identity. In the opening paragraphs of this book, we find reference to "God the Father," "being born again," "children," "fathers," "babes," "milk," and "growing up." Few of these words are used more than once but together they form a thematic emphasis on kinship. Verse 3 begins "Blessed be the God and *father* of our Lord Jesus Christ! According to his great mercy he has *caused us to be born again* to a living hope through the resurrection of Jesus Christ from the dead, to an inheritance that is imperishable, undefiled, and unfading, kept in heaven for you, who by God's power are being guarded through faith for a salvation ready to be revealed in the last time" (ESV).[12] The verse begins by praising God not in an abstract sense but as the father of Jesus Christ. The hearers of the letter are those who are ἀναγεννήσας "are begotten again or born again"

---

10. David A. deSilva, *Honor, Patronage, Kinship & Purity : Unlocking NT Culture* (Downers Grove: InterVarsity Press, 2000), 52.

11. Ibid., 195.

12. Emphasis added.

(v. 3).¹³ Believers have a new identity that is rooted in the fatherly activity of God that causes them to be reborn. Alongside of this masculine metaphor, as new babes (2:2) they are to long for milk—a metaphor with distinctly feminine overtones. The early parts of 1 Pet 1:1—2:10 contain metaphorical references to the God who fathers, while the later part of this passage (2:2) contains metaphors that point towards a mother who nurses her babies. In these verses, God can be understood as both father and mother. God is the father that begets believers anew. At the same time God is also the mother who supplies the milk that nourishes the newborn. The believer has a new identity that is tied to a new identification with God as both father and mother. This new identity is contrasted with a former identity that is referred to as "the useless way of behaving handed down from your fathers" (1:18).¹⁴ The previous way of life is recognized as a life that was ματαίας ("vain, useless, futile"). This was the kind of life that the believers had inherited from their earthly familial ties. In contrast to this, God the Father offers a new life with a new family identity. God the Mother offers a new life with a new source of sustenance. In the context of the Greco-Roman world, the believers are identified as people who have been fathered by the same God who raised Jesus from the dead (1:21). They are the children of the God who has the power to reverse death itself. Indeed, isn't this the meaning of being reborn? Rather than being caught in the fruitless ways of living that they inherited—ways of living that could only lead to death—they are given new life in a new family. In 1 Peter 1:3 God is praised because it is out of God's great mercy that people are given new life. Just as babies are born into particular environments (e.g., a hospital, a home, a geographical location) and realities (a family, access or lack of access to resources), so too, God's children are born into particular realities. These are enumerated by three phrases that follow. Each of these phrases comes after the preposition εἰς (vv. 4–5). God's children are born into a hope, an inheritance, and into salvation. The new birth is accompanied by new contextual realities that the believer participates in by virtue of a new familial identity.

---

13. The Greek word used for "begotten or born again" occurs only in 1 Peter (vv. 3, 23) and nowhere else in the NT or LXX. It is a compound word derived from the suffix ἀνα (with the general meaning of "up" and the more specific meaning here of "repetition" (BDAG) thus "again") + γεννάω (mostly referring to the male activity of begetting but also to the female activity of giving birth (BDAG)).

14. My translation. All translations from the Greek NT are my own unless otherwise indicated.

## Hope

The first reality that God's children encounter is rebirth into a living hope (v. 4). The implication is that prior forms of hope, if they existed, were based on a different reality—the futile reality associated with prior (familial?) connections. And even those prior realities that may have been encouraging for a time were not based on the same reality that these children now enter into. In this family, hope is based on the resurrection of Jesus Christ from the dead. The hope that these children have is deliberately referred to as "living" hope implying a contrast with "dead/futile" hope (e.g., despair). It is appropriate that this living hope derives its reality from the resurrection. For just as these believers have been reborn by God, so too Jesus serves as the ultimate example of one who has been raised from death by God and now lives and reigns in the very presence of God. The believer's hope is based on one who has known suffering and death, but who has also experienced the full vindication and affirmation that came when God raised him from the dead. They too can hope that the God who has birthed them into this new reality will see them through to the place of resurrection. Resurrection is not immediate. It is not the immediate result of rebirth but rather the goal. Instead, rebirth begins the work of change and transformation. Resurrection is the completion of that change and transformation as the believer is raised to the fullness of life we anticipate in the future in the presence of God. This is a reason for hope even in the face of realities in this world that might tempt one to despair. In a context where the people of 1st Peter are surrounded by those who would verbally insult and degrade them, their identity as part of the family of God is a source of hope as they participate in the transformation that begins with rebirth.

## Inheritance

The second reality that God's children experience is that they now belong to a family that is able to provide them with an inheritance. In v. 4 the inheritance is described as "imperishable, undefiled, and unfading." In contrast to transitory human inheritances (whether ancient or modern)—stocks that collapse in value, money acquired by unsavory activity, buildings that burn down, business ventures gone awry, currencies devalued in the global market—the inheritance from this parent does not pass away, and it is pure and stable. This inheritance has not been obtained by use of deceit or manipulation or by any other tainted means. And nothing can destroy it. But what is this inheritance? The inheritance is specifically identified as something that is "kept in heaven." In the ancient world, land was a significant means of conveying inheritance. Jobes writes, "In light of the role that land played in inheritance in both the Greek and the Semitic worlds, Peter's teaching about the nature of their new inheritance invites a comparison of the new 'land' in which they hold inheritance (their share in the kingdom of God) with the land rights of their birth. This comparison might have been especially meaningful to Christians displaced from their homeland. . . ."[15] In contrast to land that can be taken, sold, destroyed, or overrun, the inheritance that they receive is one that is kept in heaven where nothing perishes. In addition, this inheritance is kept "for you," and the "you" are further described as those "guarded by the power of God through faith" (v.5). Michaels summarizes this nicely when he says, "God protects his people by his power as they wait to come into their inheritance, but what is required of them in the meantime is faithfulness to their 'Lord Jesus Christ' (v. 3) and (as they will find out) the steadfast endurance of suffering."[16] This family's inheritance can never be destroyed only rejected by the children for whom it is designated.

## Salvation

Finally, children in this family enter into the reality of salvation.[17] This salvation is described as one that is ready to be revealed in the last time. 1 Peter sees salvation as something that happens across the span of time. In contrast to some Christian traditions that view salvation as a one time event into which the believer enters, here 1 Peter associates salvation with what happens "in the last time" (καιρῷ ἐσκάτῳ, 1:5). When is this last time? 1 Peter has a sense of time in which Christ was always anticipated. So for example, 1:20 talks about the Christ as "one who was known before the foundation of the world and is being made known in these last times." The last times begin with the revelation of Christ, particularly, in this section of 1 Peter, on the cross and at his resurrection (1:19–21). These last times extend into the time when Christ will be fully revealed, for 1 Peter indicates that the audience experiences Jesus as one whom they love (1:8), are currently ransomed by Jesus as the perfect sacrificial lamb (1:18–21), and anticipates a time when

---

15. Jobes, *1 Peter*, 86.

16. J. Ramsey Michaels, *1 Peter*, Word Biblical Commentary 49 (Waco, Tex.: Word Books, 1982), 23.

17. Some commentators do not take "salvation" as a third item into which God's children are born; rather they take "salvation" as a separate item for which the child is guarded or kept (Jobes, *1 Peter*, 84). Both are possible.

Jesus will be fully revealed as the ruler who has completed his work (1:7; 3:22). Salvation has already begun. It is evidenced by their new birth into this new family; however, it is not yet fully consummated. That will occur at the end of time. Peter recognizes that salvation is an ongoing experience that begins with the new birth, continues as the child of God follows the example set for him or her, and is anticipated as a final event in which evil will be overcome and Jesus Christ will be fully revealed in all of his glory. Believers are saved from despair and futility in this present life, but they are not told that this means that they will escape trial and suffering. Indeed, in 1 Peter 1:6, the author goes on to remind them that right now they have had to endure "various trials." From the context of the book, it seems that the trials faced by the believers addressed in 1 Peter are trials that come from their association with Jesus and his community. The temptation that the community faces is the temptation to turn away from their new familial identity and to return to their old identity—an identity that may seem safe in comparison to this new and challenging identity as a child of God. However, the audience should understand that these trials should not be a reason for believers to turn away from the faith. They are saved from futility and brought into their new life as children of God, so that they may experience faithful and loving life with Christ and his people both now and in the future. Indeed, the destination of their faith is described to the audience in the present tense. "You are receiving the goal of your faith, the salvation of your souls" (1:9). Salvation is both already attained and something that they will continue receiving until the final revelation of Jesus Christ. This is a family whose lives are marked by the rescue they have already received and by the perfect restoration and healing they will receive at the resurrection. It is a "both/and" in which deliverance has already begun and will be fully experienced at the promised time.

## FAMILIAL BEHAVIOR

Identity is often portrayed in behavior. The way in which people act (or even walk and talk) says something about who they are. People mark their identity with certain clothes (e.g., gangs or Goths), certain walks (e.g., swaggering or slinking), and certain ways of speech (e.g., profane or witty). Families too have identifying behaviors—actions and speech that identify them as members of one family and not another. These identifying behaviors may be spoken or unspoken, but they help to determine the boundaries of the family—who should be included or excluded. In the 1st section (vv. 1–12), 1 Peter focuses on the identity of those who have been born anew and the new realities that they have entered into as the children of God. In the 2nd section (vv. 1:13—2:10), Peter continues to focus on identity while also giving instruction about the appropriate activities of those who take on this new familial identity. There are five Greek imperatives in this section.[18] Often, those who read English translations of this section will find many more imperatives in English than there are in Greek.[19] These five imperatives can be understood as forming an argument for the life that believers are to follow. The first thing that believers are to do is to have their hope firmly set, then they are to respond with holiness to the holiness of God. They then begin to demonstrate that holy life through their way of living in the presence of those who oppose them. This is followed by an instruction to love one another. This good way of life is sustained by their longing for the milk that comes from tasting God's provision, and it results in the whole familial community becoming the dwelling place of God.

## Set Your Hope

Hope provides the context for holiness. Without hope, striving for holiness can become a deadly encounter with perfectionism or legalism. Hope that is not delusional must be set on something reliable. Here, believers set their hope (1:13) on the grace of Christ, which is being brought to them. Indeed, as family members they have already received grace. It is evident in their new birth into new life, and it is evident in the new realities they experience. In addition, they have already been born into a "living hope" (1:3). This hope does not have to be conjured up out of thin air; rather, this hope is already the ground for the reality in which they live. At the same time, hope

---

18. There is some debate over whether there are five or six imperatives in this passage. The word οἰκοδομεῖσθε in 2:5 can be parsed as either an imperative (cf., NRSV) or an indicative (cf., ESV, NASB). The word also has either a passive or a middle voice. If it were an imperative it would have to be either "build yourselves up" in the middle voice or it would have to be a "permissive passive" that reads "let yourselves be built up" (NRSV). Mark Dubis notes that this word is not clearly used this way in the NT or LXX (*1 Peter: A Handbook on the Greek Text*, BHGNT [Waco: Baylor University Press, 2010], 48.). Thus, it is best to take this verb as an indicative.

19. This is because some of the participles that are used in this section have been translated as if they were imperatives. Some grammarians argue that the participle can be used in an imperatival fashion; others are not as convinced of this usage. For a brief review of the argument, see ibid., 25–26. In my own opinion, Peter demonstrates the use of the imperative, and it seems to me that if he had wished all of the verbs to be in the imperative, then he would have made it so. The very fact that there are distinctions between the imperatives and the participle implies to me that they function differently within this section of the text. So this part of the essay will focus on the five imperatives in this section.

is a future oriented activity, and this family is reminded that their hope rests on what is coming—the full revelation of Jesus. The believer anticipates that everything will not continue exactly as it is but that there will be a time when the life of faithfulness that they have led (1:6–7) will result in praise and honor when the true reality of Jesus' reign is made known. This imperative is preceded by several participles that indicate this state in which this action of setting one's hope occurs. There's a very colorful metaphor here as the reader is instructed to "gird up the loins of your mind." This metaphor refers to the gathering up of the toga or cloak around the waist to free the legs to run quickly and to be prepared for battle. Similarly, while being prepared the person is also to be sober-minded. These participles help to clarify the context for hope. This is not hope on a whim or without serious thought and consideration. Rather, this hope is set with the mind prepared and in the context of an honest appraisal of the current situation. The believers can set their hope on the current grace they have received with assurance that Jesus has complete control of the future. The grace they have received through the revelation that has already taken place is just a taste of what is to come when Jesus is fully revealed at the end of time.

## Be Holy in All Your Conduct

Children should look like their parents. Here in 1 Pet 1:15 God is referred to as "the Holy One who calls you." The holiness of God can refer to his divine majesty that sets him apart from everyone and everything else. God is not us; God is not the creation. At the same time, God's holiness refers to the moral activity that God engages in—God's justice and love.[20] In addition, the meaning of holiness shades over into purity.[21] The very character of God is unadulterated, not watered down, not contaminated, not dirtied. God is "holy"—morally active in the world and acting out of the majestic purity by which God is characterized. For many the calling to be holy seems to be an impossible calling. How can I, a simple human being, be holy the way that the God of the Universe is holy? How can we, the people God has called, be holy, especially when living in community is so difficult? But notice the things that form the context of this command. The audience is identified as "children of obedience" (v. 14). These are children who are characterized by an obedient heart and manner of living. They listen to their parent and respond to the voice of the parent who is calling them to action. These chil-

---

20. J. C. Lambert, "Holiness," *International Standard Bible Encyclopedia* (Grand Rapids: Eerdmans, 1995), n.p.

21. BDAG, 10–11.

dren are "not conforming themselves to their prior pattern of living out of their desires and in their ignorance" (v. 14). They are not resisting the voice and calling of the Holy One. These are new children, with a new parent who has redeemed them, given them an inheritance, a new identity, and a new life. These children have their hope set firmly (v. 13) on the grace that they have received through encountering Jesus. As they see Jesus, the futility of their former way of life unfolds before them, and in response to the new life that they are given they turn away from the former patterns of living that controlled their lives. At the same time, they recognized that this capacity to turn away from their former life only comes about through the gift that they received as Christ has been unveiled in and among them. This is not by their own power, but by the purifying work that has changed them (1 Pet 1:2–5). In contrast (ἀλλά) to their former pattern of living, they are to take up a new pattern of living—a pattern modeled not on their earthly ancestors but on the heavenly parent, the Holy One who calls them. The command does not simply say "be holy" but specifies that the audience is to be holy "in all your conduct." Just as God's moral life is just, pure, and loving, so, too, the moral life of believers is patterned after the moral life of God. The command to "be holy in all your conduct" introduces a theme about "conduct" that is more explicitly prominent in 1 Peter than elsewhere in the NT.[22] Believers are to be characterized by a certain way of life, a way that is congruent with the holy activity of God. As the next chapters unfold, it becomes clear that living a life that is patterned after the life of God can be extremely challenging in the context where these believers live. The identity and values of the believers is not valued by those in the society around them who do not know God. Yet, they are not instructed to withdraw from the hostile society but rather to live out the way of life that God has shown them. Their way of living will become a testimony to those around them—whether to the intimates of the family (3:1) or to a society who abuses and reviles them (3:15–16). Holy conduct (right living) will be a means of witness in a world that is bent on disbelief. And that capacity for right living flows out of the redemptive, transformative, sacrificial work of the Father, the Christ, and the Spirit. Thus, the very command to be holy is enabled by the one who is holy. The call to be holy is followed by more specific commands about how those who set their hope on the grace of Jesus and who are living obedient lives in response to the calling of the Holy One are to act. The three com-

---

22. The noun ἀναστροφή occurs six times in 1 Peter (1:15,18; 2:12; 3:1, 2, 16) and twice more in 2 Peter. It occurs only five times elsewhere in the NT and is only used once in the other books in which it is found (Gal, Eph, 1 Tim, Heb, Jam). The verb ἀναστρέφω is only a little more frequent as it occurs seven times outside 1–2 Peter and twice within 1–2 Peter.

mands that follow touch on three significant aspects of life: conduct in the context of unbelieving society; conduct among believers; and the internal life of believers.

## Conduct Yourselves with Fear

The command to "be holy in all your conduct" (v. 15) is an adjective "holy" (ἅγιοι) with the imperative verb "be" at the end of the verse. Sandwiched between the adjective and the verb is a prepositional phrase "in all your conduct." If one were simply to render the words in their Greek order, they would read "holy in all your conduct be." The outward conduct that reveals holiness is not an afterthought. The noun "conduct" in v. 15 is followed quickly by the verbal imperative "conduct yourselves" in v. 17. The focus is turned even more fully toward behavior. But the context for that behavior is made clearer. There is both an external context and an internal context. Externally, the audience is reminded that the one whom they call "Father," the one who has given new life to them, and who has provided their inheritance, is also a judge. And this one judges everyone—believer and non-believer; alien and citizen; master and slave; wife and husband—impartially. This judge does not show favoritism to one party over another or accept brides to sway his judgment. Rather, this judge acts fairly, justly, and impartially. The audience cannot "call in a favor" from their Father, who also happens to be the judge of all the living, because their Father doesn't give them special regard or attention in this way. Instead, because they know that God is impartial and just, they are to act in such a way that they will find favor with the Father who also judges rightly and fairly.

In addition, this audience lives in exile. They do not have any special status. They are not at the center of society. They are not "at home" in a way that provides them security. So, at the same time that they cannot turn to their Father for special (corrupt/unfair) favors, they also cannot turn to their social-cultural context for special regard or elevation. Instead, the way they behave will show whether they align themselves with a culture that disregards God or with the one who has given them salvation, inheritance, and life. This is the external context in which they must conduct themselves well. The command to have good conduct is prefaced with the phrase "in fear" (ἐν φόβῳ). Since this follows immediately after 1 Peter's comments about the impartial judge whose judgments are based on the deeds of each individual, the phrase is often taken to mean in "fear of the coming judge."[23] However, this should not be taken to refer to "fear" as a sense of terror but

23. BDAG.

rather to a way of living out of reverence and respect for who God is.[24] The good conduct of believers is lived out in front of God and the whole of society and is characterized by a sense of awe and honor towards God. When it would be tempting to fear the culture that has the power to oppress, label, and marginalize, the right response is not fear of others but rather "fear" (reverence) of God. The focus rests on good behavior before God and within their exilic context. Might removing the focus solely from the imperative "conduct yourselves" and turning toward the larger context in which behavior happens help 21st century readers hear 1 Peter 1:17? Places of estrangement, alienation, and disjunction are marked by fear and anxiety. In contrast, 1 Peter envisions a family where there are no favorites. In such a family, there is no fear that someone else has more, gets more, or is worth more. Instead, fairness and impartiality become a mark of a trustworthy parent. And that trustworthy parent can be respected and honored. In this context, behavior does not have to be about gaining attention (at the expense of another), rebelling against unfair mandates, or marking out one's individual identity in contrast to the identity of others. Instead, out of right relationship with the parent, a relationship marked by respect, comes good behavior that honors the one who has given life and that reflects the character (holiness) of the life giver.

### Love One Another Earnestly from the Heart

The context in which good behavior is lived out is not only in the larger society but also within the narrower confines of the body of believers. In that context, the command is "to love one another fervently." But again, to understand the imperative, we need to turn to the context in which it is located. At the beginning of this sentence, 1 Peter turns again to the language of "holiness." This has been an important theme throughout this first chapter. It began in v. 2 where the audience is described as "sanctified by the Spirit," and it continues in v. 15 with the instruction to "be holy." This holiness is attained through the pure sacrifice of Christ the lamb. Now, in 1:22 the context for love is identified as holiness. The participle that opens this verse identifies the audience as a group that "cleanses their souls." How does such cleaning or purification take place? The text answers, "by obedience to the truth." As readers, we have already encountered words for purification and obedience together. The Spirit does the work of purifying and setting

---

24. Paul J. Achtemeier, *1 Peter: A Commentary on First Peter*, Hermeneia (Minneapolis: Fortress Press, 1996), 125; Michaels, *1 Peter*, 61; Joel B. Green, *1 Peter*, The Two Horizons NT Commentary (Grand Rapids: Eerdmans, 2007), 117.

apart believers (v. 2), and the Spirit does this for the purpose of assisting believers in their obedience to the person of Jesus Christ (v. 2). They receive life and an inheritance from the Father. Those who live out of the life they have received from the Father are assisted in the work of cleansing and purifying their souls by the Spirit, so that they may obey the truth that has been revealed to them in Jesus. This truth that is to be obeyed is not an abstract philosophical ideal but rather the truth born out of the familial relationship of the believer to Father, Spirit, and Christ. This forms the context for earnest love. True love is born out of purity and is authentic. So often what passes for love in 21st century western culture has been severely distorted by self-interest, jealousy, anger, disgust, and so much else that is alienating. Or, love is dressed up—it becomes associated with material gifts (diamonds, chocolates, flowers), or romantic expressions (cards, sweet words), or sexual gratification (sleeping around or being good in bed). But the love described in 1 Peter is authentic, genuine, and uncontrived. Such love is vulnerable without being needy; tender without being sappy; strong without being overbearing or domineering. The command to love one another should remind all those who hear 1 Peter that Jesus said that others would be able to identify people as his disciples by the love they had for each other (Jn 13:34–35). Such pure, other-oriented love is a welcome antidote to the portraits of love painted by western cultural media. This pure, other-oriented love could be the welcome cure for a society that sells experiences of "love" (so often attached to sex) that are often driven by exploitation (sex sells cars) or a longing for experiences (everyone's doing it) and status (isn't she/he the "hottest").

## Long for . . . Milk

1 Peter does not follow up on the commands to good behavior and other-oriented love with a long list of other activities. There are two broad instructions: have good conduct and love one another. These are followed by the next instruction: "crave." The imperative focuses on the internal longing of the one who has been reborn by the word of God (1:23). Their internal desire is to be oriented to a particular object . . . milk—pure, spiritual milk.[25] Jobes expresses it this way: ". . . God in Christ alone both conceives and

---

25. The meaning of τὸ λογικὸν ἄδολον γάλα is difficult to interpret. Many interpreters have given the phrase the meaning "the pure milk of the word" even though λογικὸν does not mean "word," (e.g., Achtemeier, *1 Peter*, 146–47). This argument is generally made from the context of 1 Pet 1:23–25 with its quotation from Isaiah that focuses on the λόγος. However, Jobes argues against this view for a position in which λογικὸν refers to the sustenance that God provides to believers (*1 Peter*, 132–35).

sustains the life of the new birth. They are to crave the Lord God for spiritual nourishment. They have tasted the goodness of the Lord in their conversion, but there is more to be had. The more-of-the-Lord-to-be-had by Peter's readers involves putting off all evil and all deceit and hypocrisies and jealousies, and all backbiting (2:1). Refusal to do so would stunt their growth in the new life."[26] God provides everything that is needed for these children, and then calls them to a new life reflecting the holy life of God. The children are to take off (ἀποτίθημι, used literally of taking off clothes and figuratively of ridding oneself of something[27]) all evil and all deceit. These things are not easily replaced, and the hope of these children is the strong internal urge to cling to God like a hungry baby who is only satisfied at its mother's breast. Such turning away, craving, and tasting will help the child grow up into the salvation that has begun with the new birth. Perhaps the 21st century could be labeled the "century of desire." One of the realities of western culture is that our lives are soaked in advertising—whether the old fashioned general advertising of radio, TV, and billboards or the newer targeted advertising of Facebook and Google. In this advertising saturated culture, people are encouraged to want, to desire, to aspire. And while advertisements entice people to buy—often the suggestion is not that the product they purchase will satisfy a material need but rather that acquiring this product will satisfy them by helping them obtain a certain image, lifestyle, partner, emotion, or experience. Repeatedly, however, obtaining the advertised product does not result in satisfaction of the desire. Instead, people often end up feeling empty and dissatisfied. This opens up the opportunity to seek new sources of satisfaction in new products—products that range from microwaves to cruises and from restaurants to spa treatments. In such a culture, the message of 1 Peter encourages rightly oriented desire turned towards One who can truly satisfy.

God wants to take these children that he has fathered and fed and grown and turn them into a family that is the very dwelling place of God (2:5). God births and sustains and builds these chosen children, these living stones, into a spiritual house. "House" (οἶκος) is an evocative metaphor in this context. In its most basic form the word simply refers to a place where someone dwells. But there are two other references that resonate here as well: the "house" as the temple of God and the "house" as the household or even the dynasty of God. The reference to the believers as the temple that God will build is expanded with the purpose statement that these believing children, the tribe and descendents of God, will offer sacrifices to God in

---

26. Jobes, *1 Peter*, 140.
27. BDAG.

the temple built out of living stones—all those alive in God now and in all the years past and in all the years to come. The God who created this family forms this family into a spiritual household where they will worship and serve God together. And the cornerstone for this temple is the one whom the children have already acknowledged as the living Lord, raised from the dead, and revealed to them as just, righteous, and holy. Though others have rejected the Word of truth, these chosen ones have become the very dwelling place of God. And this is why 1 Peter can say "you are a chosen race, a royal priesthood, a holy nation, a people for [God's] possession" (2:9a).

## THE SIGNIFICANCE OF 1 PETER FOR THE DECENTERED SELF

In an age where many of the markers of identity are clearly known as areas that can generate shame, frustration, anger, disillusionment, and a sense of abandonment or neglect, Peter speaks freshly. Here, in these chapters, the audience is invited to participate in the family life of God. Having experienced the rebirth that God fathers and having tasted the good milk that God provides, they can take up their hope, their inheritance, their salvation and live into their new identity as the children of God. This gives believers the freedom to choose goodness even in a world where such goodness is a source of mockery. This gives the believer the freedom to choose pure, holy love even in a world where love has been lowered to the lowest common denominator. And this gives the believer the opportunity to speak to others about the invitation that God extends to participate in God's family and all that family has to offer. Knowing one's family identity and history also provides the framework for weaving a unified narrative around the self. Such a narrative has the potential to bring a unified sense of identity in a contemporary world that often celebrates multiple, disconnected experiences of the self.

# 10

# Who's Stumbling on the Stumbling Stone?

*A Reassessment of 1 Peter 2:4–10 in Light of a Dynamic Understanding of Holiness and Election*

SUSANN LIUBINSKAS

## INTRODUCTION

THE OT IMAGERY OF 1 Pet 2:4–10 recalls the grand sweep of salvation history, stretching from Yahweh's election of Abraham and Israel to his incorporation of the Gentiles into the people of God. As such, it stands as the author's climactic description of Christian identity, describing the community in terms of its relationship to God, to Israel, and to the outside world.[1] However, much like Israel's tendency to rely on its privileged status as the elect, often at the expense of obedience to the divine prerogatives upon which it was premised, interpretations of Christian identity in this passage tend to emphasize the status of believers as the elect.[2] As a conse-

1. Karen H. Jobes, *1 Peter* (Grand Rapids: Baker, 2005), 142.
2. For example: Paul J. Achtemeier, *1 Peter: A Commentary on First Peter*

quence, Christian holiness is understood in predominantly static or cultic terms.³ This static interpretation of holiness is often accompanied by the view that the ἀπιστοῦσιν and ἀπειθοῦντες of 2:7-8 refer to those outside of the Christian community.⁴ In other words, the two terms are taken as signifying a soteriological dichotomy between the saved, 1 Peter's audience, and the unsaved, all others who do not accept the gospel.

However, is the author referring *solely* to non-Christians in 2:7b? As Joel B. Green observes, the life of the audience is characterized as life in the Diaspora where "the threat of assimilation and apostasy is constant."⁵ Of note in this regard are the various references that indicate that there are different reactions among members of the audience to the social rejection they

(Minneapolis: Fortress, 1996),152; John H. Elliott, *1 Peter*, AB 37B (New York: Doubleday, 2000), 411; Leonard Goppelt, *A Commentary on 1 Peter*, trans. John E. Alsup (Grand Rapids: Eerdmans, 1993), 143; Jobes, *1 Peter*, 144; and Bo Reicke, *The Epistles of James, Peter, and Jude*, AB 37 (Garden City, N. J.: Doubleday, 1964), 411. Moreover, since the election of individual believers is accomplished in tandem with their incorporation into the people of God, commentators emphasize the close tie between election and ecclesiology (Francis Wright Beare, *The First Epistle of Peter* (Oxford: Blackwell, 1947), 93; Joel B. Green, *1 Peter* (Grand Rapids: Eerdmans, 2007), 55; Ramsey J. Michaels, *1 Peter*, WBC 49 (Mexico City: Thomas Nelson, 1988), 93). Accordingly, interpretations of 2:9 focus on the transference to the church of the titles formerly applied to Israel in the OT, particularly those found in the Septuagint of Isa 43 and Exod 19:5-6 (Achtemeier, *1 Peter*, 152; Green, *1 Peter*, 55, 60-63; Edward Gordon Selwyn, *The First Epistle of St. Peter: The Greek Text with Introduction, Notes, and Essays*, 1946 repr. (Grand Rapids: Baker, 1981),168-169; Peter H. Davids, *The First Epistle of Peter* (Grand Rapids: Eerdmans, 1990), 90; Goppelt, *Commentary*, 147; Jobes, *1 Peter*, 159). This also holds true for interpretations that focus on either the honor-shame dynamics present in the letter or social identity construction (Green, *1 Peter*, 60; Elliott, *1 Peter*, 407-449; David Abernathy, "Exegetical Considerations in 1 Peter 2:7-9," *Notes* 15[2001]: 25; Barth L. Campbell, *Honor, Shame, and the Rhetoric of 1 Peter*, SBLDS 160 [Atlanta: Scholars Press, 1995], 85; J. De Waal Dryden, *Theology and Ethics in 1 Peter*, WUNT 209 [Tübingen: Mohr, 2006], 121).

3. For example, Davids argues that the reference to Christians as a priesthood (2:9) most likely points to their election by God through their conversion and baptism (1:15-23) rather than to their moral holiness (Davids, *First Epistle*, 87).

4. For example, Michaels writes that, "Peter uses the quotations to emphasize the identity of his readers as believers in contrast to the unbelievers or disobedient with whom they were in daily contact in the provinces of Asia Minor" (Michaels, *1 Peter*, 94). Also, Jobes, *1 Peter*, 146; Simon J. Kistemaker, *Exposition of James, Epistles of John, Peter, and Jude* (Grand Rapids: Baker, 2007), 88; Reicke, *Epistles*, 409, 434; and John H. Elliott, *Conflict, Community, and Honor: 1 Peter in Social-Scientific Perspective* (Eugene, Oreg.: Cascade, 2007), 31-32. According to Michaels, this soteriological dichotomy with its accompanying social tensions is the focal point of the author's interest throughout the rest of the letter (Michaels, *1 Peter*, 113).

5. Joel B. Green, "Living as Exiles: The Church in the Diaspora in 1 Peter," in *Holiness and Ecclesiology in the NT*, eds. Kent E. Brower and Andy Johnson (Grand Rapids: Eerdmans, 2007), 319.

are experiencing. Some have begun to be ashamed of their faith (4:6); others are tempted to retaliate (3:9); while still others are seeking to conform to a more socially acceptable lifestyle (1:14; 4:2). Moreover, the audience is warned that the goal of their adversary, the devil, is to lead them into apostasy (5:8, 9).[6] In addition, non-Christians are not explicitly mentioned in 2:7-8, rather the biblical writer refers more generally to those who do not believe and disobey.[7]

Accordingly, this essay will argue that a dynamic understanding of holiness and election, whereby obedience to the divine will is the means by which identity is formed and maintained, provides a better lens through which to view 1 Pet 2:4-10. Emphasis on a static notion of election creates a thematic disjunction between 1:1—2:10 and the paraenesis which follows (2:11—5:12) and between 2:4-10 and the call to holiness in 1:15-16 which many interpreters see as enjoining believers to moral holiness.[8] Moreover, both the rhetorical unity of the epistle and the larger OT context of 2:9-10 point to a broader understanding of election which encompasses obedience on the part of the elect. That is, if 1:15-16 constitutes the *propositio* then moral holiness, rather than simply cultic holiness, governs 2:4-10.[9] This is further supported by intertextual analysis of the larger OT context of 2:9-10, particularly when the phrase εἰς περιποίησιν (v. 9), which is used to translate the Hebrew סְגֻלָּה in Exod 19:5, Deut 7:6, 14:2, 26:18, Ps 135, and Mal 3:17, is considered. Consequently, if Christian identity is premised on both divine election and continued obedience to the divine will, then the ἀπιστοῦσιν and ἀπειθοῦντες in 2:7-8 refer not only to those outside of the Christian community, but also to those believers who are contemplat-

---

6. Gene L. Green, "Use of OT for Christian Ethics in 1 Peter," *TynBul* 41(1990): 278.

7. Lauri Thurén, *Argument and Theology in 1 Peter: The Origin of Christian Paraenesis*, JSNTSup 114 (Sheffield: Sheffield Academic, 1995), 128. Thurén makes the argument that the rhetorical situation and strategy of 1 Pet indicates that the addressees were encountering different types of social pressure because of their Christianity and thus, they would most likely react in several different ways. Since all these reactions are unacceptable, the author needs to modify all of them (Thurén, *Argument and Theology*, 86).

8. For example, Jobes maintains that in 1:15-16 the author is urging his readers to identify with God by being set apart and by relating to the world according to God's terms (Jobes, *1 Peter*, 112). Similarly, Achtemeir argues that although holiness is not something that a person can achieve by moral effort, it nevertheless is a separation from one's former culture for that entails certain appropriate behavior and conduct (Achtemeier, *1 Peter*, 121).

9. For example: Ben Witherington III, *A Socio-Rhetorical Commentary on 1-2 Peter*, vol. II of *Letters and Homilies for Hellenized Christians* (Downers Grove, Ill.: InterVarsity, 2007), 92, 113-21; and Campbell, *Honor Shame*, 63, 83-98.

ing accommodation that could well lead to apostasy as a means of escaping persecution and suffering.

A reassessment of 1 Pet 2:4–10 in light of a dynamic understanding of holiness and election entails both a reconsideration of how Christian identity is formed and maintained and an exploration of the biblical writer's conception of holiness. Thus, I will begin with a rhetorical analysis of holiness and identity as it is expressed across the epistle which will be followed by an examination of its particular expression in 2:4–10. Since the author roots Christian identity in the calling and election of Israel, the concept of holiness cannot be adequately understood apart from its OT context. Accordingly, I will examine the intertextuality of 2:9–10, particularly the ascription of Israel's title, εἰς περιποίησιν of God, to the Christian community. Finally, I will argue that interpretations of 2:4–10 that view the passage primarily in terms of believer's privileged status before God result in an attenuated reading which places undue emphasis on the theme of encouragement.[10]

Although the encouragement of Christians who are facing persecution is a concern that runs through the epistle, this theme must be balanced with those passages that strongly suggest that the author is seeking to prevent accommodation and potential apostasy among some members of the community. In other words, encouragement serves a double-purpose: as an exhortation to persevere; and as a warning against seeking honor outside of that conferred by God through Christ.[11]

## THE RHETORIC OF HOLINESS AND IDENTITY

### Across 1 Peter

The issue of identity arises in the *exordium* (1:3–12) in relation to suffering as a Christian for/with Christ.[12] Here, the audience is identified both as belonging to a new kinship group via the new birth (1:3) and as the future heirs of an imperishable, heavenly inheritance kept in heaven until the eschaton (1:4–5). However, presently they are undergoing suffering as a result of this identity (1:6–8). Thus, a major concern for the biblical writer is to portray both Christ and believers as honorable despite the suffering that appears to indicate otherwise (cf. 2:4–10). Accordingly, the problem of suf-

---

10. For example: Elliott, *1Peter*, 412, 448; Reicke, *Epistles*, 449; and Campbell, *Honor Shame*, 94.

11. Thurén, *Argument and Theology*, 128.

12. Campbell, *Honor Shame*, 50, 56. Moreover, 1 Pet 1:3–12 could be read as containing both an *exordium* and a *narratio* (Witherington, *Socio-Rhetorical*, 93).

fering as a consequence of one's identity as a Christ-follower constitutes the rhetorical exigence.[13]

Moreover, although Christians have received salvation via the new birth, this salvation will be fully revealed only at the *parousia* (1:5), indicating a progressive, climactic unfolding of a salvific state that includes the experience of trials and tribulations. Directly related to this is the writer's concern to encourage believers to persevere in godly living and to warn them not to eschew the values and norms of the Christian family in order to conform to those of the empire in an effort to either assuage or escape suffering. In other words, the author seeks to persuade his audience to seek honor in God's eyes, rather than in the eyes of larger society. Accordingly, the major sections of the letter are characterized by exhortations aimed at directing future action and as such represent deliberative rhetoric. Specifically, the discourse draws on the topics of honor and advantage in an effort to persuade the audience to embrace honorable things;[14] in this case, the author exhorts his audience to embrace the way and example of Christ in his suffering.

The theme of Christian identity is carried over into the *propositio* (1:13–16)[15] which is directly connected to the *exordium* via the causal connective διό. Thus, the theme of identity, intertwined with perseverance toward the eschatological goal introduced in the *exordium* is linked to holiness and ethical conduct in the *propositio*. Since God has given believers a new birth through Christ (1:3), therefore (διό) they are to prepare their minds for action, discipline themselves, set their hope on Christ, not be conformed to former desires, and be holy as the Father is holy (1:13–16). What this suggests is that Christian identity defined as being holy or set-apart for God, will most likely result in suffering, because this identity, which is expressed by an ethically holy life, will conflict with many, if not most, of the social values and norms that define the broader culture. In other words, to persevere in faith towards final salvation requires perseverance in exemplifying that holiness that characterizes a follower of Christ. Identity is defined by obedience to God's norms and values, while obedience to divine standards constitutes one's identity as a member of God's household.

Consequently, each of the five arguments works to solidify the connection between identity and obedience, including the first, within which 2:4–10 falls and which will be discussed in the following section.[16] With re-

---

13. Witherington, *Socio-Rhetorical*, 75.
14. Cicero, *Inv.* 2.155–58.
15. Witherington, *Socio-Rhetorical*, 49. Also, Campbell, *Honor Shame*, 58.
16. Similarly, Witherington, *Socio-Rhetorical*, 49. Witherington is probably correct

spect to the second through the fifth arguments,[17] in the second, the author exhorts believers to give due honor to those person who comprise human institutions and authority structures, including the emperor (2:11–17). Slaves are to honor even abusive masters (2:18–25); wives are to honor unbelieving husbands (3:1–6); while Christian husbands are to honor their wives (3:7); and all are to do good to those who persecute them (3:8–12), according to the example of Christ (2:21–23). They are to do this despite persecution for their identity as Christ-followers.

In the third argument, Christ is again offered as a historical *exemplum* for a paraenetic purpose (3:18–22, 4:1–11). Here, believers are to identify with their model by embracing suffering, rather than reverting back to their pre-Christian behavior (4:3–6), regardless of the fact that they are suffering shame as a result of refusing to join the rest of society in its excesses (4:4). Instead, they are to conduct themselves in accordance with the values and norms of their new identity as members of the Christian family: by praying; loving one another; showing hospitality without grumbling; and exercising their spiritual gifts for the benefit of the assembly (4:7–11).

The fourth argument constitutes an *expolitio* which develops the theme of honorable suffering from a variety of angles.[18] Here, the author holds before the audience not only the prospect of future glory, as long as they persevere in suffering for and like Christ (4:13–14), but also the prospect of judgment (4:17–18).[19] Accordingly, believers are to entrust themselves to God (4:19). Finally, in the last argument elders are exhorted to tend their flock in an exemplary, humble fashion (5:1–4), and all are to clothe them-

---

to critique Campbell for viewing 1:13—2:10 as the first argument beginning with its own *propositio*, in that normally the main or over-arching proposition(s) for the entire discourse comes after the *exordium* and before all of the arguments (Witherington, *Socio-Rhetorical*, 48). Moreover, if Campbell's structure were followed, we would be left without a *propositio* that governs that entire discourse. In addition, Witherington is correct in critiquing Campbell's assessment of 4:12—5:14 as the peroration, since the arguments appear to continue through 5:5. Moreover, Campbell's division ignores the presence of a distinct epistolary postscript (Witherington, *Socio-Rhetorical*, 208–210).

17. Similarly, Witherington: first argument (1:17—2:10); second (2:11—3:12); third (3:13—4:11); fourth (4:12–19); and fifth (5:1–5) (Witherington, *Socio-Rhetorical*, 49).

18. Campbell, *Honor Shame*, 200. Campbell notes that, although each verse in this section could stand independently as a maxim related to the topic of suffering, restatement, synonymy, contrary (vv. 15–16), and example (v. 17) are used to structure the passage. As examples of restatement we have: 4:14 which refers back to 2:12 and 3:16 (suffering slander); 4:15–16 to 2:19–20 and 3:14 (just and unjust suffering); 4:19 to 3:17 (suffering and the will of God); 4:14 to 3:14 (blessedness of suffering); and 4:13 to 1:6, 8 (joy in suffering). In addition, there is the quotation from Prov 11:31 and a conclusive statement in v. 19 (Campbell, *Honor Shame*, 199–200).

19. Witherington, *Socio-Rhetorical*, 210.

selves with humility in view of God's grace (5:5); humility being an identifying characteristic of the family of God.

The writer's concern for ethical conduct is evident once again in the *peroratio* (5:6–9), which recaps the main themes developed in the discourse. Thus, believers are to persevere in godliness in the face of suffering by humble reliance on God (5:6–7). This is accompanied by an exhortation to stand fast against the devil (5:8–9), which implicitly recalls the exhortation to obedience. Here, the devil is described in metaphorical terms as a roaring lion, seeking to devour believers, which evokes the idea of salvation as a journey wrought with danger, beginning in the present and reaching fulfillment only at the eschaton, introduced in the first chapter.

In summary, the above analysis demonstrates that the epistle as a whole is concerned with ethical conduct, congruent with divine holiness (1:15–16), and not simply with identity, although this is important, since identity with Christ is the source of believers' obedience. As we will see, this is also true of 2:4–10 where the idea of believers' election in Christ (2:6–7a) and their identity as a chosen race, a royal priesthood, a holy nation, and God's own people (2:9a) is related to: the previous material, that is, the new birth (1:3), the general call to holiness (1:15–16), including the metaphor in 2:2–3; and the paraenesis that follows (2:11—5:11), which consists of specific directives for holy living that are in accordance with a holy identity.

## Holiness and Identity in 2:4–10

This section of the discourse functions as an *iudicatio*, whose source is the OT, and as such constitutes a divine pronouncement or supernatural oracle.[20] As a divine word, it amounts to the weightiest type of authority that can be used to support an argument or case.[21] Moreover, 2:6–10 substantiates (διότι) 2:4–5 which suggests that the same idea of perseverance in obedience linked with identity in 2:4–5 continues in these verses. The ἵνα clause in the milk metaphor (2:2–3) indicates that believers are to partake of Christ as unadulterated, spiritual milk, *so that* they might grow (αὐξηθῆτε) into salvation. Of note is the first class conditional, εἰ ἐγεύσασθε ὅτι χρηστὸς ὁ κύριος (2:3), which assumes that believers have indeed tasted that the Lord

---

20. Campbell, *Honor Shame*, 79, 83.

21. Quintilian, *Inst. Or.* 5.11. 36–37, 42–44. According to Quintilian, an *iudicatio* is an authoritative opinion rendered by nations, peoples, philosophers, distinguished citizens, illustrious poets, supernatural authority derived from oracles, or the gods that is used to support an argument or case.

is good and thus, are to continue coming to him.[22] He is both the basis of their identity and the source of their continuing obedience which results in their growth.

This idea of progression in spiritual maturity, rather than a static state, is continued in 2:4 where there is implied causation. Since, you are coming (προσερχόμενοι) to him (Christ), the living stone, you yourselves are even being built-up (οἰκοδομεῖσθε) to be a spiritual house in order to be (purpose, εἰς) a holy priesthood, in order to offer (ἀνενέγκαι, purpose infinitive) spiritual sacrifices acceptable to God (2:5).[23] This offering is continuous. In other words, believers do not offer a sacrifice one time (for example, at their conversion or baptism) but are to do so as part and parcel of their identity as holy priests.

---

22. Most interpreters argue that the "spiritual milk" in 2:1–3 refers to believers partaking of the word of God (Scripture) rather than of Christ. However, Jobes argues that the metaphor needs to be understood within the context of Ps 33 LXX where the word of God is not mentioned. Thus, believers are to crave the Lord by adopting the attitudes and behaviors that will allow progression towards spiritual maturity. By hearing the word, believers enter into the new birth, but they "do not truly ingest God's life-transforming grace until they have put off ungodly attitudes and behaviors (Karen H. Jobes, "Got Milk? Septuagint Psalm 33 and the Interpretation of 1 Peter 2:1–3," *WTJ* 63 [2000]: 12–14). Campbell finds an enthymeme in 2:1–3. Major premise: newborn infants crave milk. Minor premise: believers are like newborn infants. Conclusion: they are to long for spiritual milk (Christ), so that they might grow into salvation (Campbell, *Honor, Shame*, 82–83).

23. Οἰκοδομεῖσθε may be read as an passive imperative indicating that the participle προσερχόμενοι should also be read as an imperative. Although one could also take οἰκοδομεῖσθε as a middle, "let yourself be built," which suggests that although God is doing the building, believers must cooperate, the emphasis in the verses that follow is on divine action, which suggests that it is best taken as a passive (Witherington, *Socio-Rhetorical*, 114). Also, Elliott, *1 Peter*, 412 and Goppelt, *Commentary*, 139–40. Elliott maintains that "spiritual house" should be understood as "house" or "household" rather than "temple" (John H. Elliott, *The Elect and Holy: An Exegetical Examination of 1 Peter 2:4–10 and the Phrase 'Basileion Hierateuma'* [Eugene, Oreg.: Wipf and Stock, 2005], 157–59). Similarly, Beare notes that the use of οἶκος rather than ναός suggests that Peter did not have a cultic sense in mind (Beare, *First Epistle*, 9). However, the use of ἱεράτευμα in 2:9 argues for a close connection between οἶκος πνευματικος and εἰς ἱεράτευμα ἅγιον, with the second phrase introducing the new idea of priesthood, identifying the "spiritual house" more specifically as a priesthood. As Michaels notes, "It is difficult to imagine a house intended for priesthood as being anything other than a temple of some sort" (Michaels, *1 Peter*, 100). Moreover, the metaphor should not be pressed too far. That is, believers can be imagined to be both the structure itself and the persons in it, since metaphors speak to realities that cannot be adequately described using purely denotative language. In addition, Witherington notes that οἶκος is clearly enough used in reference to the temple in 2 Chr 36:23, Ps 68:10 LXX, and Isa 56:7. Thus, 1 Peter is probably building on these texts as 4:17 suggests (Witherington, *Socio-Rhetorical*, 114–15).

In addition, God's prior election of Christ, the living cornerstone (2:4-6), forms the basis for the divine election of believers.[24] This is meant to encourage the audience to continue in their faith. In other words, they, as a community, are deemed honorable in God's eyes, as Christ is, and are to eschew seeking honor from society at large, as Christ did. In addition, the repetition of the words ἐκλεκτός (2:4, 6, 9) and ἔντιμος (2:4, 6) suggests an emphasis on election and honor and links to the use of ἐκλεκτός in 1:1 and τιμή in 1:7. In this way, Peter reminds his audience again of their honor and privileged position before God.[25] However, believers maintain their identity as God's people, his spiritual temple and holy priesthood, by eschewing the seeking of honor according to culturally defined mechanisms.

In this sense, 2:4-10 functions as a source of encouragement both for those who are intent on persevering and for those contemplating accommodation. The latter are implicitly urged to turn back from penultimate sources of honor to the ultimate source. This recalls the idea of salvation as a journey toward future glory, introduced in chapter 1, which runs through the discourse. Deliberative discourse requires that the orator show the benefit of engaging in the behavior he or she proposes, in this case perseverance in faith and obedience in the face of persecution and resultant suffering.[26] The author does this not only at the beginning of his address where he emphasizes the glory and the imperishable promised inheritance awaiting believers at the eschaton (1:4, 9), but also in this passage where he gives believers an alternative, Christologically-based identity (2:4-7a), bestowing honor on them by ascribing Israel's honorable titles to them as a community (2:9-10). In this sense, manipulation of the honor-shame categories in 2:4-10 works to "sculpt" the identity of the audience, so that human valuations, in this case slander by unbelievers, are dismissed in favor of divine assessments of honor.[27] Thus, believers' identity is linked to the elect Son, Jesus Christ. Moreover, just as Jesus was rejected, they too will be rejected.[28]

---

24. For example, Achtemeier, *1 Peter*, 152; Elliott, *1 Peter*, 411; Goppelt, *1 Peter*, 143; Jobes, *1 Peter*, 144; and Kistemaker, *Exposition*, 84.

25. Campbell, *Honor Shame*, 81.

26. Witherington, *Socio-Rhetorical*, 76.

27. Joel Green, *1 Peter*, 56.

28. Dryden, *Theology and Ethics*, 121.

## HOLINESS & IDENTITY IN THE OT AND 1 PETER 2:9

As 2:4–10 makes clear, the attainment of spiritual maturity is accomplished in tandem with incorporation into a spiritual house (2:5).[29] Accordingly, the community takes on the role of the priesthood and the titles applied to Israel in the OT, particularly those found in the Septuagint of Isa 43 and Exod 19:5–6. Although the identity of believers gives them a privileged and honored position before God, thus serving as encouragement to the community to continue in holiness regardless of their circumstances, the wider context of these OT passages suggests that this elect status is inextricably linked to the responsibility to continue in holiness.[30] That is, those who are currently enjoying an elect status before God could just as easily become those who are disobedient if they should choose to accommodate to pagan norms in order to escape persecution and suffering. Like Israel, who was judged for disobedience, despite being God's own special possession, judgment begins with the household of God (1 Pet 4:17).[31]

## "God's Special Possession" in the OT

The identification of the believers in Asia Minor with God's chosen people is a prominent motif in the epistle beginning with the epistolary prescript: ἐκλεκτοῖς παρεπιδήμοις διασπορᾶς (1:1). The terms γένος ἐκλεκτόν (Isa

---

29. See, Beare, *First Epistle*, 93; Green, *1 Peter*, 55; and Michaels, *1 Peter*, 93.

30. Although Beare notes that the phrase, "a people of God's possession," is used in Mal 3:17, he nevertheless concludes that the author uses the term in order to emphasize election (Beare, *First Epistle*, 105). Similarly, Kistemaker, *Exposition*, 93. This is also true for Reicke who sees the phrase as also alluding to Deut 7:6, 14:2, and 28:16. Yet, he concludes that this title functions to make clear the concept of divine election (Reicke, *Epistles*, 439). In addition, although Campbell lists Deut 4:20, 7:6, 14:2 and Mal 3:17 as allusions, he does not comment on these passages (Campbell, *Honor Shame*, 96). The same is true of the reference to Hos 2:23 in v.10. Thus, most commentators see this as an allusion to the electing love of God and the Christian community as the fulfillment of prophecy through their conversion to Christ (e.g.: Kistemaker, *Exposition*, 93; and Jobes, *1 Peter*, 163–164). In other words, the larger context of Hosea and the fact that the prophetic indictment is directed toward insiders, that is Israel, is not considered. The larger context of Hos 2:23 is similar to what is seen in Isa 43. In this chapter, God condemns Israel for covenant infidelity and at the same time promises to restore his unfaithful people. Tellingly, in 2:20 Yahweh tells his wayward people that they will know him again, meaning that they will again be both obedient to his covenant and have intimacy with him (Deut 7:9; Gen 19:8, 24:16).

31. It is important to note that 1 Peter refers to God as an impartial judge of people's deeds, including those of his own people (1:17).

43:20), βασίλειον ἱεράτευμα (Exod 19:6), ἔθνος ἅγιον (Exod 19:6), and λαὸς εἰς περιποίησιν (Exod 19:5, 23:22; Deut 4:20, 7:6, 14:2; Isa 43:21; Mal 3:17) in 2:9 recall this earlier identification. This conflation of OT titles exemplifies *amplificatio* which serves rhetorically to intensify the honorable nature of the attributes conveyed by these epithets. Moreover, the appellations are synonymous in the sense that they are not arranged in an ascending order of value.³² Consequently, a detailed analysis of one of the terms should shed considerable light on the whole.

An examination of λαὸς εἰς περιποίησιν, which translates the Hebrew סגלה, shows that when the term is examined within its greater context, the election of Israel as God's special possession is inextricably linked with the community's continuing obedience to the covenant. Gene Green has made a compelling case that the author of 1 Pet bases his selection of OT texts upon a correlation between the situation of his audience and the situation of Israel. After extrapolating the pertinent teaching from the OT, the biblical writer then develops it in his own terminology to show its relevance for the Christian communities in Asia Minor, taking into account "the whole of its thought and teaching."³³ The table below summarizes the occurrences of the term סגלה in the MT and LXX.

| Secular Use: 1 Chr 29:3 and Eccl 2:8 | Theological Use: Exod 19:5; Deut 7:6, 14:2, 26:18; Ps 135:4; Mal 3:17 |
|---|---|
| Hebrew:<br><br>• 1 Chr 29:3 סְגֻלָּה<br>• Eccl 2:8 סְגֻלָּה | Hebrew:<br><br>• Exod 19:5 והייתם לי סגלה מכל־העמים<br>• Deut 7:6 להיות לו לעם סגלה מכל העמים<br>• Deut 14:2 להיות לו לעם סגלה מכל העמים<br>• Deut 26:18 להיות לו לעם סגלה<br>• Ps 135:4 ישראל לסגלתו<br>• Mal 3:17 אני עשה סגלה |

---

32. Campbell, *Honor Shame*, 96. Βασίλειον ἱεράτευμα is best translated as "a kingdom of priests" in light of Exodus 19:6 as translated in the LXX. The MT reads "a kingdom of priests," which is translated in the LXX as two nouns in apposition (Witherington, *Socio-Rhetorical*, 120). Thus, the LXX reflects a Hebraism that is best rendered as a noun with its qualifying genitive.

33. Green, "Use of OT," 276, 281.

| LXX: | LXX: |
|---|---|
| • 1 Chr 29:3 περιπεποίημαι "I have aquired for myself" silver and gold <br> ... <br> • Eccl 2:8 περιουσιασμός | • Exod 19:5 λαὸς περιούσιος <br> • Deut 7:6 λαὸν περιούσιον <br> • Deut 14:2 αὐτῷ λαὸν περιούσιον <br> • Deut 26:18 λαὸν περιούσιον <br> • Ps 134:4 περιουσιασμὸν ἑαυτῷ <br> • Mal 3:17 εἰς περιποίησιν |
| English Translation: | English Translation: |
| • 1 Chr. 29:3 "I have a treasure of my own of gold and silver" <br> • Eccl. 2:8 "the treasure of kings and provinces" | • Exod 19:5 "you shall be my treasured possession from all the peoples" <br> • Deut 7:6 "to be for him a treasured possession from all the peoples" <br> • Deut 14:2 "to be for him a treasured possession from all the peoples" <br> • Deut 26:18 "to be for him a treasured possession" <br> • Ps 135:4 "Israel as his own treasured possession" <br> • Mal 3:17 "I shall make you a treasured Possession" |

In the MT, the term סגלה, simply translated as "possession" or "property," is used in reference to David's treasure (1 Chr 29:3) and the king's treasure (Eccl 2:8) that each has acquired. As specifically royal treasure, it connotes a special type of possession belonging to David and the Davidic line. The term takes on theological significance when it is predicated of the people of Israel who are described as the עם סגלה of Yahweh, the connotation being that, Yahweh is the king whose especial, royal treasure is Israel.[34] In other words, Israel is God's "dear possession," a "treasure" in the sense of that which is cherished, not through inheritance, but through the putting aside of a reserve from the possessions of the divine king.[35] In other words, although Yahweh possesses the entire universe and everything in it, he nevertheless chooses Israel for his own special purposes.

The connotation of chosen-ness inherent in the term סגלה is given further nuance in light of the fact that Israel is not God's possession in the same sense that a treasure, as an inanimate object, is. Rather, what is described in the OT is a relationship between the divine king and his *living* treasure, which suggests that the term "treasured possession" is best understood in a

---

34. BDB, "סגלה," 688.

35. Moshe Greenberg, *Studies in the Bible and Jewish Thought* (Philadelphia: Jewish Publication Society, 1995), 277. Also, TDOT, "סגלה," 10:147–48.

dynamic, relational way. The metaphorical use of the Hebrew noun and its analogues in Akkadian and Ugaritic in terms of vassalage demonstrate such an understanding.[36] According to Samuel E. Loewenstamm, epigraphical evidence shows that both the Hebrew סגלה and the Ugaritic *sglt* belong to the sphere of covenant-making and are used to denote the status of a vassal who is especially favored by his suzerain.[37] Thus, the term as it appears in the OT in a theological context may be construed as a term of endearment used by God in addressing his vassal Israel and admonishing his people to obey his voice.[38]

Accordingly, Loewenstamm's proposal allows for a more relational understanding of Israel as Yahweh's treasured possession in that it links the term סגלה with the *topos* of covenant and covenantal responsibility.[39] This linking of identity with covenantal obedience is evident in the biblical texts. Exod 19:4-5 relates God's action in bringing the Israelites out of Egypt in order to make them his treasured possession. While v. 4 emphasizes Yahweh's election of Israel, v. 5 states an explicit condition: if you obey my voice and keep my covenant, you shall be my treasured possession . . . a priestly kingdom and a holy nation. Obedience to the stipulations of the covenant (19:10—31:18), accompanies election and is followed by judgment when Israel twice disobeys (32:1-35; 33:1-6).

Similarly, the three instances of סגלה in the Book of Deuteronomy occur within the context of the covenant relationship. Here, Moses is portrayed as reiterating the law given at Sinai for a new generation poised to enter into the land promised to its ancestors (1:8). The first occurrence (Deut 7:6) appears within the context of the giving of the Moab covenant. The second occurrence, Deut 14:2, falls within the context of the covenant stipulations themselves. In both instances, Israel's favored status is to be maintained by

---

36. Samuel E. Loewenstamm, *From Babylon to Canaan: Studies in the Bible and Its Oriental Background* (Jerusalem: Magnus, 1992), 279.

37. Loewenstamm, *From Babylon*, 276.

38. Loewenstamm, *From Babylon*, 276.

39. Yet, one must keep in mind the differences between Yahweh's covenant with Israel and the covenants drawn between ancient Middle-Eastern human kings and their human vassals. For one, suzerain-vassal covenants drawn between human parties were instituted primarily as a means of addressing nationalistic concerns, either for self-aggrandizement, or political and economic security, or both. God's choice of Israel, however, does not reflect any consideration of political, military, or economic advantage. Rather, it is born out of a divine decision to choose and to love a relatively obscure group of former Egyptian slaves (Deut 7:18-19). Ultimately, Israel's understanding of itself as God's סגלה is premised not only on the ancient Middle-Eastern understanding of covenantal relationships, but also on the Israelites experience of a suzerain unlike any other who defies human constructs and understanding and whose decisions and actions remain, to some extent, a mystery.

engaging in behavior that is pleasing to God. Moreover, the reason given for obeying these stipulations is that Israel is to be a people holy to the Lord (7:1, 21). This is made explicit in Deut 26:18, which falls within the context of the ratification of the Moab covenant. Here, it is Yahweh who sets Israel above the nations and it is Israel who promises to keep his commandments in response.

A similar idea is also present in Ps 135:4 where Israel is contrasted to the nations who trust in idols and who are destined to become like these things, inanimate objects unable to praise their true creator (vv. 15–18). Israel, on the other hand is to fear, praise and bless the true God (vv. 19–21). Finally, the reference to Israel as "my special possession" in Mal 3:17 occurs within the context of a prophetic lawsuit (ריב) indicting the temple priesthood for violation of the covenant. The text is rich in covenantal imagery, and the prophet explicitly states that those who will be the Lord's "special possession" are precisely those who have kept covenant with him, while those who have failed to do so will be destroyed (3:16—4:6).

In summary, all of the OT texts which speak of Israel as Yahweh's "special possession," apart from Ps 135 where the themes of obedience and judgment are implicit, Israel's elect status is linked with the *topoi* of godly living/holiness and judgment within the context of covenant. Similarly, in the NT texts, where Christians (Jew and gentile) are designated as God's "own special possession," the privilege of election is inextricably intertwined with responsibility for living a life according to the will of God.

## "God's Special Possession" in 1 Peter 2:9

The above analysis suggests that the interpretation of περιποίησις in 1 Pet 2:9 must hold in tension both privilege and responsibility, divine action and human response. Accordingly, although it is correct that the phrase εἰς περιποίησιν indicates that Christians belong particularly to God as his elect,[40] this notion of chosen-ness is linked with obedience in the biblical texts. Moreover, although this status is freely conferred upon believers, it is given so that they might exemplify the character of the one to whom they belong.

However, J. De Waal Drydan maintains that the multiple titles in 2:9 function rhetorically to reinforce the reality of a divinely conferred identity derived from election since nothing has been said explicitly about how believers are to relate to outsiders. This, he argues, suggests that the focus

---

40. Davids, *First Epistle*, 92.

is not on social ethics but on communal identity.[41] Yet, emphasis on the unique position of believers before God without an equal emphasis on the responsibility that comes with that status accounts neither for the author's overriding concern for holiness nor for his choice of OT texts. Thus, although it is plausible that the titles are used to emphasize the unique identity of believers, it is this identity expressed in a holy life-style that especially concerns the biblical writer.

Accordingly, an important corollary to viewing 2:4–10 in light of a dynamic understanding of holiness and election is that the ἀπιστοῦσιν and ἀπειθοῦντες mentioned in 2:7–8 refer not only to those outside of the Christian community but also to those believers who are seeking to escape persecution and suffering by means of accommodation, which could well lead to apostasy.

## WHO'S STUMBLING ON THE STUMBLING STONE?

In general, the Roman Empire tended to view foreign religions with suspicion, as potentially disrupting social order. Imagined threats of the Christian sect would have included such things as: Christian slaves and wives choosing their own religion apart from the *pater potestas* (2:18—3:6); the reputed character of Christianity as a superstition; and a perception that the sect was promoting sexual immorality, cannibalism, magic, sedition, and/or atheism.[42] Given this cultural climate it is conceivable that the Christian communities in Asia Minor could well have experienced social ostracism and slander for their perceived involvement in a foreign sect. This form of persecution would have functioned as a means of shaming them into submission to the cultural expectations of the Roman state (2:12; 3:9, 16; 4:4). Given that this area was more thoroughly Romanized than many other regions of the empire, it is no wonder that the author refers to these believers as παροίκους and παρεπιδήμους (2:11).[43] In a sense these Anatolian believers are exiles of the Roman body politic, since their membership in the Christian community by virtue of their new birth (1:23) entails that they live according to a new set of values and beliefs largely in conflict with those endorsed by the broader culture.

Of note in this regard is the author's reference to non-retaliation in the second argument. Here Christ is presented as an example of one who

---

41. Dryden, *Theology and Ethics*, 125–26.
42. Campbell, *Honor Shame*, 29.
43. Green, *1 Peter*, 192.

did not abuse his abusers (2:23), while believers are urged to take up his example and not repay evil with evil (3:9–12). Grumbling against and maligning abusers would have been common responses to political authorities, masters, unbelieving husbands and others who may have been engaged in either the social ostracism of believers or their defamation.[44] Accordingly, the biblical writer addresses those who are contemplating non-Christlike retaliation against their abusers.

Further evidence of this is present in the third argument which opens with a rhetorical question. Although interpreters tend to view 3:13–14 as an answer to objections that the audience might raise as a result of the exhortation to non-retaliation in the preceding argument,[45] the use of the optative πάσχοιτε (v. 14) suggests otherwise. The presence of the optative is unusual, given that there are strong indications that the Christian communities are in fact suffering persecution to some degree or another. This suggests that there are some members of these communities who are in fact engaging in retaliation. Thus, what follows is an implicit warning to stop.

The rhetorical question: "Who will harm you, if you are eager to do good?" (3:13) expects the answer: "No one." However, in v. 14 the author adds that even if believers should suffer for doing right, they are blessed. What is being emphasized here is that while the choice not to retaliate in imitation of Christ, which would not necessarily be deemed as doing "good" in an agonistic society, is nevertheless blessed in God's sight, even if it results in suffering. In other words, retaliation, which is honorable in the eyes of society, does not result in divine blessing. Conversely, if one should suffer for doing what is honorable in God's sight, one is in reality blessed. The exhortation not to fear what they, those outside the Christian community, fear (3:14) further suggests that the author is exhorting those who are either engaging in retaliation or contemplating it in fear of being dishonored to refrain from such action, since their fear is ultimately groundless, given their real status before God.

Several references to this notion are also present in 2:6–8. Verse 6 contains an allusion to Isa 28:16. The larger context describes an oracle against Ephraim (28:1–6) and Judah (28:7–29) condemning them for making a military alliance with Egypt against Assyria, rather than trusting in God. Here, God lays a foundation stone for the purpose of annulling their ungodly

---

44. Campbell, *Honor Shame*, 104.

45. For example: Campbell, *Honor Shame*, 172–73; Witherington, *Socio-Rhetorical*, 172. Campbell notes that these objections might have included such comments as: "If we do good, we will still suffer;" "our Christian identity will still make us a target of persecution;" and/or "people will still think of us as evil-doers" (Campbell, *Honor Shame*, 172).

covenant with the foreign powers and destroying them. However, although the cornerstone, God's presence in Jerusalem, will shatter the scoffers and their plans, it will protect those who trust in the Lord (28:16–17). Thus, the larger context of Isa 28 relates to the NT author's concern to encourage believers to maintain their trust in God, rather than placing it in human systems of procuring and maintaining honor. God's promise to shatter the scoffers and their plans is akin to the eschatological hope of the believers in Asia Minor.

A similar idea is present in 1 Pet 2:7 where the writer cites Ps 117:16 (LXX). This psalm is a song of thanksgiving which celebrates the Lord's enduring love and his deliverance of the psalmist from distress (vv. 5, 11–14). In this case, the NT writer equates the distressed psalmist with Jesus, thereby emphasizing that God's preeminent role in delivering him from his dishonorable death. Moreover, the reference to honor being to those who believe (1 Pet 2:7a) in turn equates believers' honor with Jesus'. As Jesus triumphed over those who persecuted him, so will believers, if they take refuge in the Lord. The latter condition is an important caveat to which the NT author makes continual reference throughout the discourse. In other words, honor, glory, and final triumph come from God and consequently, those who believe in him are to trust him and not take matters into their own hands. Rather, they are to bless those who persecute them, following the example of Christ. Thus, within the larger context of Ps 117, the NT author's reference to the ἀπιστοῦσιν (2:7a) serves to contrast (δέ) those who seek deliverance from the Lord and take refuge in him to those who do not.

Finally, in 1 Pet 2:8 there is an allusion to Isa 8:14. Here, the prophet relates an oracle against Israel (destruction of Israel by Assyria) and a promise of Judah's deliverance (8:5–10). In 8:12–13 the prophet urges Judah not to fear what the world fears (invading armies), but instead to fear the Lord of Hosts, who is holy. Here, there is the implicit idea that the Lord is a sanctuary for those who trust in him and regard him as the ultimate measure of everything honorable and worthy. Conversely, for the house of Israel, who does not trust him and does not regard him as holy and to be feared, Yahweh is a stumbling stone. In other words, that God "is" either a refuge or a source of judgment, depends on whether persons see him as he truly is and thereby place all trust in him.

In summary, the larger context of these OT texts indicates that those who stumble include all persons, especially and including members of God's elect, who fail to fear the Lord, disregard his holiness, and trust either in themselves or other earthly powers rather than in him. This group is larger than that comprised of those who are outside of the believing community; that is, those who fail to accept the good news of Jesus Christ.

Thus, although it is true that the NT writer is concerned with establishing an honorable identity for his audience as a source of encouragement, readings which view 2:7–8 exclusively in terms of a soteriological dichotomy (the saved and the unsaved) cannot adequately account for the exhortations to progress in spiritual maturity and holiness which run throughout the letter and are directed at believers.

The fact that these Christians need to be encouraged to persevere in trust, given their difficult circumstances, implies that there is the possibility that they may choose to do otherwise. In other words, the author is concerned with more than soteriological differences. He is equally, if not more, concerned with believers achieving the full measure of their salvation as they live out the identity given to them by God in imitation of the Christ who suffered unjustly. For this reason his exhortations provide an implicit warning for those seeking to imitate cultural *exempla*.

## CONCLUSION

In conclusion, interpretations of 1 Pet 2:4–10 which view this passage primarily in terms of believers' privileged status before God result in an attenuated reading which places an undue emphasis on a static conception of election. The rhetorical unity of the epistle points to a broader understanding of election which encompasses obedience on the part of the elect. Moreover, analysis of the broader OT context indicates that the catena of citations in 2:4–10 points to a dynamic, rather than a cultic/static, understanding of election.

This is not to say that the ascription of an alternative, Christologically-based identity to the beleaguered communities in Asia Minor is not of concern to the author. Rather, it is to say that identity and obedience are inextricably tied in his theology, making it problematic to view 2:4–10 as being solely concerned with establishing identity. The wider angle of vision provided by viewing identity and obedience as interdependent brings into sharper focus the implicit warning against accommodation which lies directly below the more explicit exhortations to eschew the norms and values of Caesar's household that clash with those of the divinely constituted family of God. Thus, the intent of the author is both to encourage perseverance in the face of persecution and to discourage those members who are either considering or engaging in some form of accommodation.

This suggests that the reference to unbelievers and the disobedient in 2:7–8 includes those believers in the community who are choosing accommodation as a means of escaping persecution and suffering. According to the biblical writer, one's identity as a Christian is premised in and on Christ's identity. To be a follower of Christ means to embrace his example of non-retaliatory suffering, persevering in the certain hope that this path is the way to eschatological glory. The possibility of veering from that path remains and those who choose to do so, and as a consequence fall away, are precisely those who do not believe and who disobey. The cornerstone is the stone of stumbling for all, including members of the household of God, who choose to reject it.

www.ingramcontent.com/pod-product-compliance
Lightning Source LLC
Chambersburg PA
CBHW062017220426
43662CB00010B/1362